A Practical Guide for Crisis Response in Our Schools

Fourth Edition

a publication of

The American Academy of Experts in Traumatic Stress®

Printed in the United States of America

Publisher's Note
The Academy wishes to thank Joseph S. Volpe, Ph.D., Mark D. Lerner, Ph.D., and Brad Lindell, Ph.D.
for their extensive contributions in the development of this publication.

Published by

The American Academy of Experts in Traumatic Stress®
Administrative Offices, 368 Veterans Memorial Highway, Commack, New York 11725
Tel. (516) 543-2217 • Fax (516) 543-6977 • Automated Fax Back System (516) 771-8103
http://www.aaets.org

ISBN: 0-9674762-0-8

A PRACTICAL GUIDE FOR CRISIS RESPONSE IN OUR SCHOOLS

Fourth Edition

a publication of

The American Academy of Experts in Traumatic Stress®

The American Academy of Experts in Traumatic Stress is a multidisciplinary network of professionals committed to the advancement of intervention for survivors of trauma. The Academy's international membership includes individuals from over 200 professions in the health-related fields, emergency services, criminal justice, forensics, law, business and education. With members in every state of the United States and over 40 foreign countries, the Academy is now the largest organization of its kind in the world. For information about membership, the National Registry, the Academy's Board Certification programs in traumatic stress specialties, the Diplomate Credential, Fellowship and other benefits of membership with the Academy, please contact:

The American Academy of Experts in Traumatic Stress®

Administrative Offices, 368 Veterans Memorial Highway, Commack, New York 11725
Tel. (516) 543-2217 • Fax (516) 543-6977 • Automated Fax Back System (516) 771-8103
http://www.aaets.org

A Practical Guide for Crisis Response in Our Schools is published by The American Academy of Experts in Traumatic Stress. It is offered with the understanding that the Academy does not practice medicine or psychology, or provide direct or indirect patient/client care. This guide should not take the place of competent professional services. Additional copies may be obtained by utilizing the order form provided in the back of this guide.

ADMINISTRATION AND MEMBERS OF THE BOARD OF SCIENTIFIC & PROFESSIONAL ADVISORS

For the children and their families...

The American Academy of Experts in Traumatic Stress®

Administrative Offices, 368 Veterans Memorial Highway, Commack, New York 11725
Tel. (516) 543-2217 • Fax (516) 543-6977 • Automated Fax Back System (516) 771-8103
http://www.aaets.org
FEDERAL IDENTIFICATION NO. 11-3285203

Dear Fellow Educator,

Welcome to **The American Academy of Experts in Traumatic Stress**—a multidisciplinary network of professionals committed to the advancement of intervention for survivors of trauma.

Today, our international membership includes individuals from over 200 professions in the health-related fields, emergency services, criminal justice, forensics, law, business and education. With members in every state of the United States and over 40 foreign countries, the Academy is now the largest organization of its kind in the world.

Our mission is to increase awareness of the effects of trauma and, ultimately, to improve the quality of intervention with survivors. In this spirit, the Academy published *A Practical Guide for Crisis Response in Our Schools.*

The collaborative relationships among members of a school family are critical and provide the foundation for this guide. Now in its fourth edition, the guide serves as a comprehensive Crisis Response Plan for school districts across the country and has become a national standard for responding to school-based crises.

A Practical Guide for Crisis Response in Our Schools conveys critical information to assist school districts in responding effectively to "everyday crises" as well as school-based disasters. It is an invaluable resource for administrators, support personnel and faculty *in preparation for*, and *during*, actual crisis situations.

This guide has established a meaningful *standard,* and additionally serves as the study guide for professionals who seek to achieve **Board Certification in School Crisis Response**™. Further information about this credential, as well as the Academy, may be found in the back of this guide. You may also visit the Academy's award-winning Internet site at **http://www.aaets.org**.

By reaching our school families early with a comprehensive Crisis Response Plan, we can potentially prevent the acute difficulties of today from becoming the chronic problems of tomorrow.

Sincerely,

Mark D. Lerner, Ph.D.
President

Table of Contents

FOREWORD

Preventing School Violence and Reducing the Frequency of Disturbing Threats

by Mark D. Lerner, Ph.D.
President, AAETS

Introduction

Not long ago the most severe problems encountered in our schools were students running in the halls, making excessive noise, cutting a line, talking out-of-turn, chewing gum or violating a dress code.

Today, we are faced with a dramatic increase in the frequency of violence including assaults and gang activity. Additionally, we are seeing an increase in the frequency of substance abuse, self-mutilation, suicide, abandonment of newborn babies, and serious injuries and deaths from automobile accidents. We are also contending with new types of trauma including hostage-taking, sniper attacks, murders, terrorist activities, "hit lists," threatening graffiti, bomb scares and real bombs.

In response to this disturbing trend, The American Academy of Experts in Traumatic Stress published *A Practical Guide for Crisis Response in Our Schools*. Since the release of the first edition, the Academy has been regularly updating and revising the document in response to the rapidly changing climate in our nation's schools.

As an introduction to the fourth edition of this guide, I would like to address what may be some of the causes of the dramatic increase in the frequency of school-based crises and offer practical strategies for preventing tragedies in our schools. Secondly, in response to a recent trend of disturbing threats in our schools, I would like to share a strategy for reducing the frequency of such threats as bomb scares, "hit lists" and threatening graffiti.

Causes of School-Based Tragedies

Although statistically rare, the frequency of dramatic, well-publicized school-based disasters is increasing. Even more disturbing is that less-publicized tragedies are impacting upon members of our school families, every day, at a significantly faster rate than ever before. In fact, we no longer question *if* a school will be faced with responding to a tragedy, but *when*.

Many factors contribute to the causes of school crises and we must not focus on only one. Research is helping us to understand the relationship between violent television programs, movies, music lyrics and violent behavior. Additionally, investigation concerning the impact of violent computer and video games is presently underway. Should we be more concerned with these media due to their interactive nature?

We hear about the availability of guns and other weapons and we cannot ignore the data. From 1992 to 1999, 77 percent of all violent deaths in schools were caused by guns (The Center for the Study and Prevention of Violence, 1999). We must develop zero-tolerance policies.

There is a dramatic increase in alcohol and substance use among our children, peer pressure and gang involvement. We are learning about children who are tormented and teased, and then go on to harm themselves and others. We are seeing the effects of divorce, "latchkey kids," parents working long hours and an absence of parental supervision, training and example-setting. Today, there are relaxed curfews, a lack of respect for authority and a lack of family involvement with schools. There is a changing family structure as well, with a large number of single parent families, grandparents and extended family living in the home. There is also a growing trend of violence related to race and/or religion. This is particularly disturbing in light of the fact that diversity in America is rapidly increasing. The extent to which these variables are related to the quantitative and qualitative changes in school-based crises will become more apparent with time and with further empirical investigation.

The inevitability of illness, accidents and loss may be accepted and even anticipated by schools that often view themselves as microcosms of our world. But why is there such a dramatic increase in deliberately-caused tragedies—those of intentional human design?

I believe that at the very core of our problem is a *fundamental communication breakdown in families*—the result, in large part, of an increasingly technological and mechanized world. We are spending less time communicating, teaching and modeling appropriate behavior with our children—we are losing the battle to the proliferation of electronic media.

Today's children all too often leave or avoid the dinner table or family room, opting for the new era in violent television, video and computer games, and Internet chat rooms. Consequently, our children lack interpersonal communication, coping and problem-solving skills to meet the challenges of our new world—one reason why an increasing number of them act-out feelings of anger and frustration in dangerous attention-seeking ways, "self-medicate" with alcohol and other substances, and commit suicide at a higher rate than ever before.

Media today offers our children a regular dose of violence and I cannot underscore the negative impact this has on our society.

Practical Prevention Strategies

While consulting in the area of school crisis prevention, I am frequently asked about the efficacy of installing metal detectors, surveillance cameras and conducting safety audits. At the end of last school year, I recall one superintendent who asked whether book bags should be permitted in schools. Although there are certainly benefits gained from taking these steps, I believe that they fail to address the root of the problem.

We must help our children and adolescents to develop and enhance their communication and problem-solving skills. We must teach them how to actively listen and to empathize when relating with others. We must help our children to understand the importance of articulating their feelings about themselves and for others, and to know that it is okay to err on the side of caution when expressing concerns about others. We must regularly remind them that they can turn to their parents and/or school support personnel who will take the time to listen and respond to them.

Too often our children and adolescents hear of disturbing ideation or plans prior to a tragedy and they do not know how to respond. It is not until the aftermath of a disaster that we see survivors interviewed and we hear them describe how the alleged perpetrator had, in some way, suggested impending doom. In cases of adolescent suicide, more than 80% of kids who commit suicide tell someone, in some way, that they are going to end their life. Our children do not know what to do or where to turn with critical information.

We must work toward improving communication in order to prevent violent school-based tragedies. Yet, we must address our problem through a multimodal approach. For instance, we can help our children and adolescents to identify physiological changes in their bodies which may precede or coincide with feelings of frustration and anger. We can help them to understand which behaviors/actions cause others to become frustrated and angry. We can teach them to become aware of and to identify negative self-statements that generate feelings of frustration and anger. And, we can help our children to learn to replace self-defeating statements with positive coping statements. Behaviorally, we must model and espouse appropriate moral behavior, set limits and be consistent with our responses to aberrant behavior. Ultimately, we must teach our children to show compassion and sincerity in relating with others.

We must help our children to understand that conflict is a natural part of interpersonal relationships. When we handle conflict well it presents an opportunity to learn, to better understand ourselves and to generate creative solutions. When we handle conflict poorly, it can lead to violence.

We must help our children to make more adaptive, goal-directed decisions when faced with feelings of frustration. For example, we can teach them that it is okay to walk away from altercations or to take a few moments to "cool down." We can teach our children to express themselves assertively, to implement relaxation techniques, and to utilize conflict resolution and peer mediation skills.

The latter areas of conflict resolution and peer mediation offer great potential. When we ask children and adolescents what they believe may help to reduce the frequency of school-based tragedies, they indicate that there needs to be more constructive opportunities for expression of feelings. On the other hand, we must keep in mind that conflict resolution techniques and peer mediation programs presuppose conflict. It is my conviction that we must reach our children when they are very young and provide an ongoing effort to develop their communication and problem-solving skills.

Finally, we must view *all* students as being "at risk." However, there are "early warning signs" to identify students who should be considered at greater risk for engaging in violent behavior (see page 55 of this guide). Let us all become hypervigilant, learn to err on the side of caution, and work toward preventing violent tragedies in our schools.

Reducing the Frequency of Disturbing Threats

In the aftermath of recent highly publicized tragedies in our nation's schools, we have experienced a dramatic increase in the frequency of disturbing threats. Through opportunities in consulting, I gained a greater appreciation of the impact of such threats in our schools. For example, when a bomb threat is made by telephone, e-mailed or written on a bathroom wall, there is an enormous impact on the school community. The potential need to evacuate a school building under such circumstances presents a host of complex decisions for school administrators. Ensuring the safety of the school family and preventing further disruption of the educational process is crucial.

Many feelings are generated from observing bomb-sniffing dogs comb a school. I recall one principal's description of how traumatized he, his students and staff were after standing outside of the building for nearly two hours while dogs searched the building. He indicated that when they reentered the school everyone was anxious, hypervigilant and startled by every closing locker.

As I spoke with administrators, I learned of other disturbing threats such as "hit lists" and threatening graffiti. For example, the traumatic stress endured by fourteen students, teachers and school administrators specifically named on a poster that was placed in the entrance area of one high school was profound. The poster described how each of them would be harmed. Furthermore, the fear that was experienced by another school family after the statement "Everyone will die on June 4th" had a far-reaching impact upon the entire community. After the building principal informed parents of the threat, nearly all of the eighteen hundred students were absent from school—many roamed the streets of the community.

Understanding what may have caused or contributed to the surge of disturbing threats in our nation's schools in the wake of well-publicized tragedies may help to mitigate against similar behavior in the future.

The reasons why some students choose to make bomb threats, develop "hit lists," or write threatening graffiti are complex, and ultimately sound research will help us to understand the relationship between these threats and such variables as domestic violence, sexual abuse, substance abuse, chronic teasing and tormenting, etc. Following is my theoretical perspective based upon many years of clinical experience in working with children and adolescents as well as my interpretation of extant literature.

There are a significant number of young people who are feeling alone and powerless in our rapidly changing world. When these individuals observe the tremendous and overwhelming attention following highly-publicized dramatic events, many of them identify with the aggressor(s). They may fantasize about an opportunity to overcome feelings of aloneness, inadequacy, weakness and powerlessness. They envision themselves acting-out and perhaps overcompensate for these dystonic feelings. Fortunately, relatively few act upon these violent impulses with significant magnitude. Apparently there is some impulse control which prevents them from going to the extent that perpetrators of violent mass casualty incidents ultimately manifest. However, in their minds, they see an opportunity to take action, of a lesser magnitude, and still draw a great deal of attention.

As I reflect upon disturbing threats experienced in our schools, I ask myself why some schools experience many threats, why others experience few, and why others seem to escape such experiences. I hypothesize that the climate established by the school staff and administration is directly related to the frequency of disturbing threats.

Educators must be careful not to challenge disturbed young people with statements like, "Our school is a safe place and we will not experience the kinds of events that you heard about yesterday...." Such statements may serve to create a double bind—a challenge for these individuals. They may incite these students to try to disprove authority figures, to make themselves feel more powerful and to help them to compensate for their feelings of inadequacy and weakness. Furthermore, educators that ignore the highly-publicized tragedies occurring in our nation's schools are missing a critical opportunity to help young people articulate disturbing thoughts and feelings, and to learn more adaptive coping strategies.

What can we do to decrease the frequency of disturbing threats? If indeed the "type" of individual or individuals who generate threats are trying to overcompensate for feelings of aloneness, inadequacy, weakness and powerlessness, we must work toward helping these young people to understand that the effect that they are trying to achieve by making a threat (i.e., to overcompensate for these disturbing feelings) will not result in the attainment of their perceived goal (e.g., to feel more powerful). Rather, the result of the threat may likely cause them to be arrested, feel very alone while incarcerated, more inadequate, weaker and truly powerless. If in fact we focus our attention on helping young people to understand and observe the CONSEQUENCES of being caught for making disturbing threats, the frequency of such threats may be dramatically reduced.

How can we focus our attention on the consequences of being caught? The responsibility here lies at a number of levels. For example, legislation could be enacted that would make reporting bomb threats a felony in all states. In addition to prosecuting perpetrators, these students could face significant school-related consequences including expulsion. Schools could establish clearly understood policies whereby all "lost time" due to disturbing threats would have to be made-up. Parents could be held financially responsible for the municipal costs of responding to threats. The media could invest more attention in showing alleged perpetrators being led in handcuffs to police vans, and less time on pictures of adolescent killers sitting and smiling among their "peers."

The bottom line is that we can take steps to help young people to understand the consequences of disturbing threats by focusing attention not on the glorification of such acts, but on the reality of their actions.

Conclusion

It is important to understand what factors may be causing the dramatic increase in school-based tragedies. Similarly, it would be helpful to comprehend the ideation of people who make disturbing threats. Ultimately, research will help us to understand the causative factors and the effects of specific interventions. However, like many events in a rapidly shifting zeitgeist, we must take initial thoughtful, realistic and logical steps to respond to the problems that we are facing in our schools by developing effective prevention and response strategies. May *A Practical Guide for Crisis Response in Our Schools* continue to serve as a national standard for responding to school-based crises.

1. What is a Crisis & What is Crisis Response?

A crisis is an event of limited duration that seriously disrupts our coping and problem-solving capabilities. It is typically unpredicted and overwhelming for those who experience its wrath. A crisis may be volatile in nature and, at times, may involve threat to the survival of an individual or groups of individuals. A crisis state may result upon exposure to drastic and tragic change in an individual's environment which has become common and familiar to them. This alteration in the status quo is unwanted, frightening, and often renders a person with a sense of vulnerability and helplessness. Ultimately, with successful intervention, the equilibrium is restored between the environment and the individual's perception of their world as a safe and secure place. The primary goals of crisis response are to:

- prevent a chaotic situation from escalating into a potentially catastrophic one,
- help those affected by the crisis to return, as quickly as possible, to pre-crisis functioning, and
- decrease the potential long-term effects of the crisis on functioning.

Noteworthy, concerning the second primary goal, is that many people demonstrate the capacity to cultivate a "mission" and grow from adversity. Therefore, they do not "return to pre-crisis functioning." Instead, they seize the opportunity a crisis brings, by finding meaning or perhaps a sense of purpose, and they grow from the experience (Lerner, 1998).

The school environment is not immune to crisis situations. There is an increasing recognition that the schools of today are experiencing a greater frequency of traumatic events, including homicide and suicide, as well as increasing levels of substance abuse. The following is evidence of this disturbing trend:

- In 1997, about one third of all victims of violent crime were ages 12 to 19 and almost one half of all victims of violence were under the age of 25. Moreover, the percent of students reporting street gang presence at school nearly doubled between 1989 and 1995, increasing from 15.3% to 28.4% (U.S. Dept. of Justice, 1998).

- Today, suicide is the third leading cause of death among young people 15 to 24 years of age, following accidents and homicide and the suicide rate for children, 10 to 14 years of age, has more than doubled over the last 15 years (American Foundation for Suicide Prevention, 1996).

- Motor vehicle crashes are the leading cause of death for 15 to 20 year olds. In 1997, 3,336 drivers 15 to 20 years old were killed, and an additional 365,000 were injured, in motor vehicle crashes (NHTSA, 1998).

- The number of cases of Acquired Immune Deficiency Syndrome (AIDS) and Human Immunodeficiency Virus (HIV) reported each year for individuals between the ages of 13 and 19 continues to increase significantly. It is estimated that half of all new HIV infections in the United States are among people under the age of 25, and the majority of young people are infected sexually (Center for Disease Control & Prevention, 1998).

Today's school districts must contend with reactions to new types of trauma. For example, hostage-taking, sniper attacks, murders, terrorist activities and bombings were almost nonexistent in the schools thirty years ago. Noteworthy is that there is a strong indication in the literature that these deliberately-caused disasters, of intentional human design (IHD), and resultant victimization are worse than naturally-caused disasters (Baum et al., 1983; Ursano et al., 1994). Despite considerable social, familial and educational changes, most educators do not receive specific training in responding to the diversity of crisis situations.

Specific events include, but are certainly not limited to:
- an accident involving a student or staff member,
- suicide or homicide,
- substance overdose,
- death of classmate(s) or teacher,
- severe violence (e.g., gang fight),
- assault on a teacher or administrator,
- hostage situation on school grounds,
- child molestation,
- abandonment of a newborn in the school,
- sniper attack,
- terrorist activities,
- fire or chemical spill at school,
- plane, train, boat, bus or automobile accident, and
- natural disasters (e.g., tornado, flood, earthquake, etc.).

It is essential that school systems maintain a course of action in the event of exposure to such unexpected events. Petersen and Straub (1992) have indicated that school administrators have legal obligations to make crisis plans and to respond appropriately to such situations. Failure to take reasonable measures when confronted with a crisis can create potentially damaging effects on the school, the community, and most significantly, the students. An organized and preconceived approach to intervention is more efficient and, ultimately, more effective than "thinking-on-the-spot" and risking a haphazard crisis response.

2. The School Crisis Response Team

The building Crisis Response Team (CRT) capitalizes on the fact that co-workers know each other, have communicated previously in some manner with one another, and can work collaboratively. If a building team is not feasible, then a district team composed of members throughout the school district should be formed. Capitalizing upon the collaborative relationships that exist among members of a school family cannot be underscored enough and will be explored further in this guide. School personnel must be educated and empowered to effectively respond to school-based crises. Notwithstanding, today there are often efforts to bring in outside teams of experts in the wake of a tragedy. The well-meaning efforts of these "strangers" are often rebuffed and their presence may only serve to exacerbate confusion.

Members of the School Crisis Response Team should include the following:

Principal

The principal maintains a critical position on the Crisis Response Team. He/She holds the most authority in the building and typically has responsibility for actions taken by team members. The principal must obtain all available facts. This process often involves speaking with families as well as outside agencies (e.g., police department and/or local hospital). The principal functions as the liaison between the school building, the superintendent and other district administration. Additionally, he/she may be involved in addressing the media. Ideally, the principal is approachable and supportive, especially during times of crisis.

Assistant Principal (Dean)

The assistant principal helps the principal by serving as a liaison between support personnel, students and the principal. He/She maintains primary authority in the absence of the principal. The assistant principal can prepare and arrange for the distribution of letters to be sent home to parents and guardians. Such letters can inform them of the facts surrounding the crisis and a summary of actions the school is taking to help students (see Practical Document F). The assistant principal can meet with parents/guardians as well as facilitate the referral process for outside support (perhaps, in conjunction with the psychologist and/or social worker). Finally, the assistant principal may serve as an alternate spokesperson for the media.

School Psychologist

School psychologists are in a position to facilitate the crisis response at several levels. By virtue of their training, they can educate the school staff and students about what to expect—physically, emotionally and behaviorally—as a result of exposure to a traumatic event (e.g., a suicide). School psychologists are trained to identify individuals who may be "at risk" or vulnerable to further psychological deterioration following exposure to a crisis situation. Additionally, they may provide coping strategies, follow-up counseling with individuals, and referrals to outside professionals when appropriate.

Social Worker

Social workers can work with school psychologists in maintaining the emotional well-being of individuals exposed to a crisis. They may conduct support groups (if indicated) and help in the identification of individuals in need of further assistance. Social workers may contact and work with parents of students to facilitate further support, perhaps, by a community mental health center, etc.

School Nurse

With his/her knowledge of physical problems, the nurse is in an ideal position to help students who are injured. Moreover, the nursing staff is typically trained to handle acute physical reactions to crisis exposure including hyperventilation, fainting, etc. The nurse may serve as a liaison between the local hospital and the school building. Nurses can document the nature of injuries and facilitate in the transport of individuals to the hospital (if necessary).

Guidance Counselor

By virtue of their relationships with many students, guidance counselors may aid in identifying those individuals who are in need of intervention. They can coordinate support groups for students and staff, provide counseling as well as notify parents and guardians of students affected by the crisis (if indicated).

Teachers

Teachers may have the difficult task of providing a stable and calm model for their students at a time when they, personally, may be experiencing considerable emotional turmoil. A careful selection of teachers should be included on the Crisis Response Team. These teachers can serve as a liaison between the team and the faculty. Moreover, these teachers may be in a position to answer questions that students have regarding the crisis situation (assuming that by doing so, the emotional well-being of the student is prioritized). Teachers can help identify and refer students who appear in need of emotional support. Specific guidelines for teachers are offered in Practical Document I.

Building Security

Some schools have security guards on campus. Security guards maintain an important role in safeguarding individuals in the building in the event of a violent or potentially life-threatening situation. Building security should maintain direct contact and work in concert with local police (if indicated). Security guards can engage in crowd control in the event bystanders gather in the wake of an event. School classrooms, halls, cafeterias and grounds may need special monitoring.

Ancillary Staff

Other building staff may serve important roles during a crisis situation. For example, secretaries likely know many parents and students, and may supply the Crisis Response Team with relevant information. They may also be helpful in documentation. In addition, paraprofessionals (e.g., teacher aides) frequently have close relationships with many students within the school environment. These relationships could be invaluable in reaching students during a crisis. Finally, it is important that all staff, including non-teaching staff (e.g., custodians), have basic knowledge of the school's crisis response plan.

3. Response to a Crisis Situation

Crisis situations often render those involved feeling confused, overwhelmed and helpless. Upon recognition of a crisis, the school Crisis Response Team moves into action. An efficient response plan makes both the physical and emotional safety of individuals a priority; this includes students, teachers, administrators and support staff. It is always important to *think before acting*. Crises are temporary experiences that produce fear, confusion and distress. In an effort to protect and help students, faculty and staff should keep in mind that *the crisis is not going to last forever*. Carefully assess each step of the plan *before* it is enacted. **Practical Document A is a Crisis Response Checklist which can serve as a useful resource *during* a crisis.**

Although crisis response plans may vary from school district to school district, as will the availability of staff, a comprehensive crisis response plan will consider the following intervention strategies upon recognition of a crisis situation.

A. Fact Gathering

The first person to become aware of the crisis should contact the principal who will then notify school district administration. The primary task for the principal at this point is the gathering of details surrounding the crisis event. In the event of a fatal accident or suicide, this may involve making contact with the parents/guardians of the student(s).

Contacting parents/guardians after such tragic loss is an uncomfortable but necessary task. For example, when calling the parents of a child fatally injured in a motor vehicle accident, it may be helpful to ascertain:

- the events surrounding the youngster's death,
- how much information the parents want disclosed to the school community,
- whether funeral arrangements have been made,
- whether the parents approve of students and faculty attending the funeral, and
- if there is anything that the school can do for the family during this difficult time.

In the event of a devastating fire or natural disaster, contact with the fire department, police department, and/or local hospital is necessary for clarification of the facts surrounding the crisis.

It is also important that the principal keep in mind that people who are involved in a crisis situation are typically quite distressed and disoriented and consequently, information about the event(s) may be difficult to obtain. School personnel must be careful when inquiring about the sequence of events surrounding a crisis situation. For example, simple questions may be perceived as an interrogation and as invasive to those who witnessed a tragic event.

Rumors may abound and, at times, exacerbate chaos and confusion. It is important that personnel avoid assumptions about the nature of a crisis. For example, unless an official determination has been made for a cause of death, it is inappropriate to assume and label the cause of death as "suicide" even if it is quite obvious (Sandoval & Brock, 1996).

The principal should meet with the assistant principal and/or the school psychologist and determine the appropriateness of assembling the Crisis Response Team. Some of the variables to consider should include, but not be limited to, the **severity** of the event, the **number** of individuals affected by the event and the **reactions** of the students and faculty. Some situations may not require a crisis team intervention. For example, if the parent of a student was killed in an accident, contact with that student, his/her close friends, and teachers who knew the family may be more appropriate. In-school counseling and support should be offered to the individuals affected by the tragedy. If necessary, referrals for outside resources should also be provided. This may include specific professionals (e.g., psychologists), local mental health agencies, support groups (e.g., bereavement groups), and/or clergy.

If, upon consultation, it is decided that the Crisis Response Team is needed, then members are immediately notified. During school hours, the school should have a signal system that will communicate a message to the Crisis Response Team that they are being summoned. For example, the principal can make a public address announcement such as, "Will the principal's discussion team please report to the faculty lounge?" This signal will indicate that the Crisis Response Team is meeting immediately at that time.

An Emergency Contact List can be utilized if the crisis occurs during out-of-school hours (see Practical Document B). If the crisis occurs on a weekend, an announcement should be made on the next school day (see Practical Document C).

B. The Call to Action

Once the Crisis Response Team is assembled, it is critical that the team maintains a "pulse" on student and faculty reactions to the event. An attempt to estimate the size of the impact on the school community must be made. Things to consider should include:

- When did the event occur (e.g., during a lunch period, over the summer)?
- Where did the event occur (e.g., on school grounds)?
- How did it happen (e.g., accidental, intentional, expected)?
- How many students and staff were affected by the event?
- Which students and staff were affected?
- How were the students and staff affected?
- How are the faculty responding?
- Should classes be suspended temporarily or assignments altered?
- Should students be released from school?
- How are students indirectly being affected (e.g., siblings/friends at other buildings in the school district, etc.)?

The school district administration (e.g., superintendent) should continually be updated as the crisis develops. A determination to seek additional support resources (e.g., personnel from other school district buildings and/or outside community) should be made and acted upon. A local community counseling center may be able to offer counseling support if needed. It may be helpful for outside professionals to wear an identification badge. School personnel and students need to be acquainted with unfamiliar faces. Finally, the principal/assistant principal should determine if substitute teachers are needed.

C. Notification Procedures

Depending upon the nature of the incident, the Crisis Response Team must determine how the students, faculty, and staff will be notified of the crisis. Some methods to consider should include:

- an **announcement** to students and faculty,
- a student **assembly**,
- a mailbox **memorandum** to faculty and staff,
- an emergency faculty **meeting** (first thing in the morning), and
- notification to students in **classrooms** by the Crisis Response Team.

Typically, the building principal will make the announcement to the students and faculty early in the day (see sample announcement, Practical Document C). He or she should state whatever facts are known about the incident in order to help prevent and/or dispel rumors. **It is important that consent (e.g., from a victim's guardian) has been granted prior to release of sensitive information.** Announcements should be simple and void of details that could be easily misinterpreted. In the case of a student suicide or death, medical details and specific circumstances should be avoided. A straightforward announcement that conveys sympathy and a statement of condolence is recommended. The principal's statement should convey the following to the school community:

- facts regarding the event,
- the location of assemblies (if applicable),
- the location of support personnel (e.g., psychologist, social worker, guidance counselors),
- resources to utilize outside of school hours, and
- the need for students to sign *out* of their assigned class and *in* at designated counseling areas (i.e., for secondary level students).

In the case of a suicide, it is important that the statement is void of glorification and/or condoning of the act. Moreover, if a student assembly is chosen as a means to announce the crisis, then it is important to consider that a primary goal is to *efficiently* serve large numbers of students.

Weinberg (1990) has suggested that additional objectives of an *assembly* should be to:

- describe and normalize healthy grief reactions,
- observe students' and staff reactions—to identify individuals who are in need of further support (e.g., counseling), and
- encourage adaptive coping strategies and discourage unhealthy, maladaptive ones.

When deciding on the mode of communication about the crisis situation with the students (i.e., public address, assembly, etc.), the Crisis Response Team should consider:

- the **nature** of the crisis situation (e.g., accidental, suicide, etc.),
- the **age** of the students,
- the availability of **support services** (within and outside of the school) and,
- the needs and concerns of **parents/guardians** of the students.

As indicated previously, *confidentiality* must remain a top priority during times of crisis. In some circumstances, for example in the death of a student, the parents of that student should be contacted by the principal and consent should be granted before an official announcement is made to the school community. Information regarding funeral arrangements (if applicable) may be shared upon consent of the family (see memorandum to the faculty, Practical Document E).

Some administrators find that commencing (and possibly concluding) the school day with an emergency faculty meeting serves as a helpful adjunct to the circulation of a memo. Additionally, it is a more personal way to address a traumatic event such as a student's (or faculty member's) death. The principal should address the concerns of the faculty and staff, receive feedback from them and answer their questions. It could be helpful for a Crisis Response Team member to review warning signs (e.g., appearing detached, confused, disoriented, agitated, anxious, depressed, etc.) for high risk students and differences between age-appropriate responses and maladaptive reactions (see Section 4). This will aid the faculty in identifying students (and/or colleagues) in need of further support.

Depending upon the circumstances, the principal may suggest to teachers that they begin their classes by discussing the event and give students an opportunity to express themselves and their concerns. In all likelihood, upon notification of distressing news (e.g., death of a peer), concentration, interest and motivation for instruction will be significantly impaired. The postponement of tests should be considered.

The responses of the faculty should be monitored. When the crisis involves the death of a student, it is important to consider that many staff members develop close relationships with students and their reactions must not be overlooked. All individuals in the school building should be informed that staff (e.g., psychologist, social worker, and/or guidance counselors) are available for them at this difficult time. The locations and availability of support personnel should be posted in a highly visible and accessible area and confidentiality should be assured. Follow-up faculty and staff meetings should be planned (if indicated).

D. Crisis Response Team in Motion

Administrators and/or security may circulate in the building to be available for, and perhaps refer, students or staff for support. The building principal may need to remove personal items from a student's desk or locker to save for parents and family (Petersen & Straub, 1992). The principal and/or district administration should prepare a letter to be sent home to parents (see sample letter, Practical Document F) that states:

- the **facts** surrounding the crisis,
- a **summary** of actions the school is taking to help students,
- a list of **reactions** to expect from their child,
- **guidelines** that can aid the parent(s) in providing support to their child(ren), and
- contact **phone numbers** within and/or outside of the school for further information and support.

Building security should maintain direct contact and collaborate with the local police and/or the fire department (if indicated). Security guards can engage in crowd control in the event bystanders gather in the wake of an event. School classrooms, halls, cafeterias and grounds may need special monitoring.

Within the classroom, **teachers** should allow opportunity for students to acknowledge and discuss their thoughts and feelings associated with the crisis. By validating their students' feelings, teachers can facilitate the grieving process. Teachers should reinforce that it could be very helpful to talk with support personnel regarding their feelings about the incident. It is important that other members of the Crisis Response Team are sensitive to a teacher's beliefs concerning the type and amount of intervention that is provided in his/her classroom. It may be helpful for Crisis Response Team members to view themselves as consultants to teachers—providing information and intervention on an as-needed basis. A detailed description of what classroom teachers can do to address the reactions of their students to a crisis situation can be found in Practical Document I. Finally, the locations of support staff should be made available in a clear manner and should be posted in a highly visible place for students and staff.

Individual and small group counseling (e.g., preferably between five and eight students) provided by **school psychologists, social workers** and **guidance counselors** can offer an appropriate forum for students to express themselves (Davidson, 1989). **All personnel who counsel individuals in crisis should keep in mind that:**

- Listening to others in a *non-judgmental*, *warm* and *genuine* manner is an important goal.
- All individuals have the right to their own opinions and feelings.
- Making effective contact with another individual involves establishing rapport.
- Lecturing, preaching and/or criticizing are barriers to effective communication.
- Cultural differences exist in the overt expression of emotions.
- Maintaining confidentiality, when possible, is crucial.
- It is important to remember that *you* have support while helping others during a crisis situation.

Rooms accessible to all students, faculty and staff should be designated, especially for the purpose of counseling. This space should be continually staffed with members of the Crisis Response Team. Given the great potential for crisis counseling to become stressful for support personnel over time, a rotation of members is highly recommended.

The principal (or assistant principal) can arrange for snacks (e.g., juice, cookies, etc.) to be provided to students and support personnel. This type of accommodation often gives students a sense of comfort at such a difficult time. Teachers should be notified when their students are absent from their class (minimal information should be disclosed). It is common during times of crisis for staff members to neglect eating meals and/or to work incessantly at helping others; in the process, fatigue and exhaustion are exacerbated by lack of nutrition—*caretakers must also take care of themselves.*

It is *essential* that individuals of all ages exposed to a traumatic event have an opportunity to ventilate, to "tell their story," and feel supported by those around them. Additionally, it is important that an educational component exists in the intervention process. For example, student's who have been involved in a school bus accident need to know that they may likely experience frequent recollections of the event—like "playing a videotape over an over in your mind." They should be informed that it is not unusual to experience difficulty sleeping, eating and concentrating and that they may experience headaches or feelings of nausea. This educational component helps to *normalize* responses to an abnormal situation, and helps survivors to know that they are not alone and that they are not "going crazy." **Age-appropriate reactions and specific intervention strategies are addressed in Section 4.**

Additionally, psychologists and social workers may work with high risk students and involve parents if deemed necessary. High risk students (e.g., suicidal) may include those:

- who were close with the victim(s),
- who have experienced prior tragedy (e.g., death in family),
- known to engage in substance abuse,
- who are depressed,
- who describe their situation as "hopeless,"
- who are experiencing sleep and/or eating disturbances,
- who talk about "not being around...,"
- who give-away possessions,
- who articulate a suicide plan, and those
- with a history of self-destructive behaviors, etc.

Referrals to appropriate outside professionals, including local community mental health clinics, hospitals and practitioners must occur if a student (or staff member) is injured, in shock, or presents with seriously adverse emotional and/or behavioral reactions (e.g., suicidal ideation and/or intent). In the event of refusal by a parent or guardian to heed the school district's recommendations for outside intervention for a student clearly in need of assistance, referral to the local child protection agency *must* be considered. Moreover, hot line information and phone numbers for community mental health clinics should be provided to all students and faculty for contact (if needed) after regular school hours.

Careful documentation of all students counseled and efforts to intervene is crucial. A detailed log should be kept because it could help in the treatment of these individuals upon referral to an outside resource. Documentation of the course of events is also necessary for proper in-school follow-up after the crisis situation has been resolved.

A forum at the school, for parents to discuss and receive support on managing the effects of the crisis on their child at school and home, should be considered (e.g., in the evening). Members of the Crisis Response Team could offer important insight at such a meeting.

On the days following the crisis, the availability of support personnel is crucial. Students and faculty should be reminded that support staff, such as the psychologist, social worker and/or guidance counselors, are available for continued help if they feel a need to talk. Oftentimes, the emotional impact of a crisis situation is experienced weeks and, perhaps, months after the event has resolved. The school district should maintain a follow-up plan to ensure that individuals affected by the crisis receive proper support and intervention. Follow-up faculty meetings can address concerns of the staff and faculty as they arise.

Members of the Crisis Response Team must always remain sensitive to how others are perceiving them. If their mood is incongruent with the general climatic mood, they will likely be perceived as lacking genuineness and may be rebuffed by the very individuals who most need their services. For example, it would not be advisable for a team member to engage in a general social conversation about extraneous issues in full view of the "victims."

E. Addressing the Media

Depending upon the nature of the crisis, a plan to deal with the media should be considered. Crisis situations, especially in the school system, tend to precipitate the interest of news stations. Knowledge of what and how much information to share with the media should be determined by administration—perhaps in consultation with the Crisis Response Team (see sample announcement to the media, Practical Document D). Factors to consider include:

- the confidentiality of those involved in the crisis,
- the wishes of the family members of victims, and
- the potential liability and confusion that could result from dissemination of erroneous information.

An individual (e.g., superintendent, building principal) should be selected in preparation for media coverage. **It is strongly recommended that other personnel be discouraged from disclosing information to the media unless permission is granted from their direct supervisors (e.g., principal).** An alternate spokesperson, knowledgeable about the facts surrounding the crisis event, should be selected in the event that the designated speaker becomes unavailable for the media.

F. Debriefing

The Crisis Response Team should reconvene before leaving the school. This *debriefing period* is a necessary part of any comprehensive crisis intervention plan (Sandoval & Brock, 1996). The debriefing permits a review of the precipitating events that may have led to the crisis situation and the manner in which the Crisis Response Team has managed the circumstances. Follow-up actions are reviewed and personnel may be selected to contact

students and their families who were most significantly affected by the event. Assuming proper consent is granted, follow-up contact with outside referral sources, such as mental health professionals, may be helpful.

The emotional reactions and thoughts of the Crisis Response Team should be addressed during the debriefing period as well. Caregivers are not immune to the traumatization that often occurs in the wake of a tragic event. Figley (1995) has described "compassion fatigue" as a potential consequence of working with individuals in crisis. In their effort to protect, assist, and heal, helpers pay a cost— emotionally, cognitively and behaviorally— and can develop posttraumatic symptoms as a result of their exposure to these events. It may be beneficial for the psychologist to provide materials to the Crisis Response Team on stress and its management as well as information on trauma and its effects on individuals (see *Traumatic Stress: An Overview,* Practical Document G). If necessary, the appropriate referrals should be made to support staff.

G. Funerals

In the event of the death of a student, attendance at the victim's funeral is a decision that should be made by all students' families. Additionally, the wishes of the family of the deceased should always be considered when individuals desire to attend or take part in the funeral. Assuming that consent is granted by family members, attendance at the funeral service may facilitate closure to very difficult and confusing circumstances. Members of the Crisis Response Team should be available to students before and after funeral services. If possible, school support personnel should accompany students to the funeral services. The age of the individual is of utmost priority in determining funeral attendance. The concept of death is vague and abstract for many elementary students and careful discretion is therefore advised.

H. Memorialization

It has been suggested that following a crisis event, some form of *memorialization* may facilitate the grieving process (Sandoval & Brock, 1996). This can take the form of a moment of silence, a plaque, planting a tree, a dedication, flying the flag at half-mast, etc. Some researchers have suggested that memorials may serve to glorify and reinforce the attention that death or tragic loss brings and should be avoided altogether (McKee, Jones, & Richardson, 1991). Ideally, the decision to establish a memorial should be made with special consideration given to the nature of the crisis (e.g., accidental death, suicide), needs of the students involved (including their age), and consensus of the school district administration.

4. Age-Appropriate Reactions & Intervention Strategies

The manner in which people react to crisis situations is dependent upon a number of variables including personal history, personality variables, severity and proximity of the event, level of social support and the type and quality of intervention. While no two people respond to situations, including crisis situations, in exactly the same manner, the following are often seen as <u>immediate</u> reactions to a crisis (age-appropriate reactions, as well as age-specific interventions, will be addressed shortly):

- shock—numbness,
- denial or inability to acknowledge the situation has occurred,
- dissociative behavior—appearing dazed, apathetic, expressing feelings of unreality,
- confusion,
- disorganization,
- difficulty making a decision, and
- suggestibility.

Initially, the most important objective in crisis response is to develop rapport. Empathy, warmth and genuineness are crucial in leading to understanding and trust and ultimately, to disclosure of thoughts and feelings (Lerner, 1988). It is important to give back, as much as possible, a sense of control that may have been lost as a result of exposure to the traumatic event. Caregivers must recognize trust issues, particularly when people have been violated. For example, a child who has been molested by an adult may have difficulty sharing thoughts or feelings about the experience with another adult. Similarly, a high school girl who has been raped may find it difficult speaking with a male counselor about the experience.

It is crucial to provide people with an opportunity to "tell their story." The goal here is not so much aimed at helping the victim to "feel better" as much as to prevent a maladaptive response. This is a critical point. Too frequently caregivers misinterpret denial experienced by the victim as a sense of coping. This seeming adaptation is dangerous because it may lead to reinforcement of further denial or worse, "running from" intervention. Finally, it is important not to be confrontational during early crisis response.

While individuals are being provided with an opportunity to articulate their thoughts and feelings in a warm and supportive climate, as well as educated about some of the common responses to traumatic events (see age-appropriate reactions which follow), it may be helpful to:

- Talk about the **facts** surrounding the experience (possibly easier and less threatening)
- Talk about **behaviors** at the time of the experience (e.g., Where exactly were you and what were you doing?)

- Talk about **physical reactions** at the time of the experience (e.g., How did your body respond?)
- Talk about **thoughts** at the time and immediately after the experience (e.g., What was going through your mind?)
- Talk about **feelings** at the time and immediately after the experience (e.g., What were you feeling?)

Finally, it may be helpful to ask "What was the worst thing about the experience for you?" One should expect considerable variability from person to person and be careful not to judge their response. Again, it is crucial to give back a sense of control and help to empower individuals.

Understanding the typical reactions of individuals exposed to a crisis situation is a critical step in identifying people who may be in need of further professional assistance. Several investigators (Greenstone & Levittown, 1993; Klingman, 1987; Pitcher & Poland, 1992; Weaver, 1995) have described age-appropriate reactions of individuals exposed to a traumatic event. Although there is heterogeneity in the reactions of individuals surrounding a crisis, most of these responses are expected reactions and subside in several weeks following the crisis. A list of possible interventions is included within each age category.

Preschool Children (Ages 1 through 5)

Engaging in behaviors that are immature and that have been abandoned in the past including:

- thumb sucking
- speech difficulties
- bed wetting
- decreases or increases in appetite
- fear of the dark
- clinging and whining
- loss of bladder control
- separation difficulties

Interventions:

Preschool children do not yet possess the cognitive skills to understand a crisis and lack the coping strategies to deal with it effectively. They therefore look to adults in their environment for support and comfort. Their own reactions to a crisis are governed by how significant adults react. They are vulnerable to sudden changes and/or disruptions in their environment which frequently results in them viewing their world as "unsafe" and "scary." The young child's main concern during a crisis will likely be if they are going to be abandoned. Interventions need to focus on offering support and reassurance, while at the same time helping the child to express his/her feelings. Because younger children typically do not have this ability to adequately express their feelings, intervention strategies must take this into account. Play activities may afford the young child an opportunity to express feelings and thoughts that are not expressed verbally. The use of clay, paint or building blocks may be a viable medium for preschool children.

Childhood (Ages 5 through 11)

- sadness & crying
- school avoidance
- poor concentration
- irritability
- fear of personal harm
- nightmares
- bed wetting
- anxiety & fears
- confusion
- eating difficulty
- physical complaints (e.g., headaches)
- regressive behavior (clinging, whining)
- aggressive behavior at home or school
- withdrawal/social isolation
- attention-seeking behavior

Interventions:

It is important to consider that children, especially younger children, typically do not have the ability to adequately express their feelings verbally. Consequently, the manifestation of these emotions are often behavioral and need a forum for ventilation. Most young children do not understand the finality of death and may deny its permanency. Children at the elementary level may develop genuine fears regarding death and fear separation from their families and friends.

Play sessions, in which feelings and thoughts can be expressed, should be considered. Planned discussion about fears and anxieties may also help. Painting or drawing, writing in a journal, reading and/or discussing stories, and exercising may all facilitate the healing process. Given the developmental level of verbal communication for most children in this age group, drawings, especially, seem to offer a safe and playful forum for the expression of emotion. The child could be asked to describe their drawing and/or tell a story. For instance, the child can be encouraged to draw what they are afraid of and the good things that they can remember about the incident (e.g., the police officer with the dog). It is important that the child is never blamed or judged for their reactions to the crisis.

Early Adolescence (Ages 11 through 14)

- sleep disturbance
- withdrawal/isolation from peers
- increase or decrease in appetite
- loss of interest in activities
- rebelliousness
- generalized anxiety
- school difficulty, including fighting
- fear of personal harm
- physical ailments (e.g., bowel problems)
- poor school performance
- depression
- concentration difficulties

Interventions:

Children at this age often exhibit concern regarding separation and non-existence. Speculation of what becomes of the deceased, once

their body has expired, is possible. Young adolescents, especially boys, may display bravado and present as cynical, perhaps as a defense against overwhelming emotional reactions.

Group discussions that encourage the children to talk about their feelings regarding the crisis may be beneficial. Students at this age often express confusion about death and seek information. Issues about personal and family safety may be discussed. Teachers may encourage students to write a letter (e.g., to the families of victims, to rescue workers, etc.).

Additionally, they can say to their students:

- "It is O.K. to have the feelings that you have today."
- "Did you know that your feelings are a normal way to feel better?"
- "Your feelings are a normal reaction to an abnormal situation."
- "It is O.K. to ask for help."
- "I am here for you if you would like to talk."

The creation of plays or stories with favorable outcomes could be beneficial. Such activities can promote a sense of mastery which helps mitigate feelings of helplessness and vulnerability which may abound at such times. Coping strategies such as relaxation techniques (e.g., deep breathing) and listening to music could be discussed and may help to further empower students. Assessment of the child's thoughts may indicate distorted perceptions and irrational beliefs (e.g., "Mom is going to die too."). Healthier and more adaptive thoughts can be developed with the youngster(s) and recorded on a piece of paper. The manner in which "happier" thoughts can create "happier" feelings can be described (for more information, see Forman, 1993; Meyers & Craighead, 1984). Temporary modification in school and homework assignments should be considered. More individualized attention may be needed for academic instruction.

Adolescence (Ages 14 through 18)

- intrusive recollections
- numbing
- anxiety and feelings of guilt
- sleep disturbance
- eating disturbance
- apathy
- antisocial behavior (e.g., stealing)
- aggressive behavior
- poor school performance
- depression
- increased substance abuse
- peer problems
- amenorrhea or dysmenorrhea
- withdrawal
- poor concentration and distractibility
- psychosomatic symptoms (e.g., headaches)
- agitation or decrease in energy level
- decreased interest in the opposite sex

Interventions:

Adolescents can usually engage in more abstract and hypothetical thinking and there is a better sense of the permanence of death. However, many teens maintain distorted cognitions regarding their own mortality; that is, they believe that something tragic will "never" happen to them and that "good things happen to good people and bad things happen to bad people." A crisis situation involving death challenges the thoughts that individuals have often developed by this age.

It is important to *encourage* discussion of feelings, beliefs and concerns regarding the crisis situation without *insisting* on this expression. Certain types of crises (e.g., death) tend to evoke memories of past loss and subsequently, negative emotions. Faulty thinking regarding the events may be addressed (e.g., "I should have saved him"). Look for common themes, beliefs and feelings among individuals. Strive to acknowledge and normalize these reactions. As indicated earlier, empathic listening to students in a non-judgmental and genuine fashion is essential. It is important to remain patient, especially when the individual is resistant to overt expression of their opinions and/or emotions. Things that faculty could say include:

- "Given what you have been through, I understand that you feel this way."

- "It's not unusual to feel alone."

- "Things may seem very disorganized and chaotic right now, but things may become clearer with time."

- "Many people tend to blame themselves for things that they had absolutely no control over; do you think that is true here?"

- "I understand that these feelings can be uncomfortable and, at times, overwhelming."

- "Keep in mind that I'm here for you if you need me."

Maintain sensitivity to the adolescent's level of understanding. Moreover, do not assume that you should have all of the answers to his or her questions; say "I don't know" when it is deemed appropriate. Remember to respond honestly and directly.

Coping strategies such as relaxation techniques and problem-solving strategies may be discussed. Expectations for specific levels of school and home performance may need to be temporarily modified. A safe forum for ventilation may be provided by a class discussion or writing assignment. Some of the topic areas to consider may include:

- Losses that we have experienced in the past.

- Personal experiences with death and how we coped in the past.

- Feelings about loss or death.

- Things that we can do to take care of ourselves.

- What are the differences between grieving and depression?

Adulthood

- shock and disbelief
- denial
- feelings of detachment
- depression
- unwanted, intrusive recollections
- anxiety
- concentration difficulty
- hypervigilance
- psychosomatic complaints
- withdrawal
- eating disturbance
- sleep difficulty
- poor work performance
- emotional lability
- emotional and mental fatigue
- marital discord
- irritability and low frustration tolerance
- loss of interest in activities once enjoyed

Interventions:

Adults who are exposed to a crisis situation often experience feelings of vulnerability and helplessness. Faculty and staff who are exposed to a crisis are at risk of experiencing emotional distress related to the incident. For example, the teacher who has just learned that her colleague has died of a heart attack in the classroom next door may need immediate support. This individual's shock at this untimely news, his/her sense of aloneness and loss, and immediate well-being should be prioritized. The teacher should have the option, if possible, to leave his/her immediate classroom and seek the support of his/her colleagues and/or professional support staff. Referrals to outside professionals (e.g., psychologists) should be made by appropriate school personnel if warranted. As always, privacy and confidentiality are essential.

Allowing the person to share their experience (i.e., "tell their story") either on a one-to-one basis or in a small group setting is a useful strategy. Beliefs surrounding the event may be distorted and precipitate feelings of guilt, anxiety and depression. Other coping strategies may include:

- temporarily altering one's work schedule to decrease demands,

- seeking social support (e.g., colleagues, self-help groups),

- exercise such as jogging, walking, bicycling,

- relaxation exercises such as yoga, meditation,

- maintaining a balanced diet and sleep cycle,

- writing about the experience,

- listening to music, and

- hot baths and massage.

Summary of Intervention Strategies

Preschool and Elementary Children

- Play activities including the use of clay or blocks
- Painting
- Drawing pictures reflecting feelings and memories
- Writing in a journal (for older children)
- Reading and discussing stories
- Writing cards or letters to the deceased or surviving family members (if applicable)
- Creating a mural or "memory board" about their experiences during the crisis
- Developing a "memory box" to process "happy" thoughts
- Develop "thoughts as they relate to feelings" chart
- Individual and group counseling

Adolescents

- Journal writing
- Art activities
- Poetry writing
- Story writing
- Writing cards or letters to the deceased or surviving family members (if applicable)
- Relaxation techniques including deep breathing and muscle relaxation
- Problem-solving strategies
- Small group discussions
- Support groups
- Exercise
- Listening to music
- Individual and group counseling

Adults

- Temporarily alter work schedule
- Seek social support
- Exercise
- Relaxation exercises such as yoga and meditation
- Writing about the experience
- Listening to music
- Hot baths and massage
- Individual and group counseling

5. Practical Information Concerning Grief Counseling

Grief refers to the feelings that are precipitated by loss. Loss may take different forms including the loss of a personally meaningful relationship or the loss of an attachment figure. Moreover, *secondary losses* include aspects of life that are lost as a consequence of another loss (Baker & Sedney, 1996). These losses involve the way in which life changes after a death such as the need to move to a new home, changes in routine (e.g., child care) and perhaps, changing schools.

Bowlby (1980) identified four factors that will affect a child's ability to grieve or mourn a loss and should be considered by school personnel who attempt to offer support to children and adolescents. A child can begin the process of mourning if they:

- maintained a secure relationship to their parents/caregivers before the death/loss,
- receive prompt and precise information about the death/loss,
- are participants (if they desire) in the social rituals following the loss/death (e.g., funeral) and
- have access to significant others in the days and months following the loss/death.

It is essential that school personnel and caregivers understand that coping with loss is a process involving a series of tasks carried out over time (Baker, Sedney, & Gross, 1992). The passage of time is a necessary but not a sufficient component of successful grieving.

Helping Preschool and Elementary Children Cope with Loss

Children must feel safe before they can begin to grieve. Grieving involves "emotional risk-taking" for the individual. Baker and Sedney (1996) have emphasized the importance of providing children with accurate information that they can comprehend. Children can benefit from knowing about the "story" of how the person or persons died, why the person or persons died, and when the death occurred. Of course, the explanation provided will depend upon the age of the child.

It is important to consider that deaths that occur through traumatic or violent circumstances may prolong the time that the child takes to feel safe in their world. Moreover, traumatic reactions including sleep and eating disturbances, concentration impairment and withdrawal must be addressed before grieving can successfully occur. Thus, referral to and support from the child's pediatrician or mental health providers in the community should be considered depending on the circumstances.

Acceptance of a loss at cognitive and emotional levels is a process that will vary considerably from individual to individual. Factors affecting acceptance of loss include the bereaved child's history of prior losses, family and social support, and the manner in which significant others react to the child. Children may ask questions repetitively in their effort to find answers for their loss. This reflects their feelings of confusion and uncertainty. It is essential to understand that a child does not fully understand the finality and irreversibility of death until 6 or 7 years of age. Consequently, asking questions regarding when the bereaved will be "returning" or seemingly "forgetting" that they were told that the dead person(s) will not be returning are common responses. At approximately 10 years of age, children begin to understand that death is universal, irreversible and inevitable (Baker & Sedney, 1996). Feelings of guilt and anger may be coupled with anxiety and depression as the child processes the loss and comes to greater acceptance of the change in their life situation.

Helping Adolescents Cope with Loss

Noppe and Noppe (1996) have suggested that adolescents may be especially vulnerable to conflict and tension that follow the death of a significant other. Adolescents understand that death eventually occurs for all living things (i.e., universality) and that death is irreversible. When a tragic death does occur, teens may exhibit a cascade of emotions ranging from rage to complete withdrawal.

It is important to understand that when teens lose a friend, for example, there is a loss of companionship, loss of an important confidant, love and personal support (Oltjenbruns, 1996). Thus, considerable challenges to one's sense of security and safety may ensue. The death of a friend or significant other may also affect the adolescent's sense of self-identity. Thus, integrating the concept of mortality into one's conceptions about their world may be a necessary but formidable task.

"Survivor guilt" may also complicate the process of bereavement and acceptance of loss for the adolescent such that a belief is maintained that one should have died with or instead of the person who died (Oltjenbruns, 1996). This may be especially relevant when one is responsible for the death of their friend or significant other (e.g., motor-vehicle accident). Again, if bereavement is complicated by traumatic reactions to a loss, referral to and support from mental health providers in the community should be considered depending on the circumstances.

Phases of the Grieving Process

It is essential to consider that there is variation from person to person concerning how quickly an individual will move through the tasks associated with grieving or mourning. The following is a brief outline describing some of the reactions by people who experience a significant loss (Bowlby,1980; Kubler-Ross, 1969). Hill and Foster (1996) indicate that people do not necessarily progress sequentially and linearly through these phases and new losses may begin the process from the beginning all over again.

I. Numbing (Initial reaction)
- Shock and denial (e.g., "I can't believe it...It's a bad dream... It's not happening to me...")
- Periods of intense emotion (e.g., anger, rage, guilt, fear)

II. Yearning & Searching (Within hours or days)
- Beginning to register reality of the loss
- Preoccupation with lost individual
- Symptoms of insomnia, poor appetite, headaches, anxiety, tension, anger...
- Sounds and signals interpreted as deceased person's presence

III. Disorganization (Weeks to months following)
- Feelings of anger and depression
- Questioning (e.g., "Why did this have to happen?")
- Bargaining (e.g., "If only I could see him just one last time....")

IV. Reorganization (Months to years following)
- Acceptance
- New patterns and goals

Assisting Students During Specific Grieving Situations

Life-Threatening Illness of a Classmate

Children and adolescents are, at times, subjected to the death of a classmate in their school system as a result of life-threatening diseases (e.g., terminal illness). Unlike other deaths, such a condition may be known to students and staff. There are several strategies to consider in preparation for a loss and after the loss of a peer.

Prior to Death

- Give careful consideration to the wishes of the child.
- Receive and clarify information about the child's health status with the permission of the child and his/her parent or guardian.
- Educate students about the disease in terms they can understand (depending upon the age of student).
- As long as possible, keep the ill student involved in classroom activities and projects.
- Assist the ill student in expressing his or her own needs.
- Be familiar with the Crisis Response Plan of the school building/district.

After Death

- Upon death of the student, have support personnel in the classroom to offer assistance.
- If possible, facilitate discussion about thoughts and feelings associated with the loss.
- Have students write a card for the student's family.

- Consider funeral attendance (use discretion and consider the age of the child).
- Consider the needs and wishes of the family regarding phone calls to the home.
- Identify students who were particularly close to the child and make referrals for outside assistance if indicated.

Death of a Parent/Guardian

A child who loses a caregiver will undoubtedly experience a significant impact on his or her functioning in the school and home settings. Some suggestions for assisting students who lose a parent/guardian include:

- Reassure the student of his/her safety and security at school.
- Modify academic expectations and assignments temporarily.
- Provide opportunities for ventilation of emotions.
- Educate the student of reactions that they may experience over the next few weeks and/or months (e.g., sleep difficulty, anger, etc.).
- Provide the student with an opportunity to reminisce and reflect on their deceased significant other.
- Offer in-school counseling (i.e., bereavement group).
- Assist with out-of-school interventions/referrals if indicated.

Concluding Comments and Summary

Loss and grief will have a tremendous impact on children and adolescents emotionally, academically and behaviorally. School performance may be hampered by shorter attention span, irritability, acting out, increased need for teacher attention, and feelings of anger, guilt, anxiety and profound sadness. In general, increased support including individual and family counseling, bereavement support groups, journalizing, poetry and art therapy should be explored as methods for assisting individuals with the bereavement process.

There are no "cookbook" approaches to counseling individuals who are struggling with loss. Perhaps, the most important factor is "being there" for the person. Attempt to develop a "helping relationship" that is characterized by empathy, warmth and genuineness. Encouragement to express feeling *without* insistence is recommended. Although relatives and friends intend to be supportive, they may be inclined to discourage the expression of feelings, particularly anger and guilt. Avoidance of such expression for individuals may prolong the grieving process and can be counterproductive. Allow for periods of silence and be careful not to lecture. It is also important to avoid cliches such as "Be strong..." and "You are doing so well..." Such cliches may only serve to reinforce an individual's feelings of aloneness. Again, allow the bereaved to tell you how *they* feel and attempt to "normalize" grief reactions by discussing (as needed) reactions that they may encounter as they attempt to recover from the loss (see aforementioned phases of mourning). Finally, do not be afraid to offer a comforting touch. A squeeze of the hand or a gentle pat on the back can demonstrate for the individual that you are there and that you truly care.

---

6. Managing "Everyday Crises" in the School Setting

I. Domestic Violence

In the past two decades, there has been growing recognition of the prevalence of domestic violence in our society. Moreover, it has become apparent that some individuals are at greater risk for victimization than others. Domestic violence has adverse effects on children, families, and society in general.

Domestic violence includes physical abuse, sexual abuse, psychological abuse, and abuse to property and pets (Ganley, 1989). Exposure to this form of violence has considerable potential to be perceived as life-threatening by those victimized and can leave them with a sense of vulnerability, helplessness, and in extreme cases, horror. Physical abuse refers to any behavior that involves the intentional use of force against the body of another person that risks physical injury, harm, and/or pain (Dutton, 1992). Physical abuse includes pushing, hitting, slapping, choking, using an object to hit, twisting of a body part, forcing the ingestion of an unwanted substance, and use of a weapon. Sexual abuse is defined as any unwanted sexual intimacy forced on one individual by another. It may include oral, anal, penile or vaginal stimulation or penetration, forced nudity, forced exposure to sexually explicit material or activity, or any other unwanted sexual activity (Dutton, 1994). Compliance may be obtained through actual or threatened physical force or through some other form of coercion. Psychological abuse may include derogatory statements or threats of further abuse (e.g., threats of being killed by another individual). It may also involve isolation, economic threats and emotional abuse.

Prevalence of Domestic Violence

Domestic violence is widespread and occurs among all socio-economic groups. In a national survey of over 6,000 American families, it was estimated that between 53% and 70% of male batterers (i.e., they assaulted their wives) also frequently abused their children (Straus & Gelles, 1990). Other research suggests that women who have been hit by their husbands were twice as likely as other women to abuse a child (CWP, 1995).

The risks of exposure to parental violence is increasing. Children from homes where domestic violence occurs are physically or sexually abused and/or seriously neglected at a rate 15 times the national average (McKay, 1994). Approximately, 45% to 70% of battered women in shelters have reported the presence of child abuse in their home (Meichenbaum, 1994). About two-thirds of abused children are being parented by battered women (McKay, 1994). Of the abused children, they are three times more likely to have been abused by their fathers.

Studies of the incidence of physical and sexual violence in the lives of children suggest that this form of violence can be viewed as a serious public health problem. State agencies reported approximately 211,000 confirmed cases of child physical abuse and 128,000 cases of child sexual abuse in 1992. At least 1,200 children died as a result of maltreatment. It has been estimated that about 1 in 5 female children and 1 in 10 male children may experience sexual molestation (Regier & Cowdry, 1995).

Signs and Symptoms of Domestic Violence in Children and Adolescents

More than half of the school-age children in domestic violence shelters show clinical levels of anxiety or Posttraumatic Stress Disorder (Graham-Bermann, 1994). Without treatment, these children are at significant risk for delinquency, substance abuse, school drop-out, and difficulties in their own relationships.

Children may exhibit a wide range of reactions to exposure to violence in their home. Younger children (e.g., preschool and kindergarten) oftentimes, do not understand the meaning of the abuse they observe and tend to believe that they "must have done something wrong." Self-blame can precipitate feelings of guilt, worry, and anxiety. It is important to consider that children, especially younger children, typically do not have the ability to adequately express their feelings verbally. Consequently, the manifestation of these emotions are often behavioral. Children may become withdrawn, non-verbal, and exhibit regressed behaviors such as clinging and whining. Eating and sleeping difficulty, concentration problems, generalized anxiety, and physical complaints (e.g., headaches) are all common.

Unlike younger children, the pre-adolescent child typically has greater ability to verbalize negative emotions. In addition to symptoms commonly seen with childhood anxiety (e.g., sleep problems, eating disturbance, nightmares), victims within this age group may show a loss of interest in social activities, low self-concept, withdrawal or avoidance of peer relations, rebelliousness and oppositional-defiant behavior in the school setting. It is also common to observe temper tantrums, irritability, frequent fighting at school or between siblings, lashing out at objects, treating pets cruelly or abusively, threatening of peers or siblings with violence (e.g., "give me a pen or I will smack you"), and attempts to gain attention through hitting, kicking, or choking peers and/or family members. Incidentally, girls are more likely to exhibit withdrawal and unfortunately, run the risk of being "missed" as a child in need of support.

Adolescents are at risk of academic failure, school drop-out, delinquency, and substance abuse. Some investigators have suggested that a history of family violence or abuse is the most significant difference between delinquent and nondelinquent youth.

An estimated 1/5 to 1/3 of all teenagers who are involved in dating relationships are regularly abusing or being abused by their partners verbally, mentally, emotionally, sexually, and/or physically (SASS, 1996). Between 30% and 50% of dating relationships can exhibit the same cycle of escalating violence as marital relationships (SASS, 1996).

Assisting Children and Adolescents Exposed to Domestic Violence

For some children and adolescents, questions about home life may be difficult to answer, especially if the individual has been "warned" or threatened by a family member to refrain from "talking to strangers" about events that have taken place in the family. Therefore the student may require an extended period of time to disclose important information. Referrals to the appropriate school personnel could be the first step in assisting the child or teen in need of support. When there is suggestion of domestic violence with a student, consider involving the school psychologist, social worker, guidance counselor and/or a school administrator (when indicated). Although the circumstances surrounding each case may vary, suspicion of child abuse is required to be reported to the local child protection agency by teachers and other school personnel. In some cases, a contact with the local police department may also be necessary. When in doubt, consult with school team members.

If the child expresses a desire to talk, provide them with an opportunity to express their thoughts and feelings. In addition to talking, they may be also encouraged to write in a journal, draw, or paint; these are all viable means for facilitating expression in younger children. Adolescents are typically more abstract in their thinking and generally have better developed verbal abilities than younger children. It could be helpful for adults who work with teenagers to *encourage* them to talk about their concerns *without insisting* on this expression. Listening in a warm, non-judgmental, and genuine manner is often comforting for victims and may be an important first step in their seeking further support. When appropriate, individual and/or group counseling should be considered at school if the individual is amenable. Referrals for counseling (e.g., family counseling) outside of the school should be made to the family as well. Providing a list of names and phone numbers to contact in case of a serious crisis can be helpful.

II. The Suicidal Student

According to the American Foundation for Suicide Prevention (1998), suicide rates vary with the age group examined. Suicide in younger children is actually quite uncommon with children under the age of 10 accounting for the smallest amount of suicides. Suicide for children between the ages of 10 and 14 accounts for approximately 7% of all deaths occurring in this age group in the United States and less that 2% of all suicides across all age groups. It is important to note that the suicide rate for children, 10 to 14 years old has, however, more than doubled over the last 15 years.

Adolescents attempt suicide at a much higher rate than they actually complete the act with suicide as the third leading cause of death among young people 15 to 24 years of age, following accidents and homicide (Range, 1996). Adolescent females are more likely to attempt suicide whereas males are more likely to successfully commit suicide (i.e., they tend to use more lethal means). Guns, especially handguns, are the most frequent cause of successfully completed suicides. Suicide attempts are typically manifested as drug overdoses and occur in the home (Kovacs, Goldston & Gatsonis, 1993).

Children and adolescents not only make suicide attempts (often referred to as ***parasuicidal behavior***) but also *think* about suicide. Between 16% and 30% of children referred for clinical services who manifest suicidal thoughts actually attempt it (Kovacs et al., 1993).

Presentation of the Suicidal Student

A review of the scientific literature indicates that a number of family and individual variables should be evaluated when determining suicidal risk (Fremouw, de Perczel & Ellis, 1990; Range, 1996). These variables follow:

Family Variables Related to Higher Risk

- Higher levels of family discord/conflict (i.e., lack of cohesion)
- Family history of depression and/or mental illness
- Lack of emotional support
- Illicit drug and alcohol use among family members
- Sexual and/or physical abuse or neglect suspected within the family
- Family stress including parental unemployment, divorce and family relocation
- Family history of suicide

Individual Variables Related to Higher Risk

- Mood disorders, especially depression
- Feelings of hopelessness
- Sleep and/or eating difficulties
- Anger, aggressive tendencies and hostility
- Conduct problems including running away
- Substance use and abuse (e.g., alcohol and illicit drugs)
- Poor problem-solving skills
- More negative life events (e.g., recent loss)
- School problems (e.g., academic failure, behavior problems)
- Prior psychiatric hospitalization
- History of self-destructive behavior/suicide attempt(s)
- Difficulty promising that they would not harm self
- Unusual neglect of personal appearance
- Impulsivity
- Anxiety/Panic-related symptoms
- Eating disorders
- Sudden tendencies toward isolative and withdrawn behavior

The student who presents with a desire to end his/her life will need immediate attention. Individuals who are actively suicidal often exhibit multiple signs of distress. These signs may include:

- saying farewell to peers
- giving away prized possessions,
- writing essays and/or notes about suicide
- verbalizing to a peer or teacher about "not wanting to be around any longer"
- excessive fatigue
- sudden changes in personality and
- self-destructive behavior (e.g., self-mutilation).

Related Information for the Management of a Suicidal Crisis

Self-mutilation, cutting and/or skin carving are not always indicative of suicidal intention. Such behaviors may be observed with concomitant psychopathology including depression, complex forms of Posttraumatic Stress Disorder and personality disorders. Thus, intervention for self-mutilating behavior should be addressed accordingly and should involve consultation with the school nurse. In-school counseling, psychotherapy and/or psychiatric consultation is typically recommended to the student and their family to address related issues.

If a student attempts suicide on school grounds, immediate contact with school administrators and the police is recommended. Building security should be involved and work collaboratively with local law enforcement to safeguard students and staff in the area. Security guards can engage in crowd control and allow emergency support personnel to intervene. Individuals who witness a suicide attempt will need careful monitoring and support to help mitigate the effects of exposure to such a traumatic event.

The Management of Suicidal Students

Threats of suicide must be taken seriously. Such verbalization and actions are not "simple" means for individuals to "get attention." These students are oftentimes, desperately seeking help and will need support. The actively suicidal student's judgement is often impaired and they may have no insight into the notion that "suicide is a permanent solution to a temporary problem" (Fremouw, de Perczel & Ellis, 1990).

It is important to always have face-to-face contact with the suicidal teenager. Do not attempt to exclusively evaluate through indirect methods (e.g., through peer observation or staff report only). Direct interview of the student in a safe and non-threatening environment is recommended.

Discussing the possibility of suicide with the student does not increase the likelihood that he or she will commit suicide. The school staff member (e.g., school psychologist or social worker) who is working with the student should never attempt to manage a suicidal student alone. They should work in a collaborative fashion with a colleague, perhaps, the school administrator, school nurse, guidance counselor, teacher or adult who may be more familiar with the student to facilitate the evaluative process.

Questions and interaction with the student should be made in a calm and quiet manner and without overt expressions of shock or disbelief conveyed to the student. Do not portray questions euphemistically (e.g., "Why do you want to meet your maker?" or "Why do you want to go to Heaven?"). Start questions out relatively general and then get more specific. Be direct (e.g., "Why do you want to kill yourself?"). Practical interview questions include:

- Have you been feeling depressed? Adjust language depending on age (e.g., sad, bummed-out, blue...).
- How long have you been feeling depressed?
- Do you feel hopeless?
- Have you experienced difficulty sleeping? (e.g., falling asleep versus middle of night awakening?)
- Has your appetite changed (e.g., Have you gained or lost weight?)
- Have you found yourself turning to alcohol or other substances to help you cope?
- During this time, have you ever had thoughts of killing yourself?
- When did these thoughts occur?
- What did you think about doing to yourself?
- Did you act on your thoughts?
- What stopped you from doing it?
- How often have these thoughts occurred?
- When was the last time you had these thoughts?
- Can you promise that you will not harm yourself?
- Have your thoughts ever included harming someone else in addition to yourself?
- How often has that occurred?
- What have you thought about doing to the other person or people?
- Have you taken any steps toward acquiring the gun, pills, etc.?
- Have you thought about when/where you would do this?
- Have you thought about the effect your death would have on your family or friends?
- What help could make it easier for you to cope with your current thoughts and plans?
- What makes you want to live?
- How does talking about this make you feel?

It is essential to determine the frequency and duration of suicidal ideation and suicidal intention. If suicidal thinking is reported, then an assessment of suicidal intent must be conducted. A suicidal plan should be investigated. This will include ascertaining information regarding:

- the *means* or *method* that one would utilize to kill himself or herself
- the *availability* or *access* that the individual has to the stated means
- the *lethality* or likelihood of success given the chosen suicidal method
- the *intent* or how probable the individual is to follow through on the act

More severe risk is indicated when there is a greater magnitude of family and individual variables present and when specific plans including available and lethal means are reported (Fremouw, de Perczel & Ellis, 1990). Self-report instruments such as the Children's Depression Inventory (CDI; Kovaks & Beck, 1977) or Suicide Ideation Questionnaire (Reynolds, 1987) may be used to supplement information obtained through the interview method but should never be used as the sole criterion for determining suicidal risk.

Contact with parents or legal guardians should always be made. In such circumstances, pledges of confidentiality can not be kept (e.g., a promise not to inform a parent of the student's suicidal ideation or intent). Harboring such information can be potentially dangerous. In certain circumstances, a "No Suicide" contract may be indicated. This would be developed in an effort to delay self-destructive actions by the student. However, it should not be done as a substitute for contacting significant others. This is especially the case with the greater number of risk factors indicated. Discuss with the parent/guardian:

- the seriousness of the situation
- the specific intention or plan of the individual
- the need for close monitoring
- the need to remove weapons (e.g., firearms), illicit substances including alcohol and/or potentially dangerous prescription drugs from the house
- the need for psychiatric evaluation and/or hospitalization

If the student is presenting as a danger to himself or herself, hospital admission should be considered immediately. Using discretion, the need for support of the local police department or mobile crisis units (if available) should be evaluated. Outside counseling (i.e., individual and/or family therapy) and psychiatric consultation are typically indicated and referrals for assistance should be recommended to the family. Follow-up including in-school counseling should be available to the student, especially upon return to school following the crisis. School support staff should obtain consent from parents/guardians to work in concert with outside support professionals as the student transitions back to their regular routine. As always privacy and/or confidentiality should be a high priority. A card with "suicide hot-lines" should be provided to possibly avert future crises. School staff should be alerted of possible "contagion effects" following a suicide or suicide attempt by a student. In such situations, a peer or peers

may present with suicidal ideation/intent after exposure to a suicidal crisis (e.g., peer suicide or mass media/news stories). Intervention should be implemented as necessary.

III. The Violent Student

One in 12 high school aged students is threatened or injured with a weapon every year and individuals between the ages of 12 and 24 have the highest risk of becoming a victim of violence (APA, 1999). Violence in American society is on the increase. According to the U.S. Department of Justice (1994), young people between the ages of 16 and 24 consistently have the highest violent crime rates with the overall trend on the increase. Violent behavior is often the result of numerous contributing factors including faulty learning, poor coping skills and problem-solving abilities, anger/ hostility, attempts to control other individuals, peer pressure, exposure to abuse/neglect in the home, psychopathology including depression and impulse-control difficulties.

It is important to consider that aggression in children, if unaddressed, can become a relatively stable trait over time (Olweus, 1984). Violent and aggressive behavior produces significant social adjustment difficulties for the perpetrator and is disruptive to the school community in general.

Presentation of the Violent Student

School personnel will oftentimes learn that a student is potentially violent through:

- direct observations of aggressive or violent behavior (e.g., the teacher who observes such behavior in the classroom),
- speaking with potentially violent students (i.e., the student may report their hatred and desire to be violent toward a peer, etc.),
- indirect means (e.g., writing assignments with violent and/ or assaultive and/or homicidal themes), or
- peer reports.

It will be especially important to be aware of factors that place some individuals at higher risk for violent behavior. These factors may include:

- frequent loss of temper,
- numerous disciplinary actions at school (e.g., fighting),
- histories of aggression toward people and animals,
- tendencies toward bullying, threatening or intimidating others,
- substance use and abuse,
- isolative and withdrawn behavior,
- detailed plans to commit an act of violence,
- verbal or written expressions of hatred or anger or threats to hurt other individuals,
- deliberate acts of vandalism and destruction of property,
- gang involvement,
- feelings of rejection and/or alienation from peers,
- truancy,
- academic difficulties, and
- access to weapons including firearms and knives.

Strategies for Managing the Violent Student

Students who are violent pose a significant threat to their own well-being as well as that of the school community. These students should be seen as soon as school personnel become aware of the issue. With regard to the aforementioned risk factors, as the number of factors increases, so does the need for intervention become more imminent (See Practical Document L).

The needs of the violent student must be addressed. As always, consultation with school administration as well as parents and/or guardians is essential. If the student has a specific plan to engage in an act of violence toward another person, contact with the police or local law enforcement agency should be strongly considered. Using discretion, contact with the intended target may be necessary.

When a student (or students) presents as agitated, encourage the individual to sit down. This will reduce the probability of the student(s) striking out physically. Whenever possible, position yourself between the student and an exit. Then, provide the student(s) with the opportunity to "tell his/her story." Attempt to convey empathy (i.e., that you are trying to understand and appreciate their circumstance). In cases where students are agitated due to interpersonal conflicts, make every effort to separate the disputing parties.

Physical force or restraining of students should only be utilized when the safety of the student or others is compromised and there are no other options. As always, make every effort to work collaboratively with school personnel when working with the agitated and potentially violent student. After the immediate crisis is resolved and a potentially violent situation is defused, then a referral to school administration should be entertained for possible disciplinary action.

In-school counseling and outside professional counseling are typically recommended as a means for intervention. The individual may have an opportunity to explore:

- anger control techniques,
- social skills training,
- assertion skills,
- self-management skills including training in self-talk or self-instruction,
- communication skills, and
- relaxation techniques.

Family counseling is often suggested as a means to assist communication styles and/or conflict that may exist in the homes of "at risk" students. If substance abuse is a related factor, then treatment should also focus on abstinence and relapse prevention training. In-school counseling as well as group counseling should be considered as means of developing alternate coping strategies. Recognize that not all violent students and their families will be receptive to the school's efforts to intervene. Under such circumstances, administrative action (e.g., expulsion, home-bound instruction) may need to be implemented.

Students who are the victims of violence may need special attention as well. Beginning in the elementary level, students should be educated about factors (i.e., warning signs) related to violent behavior. Students need to learn the signs or "red flags" for violent behavior to help themselves if they encounter these problems or know of someone who does. They should be informed that they have the right to feel safe in their school environment and that intimidating or bullying behavior is not tolerated at school. Students should be informed that there are school staff members that they can privately approach in the event that they are victims of violence or suspect that a peer is potentially violent. Students should be advised to avoid conflict by minimizing their exposure to violent peers. They should be reminded that being alone with such individuals is a possible risk for them especially if the person exhibits various warning signs for violent behavior.

IV. The Substance Abusing Student

After a decade of decreasing trends, since 1992 drug use appears to be increasing among teenagers and young adults (NIDA, 1994). In a large scale survey conducted by the Substance Abuse and Mental Health Services Administration (1994), it was reported that marijuana, tobacco and alcohol account for a large proportion of reported drug use. It was also reported that many users abused a variety of illicit drugs including cocaine, crack, crank, heroin, MDMA or "Ecstasy," phencyclidine, methaqualone and hallucinogens as well as legal drugs not prescribed by a physician including amphetamines, benzodiazepines, barbiturates and anabolic steroids. Inhalants were also used including amyl and butyl nitrite, gasoline, nitrous oxide, glue and other solvents.

Among high school seniors reporting usage in the past month (prior to survey) in 1994, data indicate that 22% reported use of an illicit drug, 19% reported marijuana use, 4% reported stimulant abuse, 3% reported inhalants, 3% reported hallucinogens and 1.5% reported cocaine use (NIDA, 1994). In younger adolescents, the abuse of inhalants is a leading drug problem (NIDA, 1994). National data have also shown individuals as young as 11 beginning to use alcohol and marijuana, and other illicit drugs as early as age 12 (Harmon, 1993). Almost two-thirds of all American youth try illicit drugs before completion of high school and almost 90% have tried alcohol, a very popular "gateway" drug for many adolescents (Anderson, 1998). It has been estimated that there are over 3.3 million teenage problem drinkers (Anderson, 1998).

Presentation of the Substance Abusing Student

The drugs that young people are using today are stronger, purer, cheaper to produce and purchase (Gonet, 1994). Moreover, they are more readily available. The student who presents as substance abusing will oftentimes, show evidence in the school setting of deterioration in academic and social functioning. Warning signs include:

- School failure
- Frequent lateness
- Frequent absences
- Forgetfulness
- Concentration difficulties
- Blackouts (or drug-induced amnesia)
- Excessively and easily angered and hostile
- Erratic mood swings
- Depression
- Changes in friends and relationships
- Defiance of rules
- Unkempt physical appearance
- Excessive weight gain or loss
- Frequent lying
- Legal problems
- Excessive disciplinary referrals at school
- Loss of initiative
- Isolation and secretiveness
- Argumentativeness and defensiveness
- Paranoia
- Family discord
- Parental substance abuse
- Disappearance of money or valuables from home or from others
- Watery or red eyes with dilated pupils
- Excessive use of eye-drops (e.g., Visine® or other over-the-counter products)
- Deodorizers for room
- Drug paraphernalia including matches, pipes, screens, rolling paper, scales, seeds and small bags

Strategies for Managing the Substance Abusing Student

In order to assess the needs of a student suspected of abusing drugs, at the very least, a careful diagnostic interview should be conducted. The school psychologist or social worker is in the best position to perform this evaluation given their training and expertise. Information about the type(s) of substance(s) that are being used, frequency of use, amounts being consumed and effects that the substance(s) has had on functioning should be addressed. The student may present as guarded and defensive in light of your questioning. Remain calm and make every effort to protect the individual's confidentiality and privacy.

If an individual is impaired and not fit for educational instruction, schools should evaluate their district policy regarding the handling of such matters. Teachers should consult with the school psychologist, social worker, nurse and/or administrators so as to be informed on how to proceed with the youngster. An evaluation by the school nurse for vital signs including heart rate, blood pressure, temperature and pupil response should be routine. Contact with parent or guardians is usually indicated in these circumstances. The student may need further assessment by their family physician or pediatrician. Although substance use during the school day is a violation of school rules/policy, disciplinary action should be deferred until the substance abuse is addressed with the family of these youngsters.

Some students may exhibit behaviors (e.g., poor school performance, mood lability) consistent with drug use or abuse. However, the student may deny any usage. In these situations, parent involvement is essential in order to address the problem. A parent conference is recommended to discuss intervention strategies. Recommendations for intervention may include:

- Medical assessment
- Toxicologic tests [using radioimmunoassays (RIA) or enzymatic immunoassay (EIA)]
- Individual and group counseling within school setting
- Substance abuse counseling (outside of school)
- Family counseling
- Drug education courses
- Day treatment programs
- Residential programs

By intervening early with substance abusing students, the long-term costs to the individual, his or her family and society can be kept to a minimum. Many students will relapse and go through treatment several times before they have a full recovery. Individuals who follow treatment plans as prescribed by professionals have better prognoses for a more efficient recovery. For those students who return from outside substance abuse programs, a supportive recovery environment involving family and non-substance abusing peers, is strongly indicated. The school district should work collaboratively with such programs to facilitate transitioning back to the regular school routine. In-school counseling and support should be available as needed to help with relapse prevention.

V. The Pregnant Adolescent

According to national statistics, by age 19, 77% of females and 85% of males report having had sexual intercourse with over one million teen girls (approximately 1 in 10) becoming pregnant each year (APPI, 1998). Each day, over 1400 teenage girls give birth with more than 85% of these births unplanned.

Abstaining from sexual intercourse is truly the most effective method of preventing pregnancy and sexually transmitted diseases (STDs) according to Planned Parenthood (1998). However, given that experimentation, impulsivity and curiosity often guide adolescent decision-making, abstinence is often not the chosen course of prevention by many teens. Sexuality education is a viable but controversial topic in the United States. In the United States, almost half of teens report that they personally need more information on how to prevent AIDS and STDs (Princeton Survey Research Associates, 1996). Currently, there is no federal law or policy that mandates sex education or HIV education in the school (Sexuality Information and Education Council of the U.S., 1995).

Strategies for Assisting the Pregnant Adolescent

It is important to consider that younger mothers are at greater risk of health complications. This is typically due to inadequate prenatal care, poor nutrition, and unhealthy lifestyles (Planned Parenthood, 1998). Pregnant teens are at high risk for academic failure, social difficulties and financial problems. When a school staff member becomes aware of a pregnancy with a student, contact with the student is essential. Consultation and perhaps, collaboration with the school nurse is strongly suggested given the expertise of the nurse with physical and/or medical-related issues. Interview of the student should include:

- obtaining information about the student's last menstrual cycle

- assessment of nutritional intake

- an evaluation of the student's health and psychological well-being

- physical examination

- plans of the individual regarding her pregnancy (e.g., keeping baby, etc.)

Laws in the United States governing parental contact for students under age 18 may vary and depend upon the state. As with any student who presents with risk of their health and/or well-being, contact with parents or guardians may be critical. It is best to first encourage the student to inform their parent. If student compliance is difficult, school contact may be indicated, especially with students under age 16.

Most teens who become pregnant will involve a parent in their decision to keep, adopt or abort their unborn child (Planned Parenthood, 1998). Twenty-five states currently have laws that mandate parental consent, parental notice or professional counseling for a minor to receive an abortion (Planned Parenthood, 1998). Students who elect to have an abortion will likely need additional support.

Empathic listening with the pregnant adolescent is critical. Emotionally, they are likely to be quite fragile and perhaps, irritable and moody. It is important to remember that this is an unexpected ordeal for most teenagers. The student and their family will need consistent support and counseling as they choose the best course of action. In some cases, alternate programs for pregnant teens can be considered.

VI. The Student Experiencing a Divorce

Divorce often comes unexpectedly for children and is often associated with intense emotions for those involved with the divorce process. Between a third and half of all children born in marriages will encounter a divorce and reside with a single parent prior to turning 18 years old (Acklin, 1998). The average divorce occurs within the first 7 years of marriage and consequently, many of these children are under the age of 6 (American Academy of Pediatrics, 1994). Children can thrive in a divorced home when provided with proper support and attention.

Presentation of the Student Experiencing a Divorce

When parents present to their children that they are divorcing, children, depending on their age, will need time to process this potentially overwhelming information. Divorce is traumatic for many children. Although the details will typically be unclear, especially for younger children, the process of accepting this dramatic change will be manifested in a variety of ways.

According to the American Academy of Pediatrics (1994), a critical factor governing the effects of divorce on a child is how the parents are treating one another and the children during and after the divorce. Some parents will not put their children first in these matters and force a child to take sides in the divorce. Some parents will criticize each other in front of the children or have hostile conversations with the children present. Other parents will involve their child in their arguments between them. All of these circumstances will add a tremendous amount of unnecessary stress to an already traumatic situation.

Preschool children may experience the following reactions:
- Self-blame and a sense of responsibility
- Nightmares
- Anger and/or hostility
- Defiance
- Regressive behaviors including bed-wetting
- Fearfulness and/or separation anxiety
- Eating and/or sleeping difficulty
- Outbursts or tantrums

Elementary age children may experience the following reactions:
- Sleeping and/or eating difficulty
- Moodiness and irritability
- Feelings of rejection by parent(s)
- Distractibility
- Forgetfulness
- Academic difficulties
- Fantasies about their parents reuniting
- Excessive anger and hostility
- Feelings of abandonment

Adolescents may experience the following reactions:
- Depressed feelings
- Suicidal ideation
- Loneliness
- Excessive aggressive behavior
- Eating and/or sleeping difficulty
- Worry about the financial status of the family
- Risk-taking behavior including sexual and/or drug experimentation
- Withdrawal or isolative behavior
- Academic difficulties
- Concentration problems

Strategies for Assisting Students Experiencing a Divorce

School support staff can play a very helpful role in helping students adjust to the divorce process. By meeting with students individually or in small groups (i.e., with other similar-aged peers also going through divorce), school psychologists, social workers, and/or guidance counselors can make a difference for children. It will be useful for children to address through discussion, drawings, art work and the like feelings that may be associated with their parents' divorce. Discussion of the fears, anxieties, guilt feelings as well as possible somatic reactions including sleep and eating problems may help children to realize that what they are experiencing is very "normal" under the unusual circumstances. Coping and relaxation strategies can also be explored.

Teachers should work with support personnel and be appraised of the emotional and cognitive status of the child. Academic demands may need to be lessened or modified temporarily. Signs and symptoms that the student may encounter should be discussed with teaching staff. Teachers have a beneficial vantage point as they see the child on a daily basis and monitor their interactions with peers and other adults.

Parent conferences can be helpful as an adjunct to counseling and support at school. Parent meetings should offer emotional and informational support to the parent which could ultimately benefit the child. Parents can be offered several suggestions to assist their child or teen at home including:
- Spend more quality time with the child or children
- Convey a sense of safety and security
- Encourage the child to talk without insisting on expression
- Encourage outside school activities
- Respect the child and his or her privacy
- Do not involve the child in arguments or disputes
- Have and maintain household rules
- Attempt to keep the child's daily routine simple and predictable
- Offer extra-help or tutoring for extra academic help (if needed)
- Provide close monitoring, especially if you suspect risky behavior (primarily for adolescents)

- Keep communication open and encourage family discussions
- Allow the child to remain a child (i.e., do not use them as a "spouse replacement")
- Do not expect the child to make the adjustment quickly
- Be patient when the child asks questions, especially about the other parent
- Give reassurance to the child that he or she is loved

Helping and nurturing a child's strengths and resiliency will foster a return to more adaptive functioning. However, other factors that can complicate the divorce process include difficulties with child support that may ensue, physical and/or verbal violence in the home between family members and custody disputes. In such cases, professional counseling outside of the school should be recommended to parents. Collaboration between outside support services and school staff is suggested with confidentiality maintained as a high priority.

VII. Working with Student Survivors of Motor Vehicle Accidents

Involvement with motor vehicle accidents is an unfortunate but common experience in the United States. According to the National Highway Traffic Safety Administration (1998), motor vehicle crashes are the leading cause of death for 15 to 20 year olds. Moreover, 17% of all drivers involved in police-reported crashes were young drivers. In addition to the physical difficulties encountered by survivors, emotional and cognitive problems are also commonly produced by an automobile accident.

Presentation of the Student Survivor of a Motor Vehicle Accident

The impact that a car accident has on the student will vary considerably from individual to individual and may vary with the age of the student. Vehicle accidents have the potential to leave people feeling powerlessness and vulnerable. Moreover, such students are at risk of developing numerous acute stress reactions (Matsakis, 1996). Some of these symptoms may be manifested as the following, depending on the age of the student:

Preschool and Elementary Age Students:
- sadness & crying
- school avoidance
- physical complaints (e.g., headaches)
- poor concentration
- irritability
- fear of personal harm
- regressive behavior (clinging, whining)
- nightmares
- anxiety and excessive fears
- confusion
- eating difficulty
- withdrawal
- repetitive play (e.g., crashing objects)

Adolescent Students:

- sleep disturbance
- withdrawal
- eating problems
- loss of interest in activities
- rebelliousness
- anxiety
- fear of personal harm
- physical pain
- poor school performance
- depression
- concentration difficulties
- survivor guilt
- Intrusive recollections of the accident
- fears of cars and driving
- exaggerated startle response
- difficulty driving or being near the accident site
- apathy
- aggressive behavior and anger
- agitation or decrease in energy level

Strategies for Assisting Student Survivors of a Motor Vehicle Accident

Interview of the student who was involved in the motor vehicle accident by school staff should be considered (if the individual is amenable and/or physically able). Blanchard and Hickling (1997) have indicated that there are several variables that should be considered when trying to assist survivors. These include:

- Is the individual having re-experiencing symptoms including intrusive recollections, nightmares, flashbacks or distress when reminded of the accident?

- Is the person actively trying to avoid thoughts or reminders of the accident?
- How serious were the physical injuries?
- Was the individual brought to an emergency room and/or hospitalized?
- How frightened or horrified was the individual regarding the possibility of dying?
- Does the individual have a history of prior psychopathology (e.g., depression, anxiety)?
- Does the individual have a history of prior traumatization?
- Was anyone killed in the accident?

It has been estimated that over 35% of individuals involved in a motor vehicle accident may develop Posttraumatic Stress Disorder (Blanchard and Hickling, 1997). Providing a supportive recovery environment at school and recommending such support for parents is essential. Students and parents or guardians should be educated about the signs and symptoms of traumatic stress typically experienced by survivors of accidents. Students should never be told to "get over it already" or "it was just a car accident." They should know that what they are feeling are "normal" reactions to an abnormal situation.

Modification of academic instruction may be necessary. Extra academic support or tutoring can be helpful if academic deterioration is observed. In-school counseling (individual or small group) may be indicated. Coping strategies to consider using include deep breathing exercises, journalizing, art and drawing, poetry writing, exercise and listening to music. It is important to consider that some students will have a "delayed-onset" of traumatic symptoms, perhaps, weeks or months following the accident. If decompensation is noted (i.e., there is a progressive worsening of symptoms or symptoms do not seem to be improving in the weeks following the accident), professional counseling and/or psychiatric consultation outside of school is strongly recommended.

7. Summary

The immediacy and unpredictability of crisis situations often leave individuals with a sense of worry, vulnerability and distrust. A school system is unique in that it brings together individuals of all ages and professionals from numerous disciplines. Capitalizing upon the collaborative relationships that exist among members of a school family provided the foundation of the structure and process described in this guide. It is crucial that school personnel are educated and empowered to effectively respond to school-based crises—rather than relying upon outside teams of experts. The well-meaning efforts of such "strangers" are often rebuffed and their presence may only serve to exacerbate confusion. *A School Crisis Response Team that identifies and responds to a crisis in a unified and collaborative manner can alter the aftermath of a crisis.*

Appropriate intervention makes the physical and emotional well-being of the individuals within the system a priority. An understanding of the reactions of people exposed to a crisis situation is essential, and addressing emotional needs is paramount when striving for successful resolution of a crisis state.

Heterogeneity exists in the reactions of individuals surrounding a crisis, and most of these responses subside in several weeks following the event. A referral for outside intervention should be considered for individuals who continue to experience symptoms, especially when they appear to interfere with the individual's daily functioning. Studies have shown that a percentage (approximately 25% to 30%) of individuals who are exposed to a traumatic event develop Posttraumatic Stress Disorder (PTSD; Yehuda, Resnick, Kahana, & Giller, 1993). For an overview of traumatic stress and PTSD, see Practical Document G.

Crises are occurring in our schools on a daily basis with a greater frequency than ever before. It is crucial to have an understanding of the nature of these "everyday crises" as well as knowledge of practical strategies for effective intervention.

By reaching people early following a traumatic event, we can potentially prevent *acute* stress reactions from becoming *chronic* stress disorders (Lerner, 1997).

PRACTICAL DOCUMENTS

A. Crisis Response in Our Schools: A Practical Checklist

There has been a dramatic increase in the frequency of crises in our schools. The following checklist was developed to facilitate an effective crisis response in the wake of a tragedy. This list will require modification to address the nature of the crisis situation and should not take the place of competent professional services. By reaching our school families early following a traumatic event, we can potentially prevent the *acute* difficulties of today from becoming the *chronic* problems of tomorrow (Lerner, 1997).

I. Fact Gathering

- ❏ Notify building principal
- ❏ Clarify facts surrounding the crisis
- ❏ Contact school district administration
- ❏ Contact parents/guardians (of individuals involved/affected)
  - • Obtain consent for release of information
- ❏ Contact police and/or fire department
- ❏ Principal consults with assistant principal and/or school psychologist
- ❏ Determine the need for assembling the Crisis Response Team

II. The Call to Action

- ❏ Assemble the Crisis Response Team
- ❏ Share facts with team members and assess the impact of the crisis
  - • When did the event occur (e.g., during a lunch period, over the summer)?
  - • Where did the event occur (e.g., on school grounds)?
  - • How did it happen (e.g., accidental, intentional, expected)?
  - • How many students and staff are affected by the event?
  - • Which students and staff are affected?
  - • How are the students and staff affected?
  - • How are the faculty responding?
  - • Should classes be suspended temporarily or assignments altered?
  - • Should students be released from school?
  - • How are students indirectly being affected (e.g., siblings/friends at other buildings in the district, etc.)?
- ❏ Determine if additional support services are needed (e.g., psychologists/social workers/counselors from other buildings)
  - • Weigh efficacy of "unknown" professionals
  - • Provide identification badges for these outside professionals
- ❏ Update school district administration

III. Notification Procedures

- ❏ Consider:
  - • Announcement to students and faculty
  - • Announcement should not give too many details that could be misinterpreted
  - • Location of support personnel (e.g., library)
  - • Need for students to sign out of class and in with support personnel
  - • Mailbox memorandum to faculty and staff
  - • Emergency faculty meeting (first thing in the morning)
  - • Notification of students in classrooms by Crisis Response Team

IV. Crisis Response Team in Motion

❏ Administrators and security circulate through the building.
  • "Pockets" of grieving students should be directed to location of support personnel
❏ Consider letter to be sent to students' homes — facts, summary, reactions, guidelines, contact numbers.
❏ Team members should visit selected classrooms to provide opportunity for discussion.
❏ Teachers should allow opportunity for students to ventilate.
❏ Counseling with individuals and small groups by psychologists, social workers and/or guidance counselors.
  • Attempt to cultivate a "helping relationship" characterized by empathy, warmth and genuineness.
  • Encourage people to express their feelings.
  • Be careful not to lecture and allow periods of silence.
  • Avoid cliches such as, "Be strong..." and "You're doing so well..."
    Such cliches may only serve to reinforce an individual's feelings of aloneness.
  • Attempt to "normalize" grief reactions.
  • Remember that cultural differences exist in the overt expression of emotions.
  • Maintaining confidentiality, when possible, is crucial.
  • Provide snacks (e.g., juice, cookies, etc.) to students and support staff.
  • It is important to remember that *we* have support while helping others during this difficult time.
❏ Identify high risk individuals.
❏ Contact parents/guardians of high risk students.
❏ Provide referrals for outside support (if indicated).
❏ Provide hot-line numbers to parents/guardians for after school hours (if necessary).
❏ Carefully document events.
❏ Consider open forum for parents (after school hours).
❏ Schedule follow-up by support personnel for high risk individuals.
❏ Schedule faculty meeting.
❏ Remain sensitive to how team members are being perceived.

V. Addressing the Media

❏ Develop a response - consider confidentiality, family wishes, liability of erroneous information.
❏ Designate a spokesperson - "no one else talks."
❏ Designate alternate spokesperson.

VI. Debriefing

❏ Review the events of the day.
❏ Revise the intervention strategies (e.g., plan for upcoming days).
❏ Monitor reactions of crisis team members - "compassion fatigue."

VII. Funeral

❏ Consider the wishes of the students' family.
❏ Consider the wishes of the victim(s) family regarding attendance.
❏ Consider the age of the attendants.
❏ Consider the number of staff attending.
❏ Have support personnel available there.

VIII. Memorialization

❏ Consider appropriateness.
❏ Consider a method:
  • a moment of silence
  • a plaque
  • planting a tree
  • a dedication
  • flying the school flag at half-mast

B. Emergency Contact List (For Out-of-School Hours)

Sample

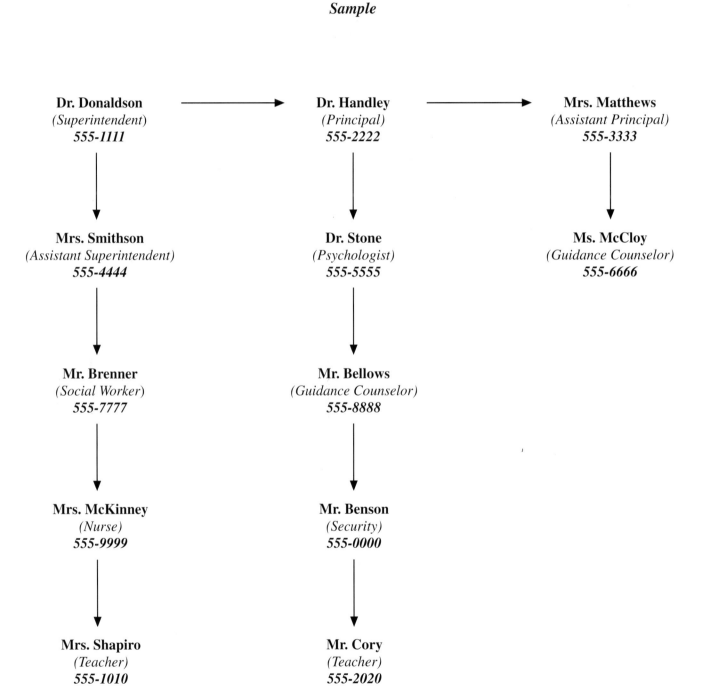

Dr. Donaldson
(Superintendent)
555-1111

Dr. Handley
(Principal)
555-2222

Mrs. Matthews
(Assistant Principal)
555-3333

Mrs. Smithson
(Assistant Superintendent)
555-4444

Dr. Stone
(Psychologist)
555-5555

Ms. McCloy
(Guidance Counselor)
555-6666

Mr. Brenner
(Social Worker)
555-7777

Mr. Bellows
(Guidance Counselor)
555-8888

Mrs. McKinney
(Nurse)
555-9999

Mr. Benson
(Security)
555-0000

Mrs. Shapiro
(Teacher)
555-1010

Mr. Cory
(Teacher)
555-2020

C. Sample Announcement to Students & Faculty

Note: *This sample is fictitious and is provided as an example to be used by the school principal, or his/her designee, to formally address the students and faculty. This announcement will require modifications based upon the nature of the crisis, age of the student population, wishes of the victim's family, etc.*

"You may have noticed that our flag is flying at half-mast. Last night, two of our students were involved in an automobile accident on Oak Ridge Drive. Barry Roth and Steven Kent, who were driving together, both died as a result of their injuries. As more information becomes available, including funeral arrangements, I will speak to you again. This is a terrible tragedy for the Kennedy High School community and our thoughts are with the Roth and Kent families.

We need to be here for each other at this difficult time. Anyone who feels the need to talk should report to our school library, where you can speak with our school psychologists, social workers and guidance counselors. Please sign *out* of your assigned class and *in* at the library. Should you need to speak with someone after school hours, you can contact the Middle Earth Crisis Counseling & Referral Center at (516) 679-1111. Their services are confidential and free of charge.

I am requesting that seniors who have driven to school remain on campus for the next few days so that we can all be here to help each other. If you see someone in need, please reach out to support and comfort them—and encourage them to speak with someone in the library."

D. Sample Announcement to the Media

Note: *This sample is fictitious and is provided as an example to be utilized by the school principal, or his/her designee, to address the media. This announcement will require modifications based upon confidentiality issues, wishes of the victim's family, nature of the crisis (e.g., will the crisis draw national attention), etc.*

"My name is Dr. Jonathan Miller and I am the principal of Cedar Creek Middle School. We learned that one our seventh grade students, Melanie Cole, was abducted this morning by two men as she stepped-off of her school bus in front of the school. We subsequently learned that the police found and identified Melanie's body near Cedar Creek just two blocks east of the school. This is a terrible tragedy for Melanie's family, our school and our community. We have been in contact with Melanie's parents and they have requested that we all understand their need for privacy at this difficult time.

Our school implemented our Crisis Response Plan. District psychologists, social workers, guidance counselors, administrators and teachers who are members of our school's Crisis Response Team immediately went into action and are providing help for our students and faculty. Fortunately, our school family is pulling together at this difficult time. Thank you."

E. Sample Memorandum to the Faculty

Note: *This sample is fictitious and is provided as an example to be utilized by the school principal, or his/her designee, in writing to the school faculty. This memorandum will require modifications based upon confidentiality issues, wishes of the victim's family, nature of the crisis, age of student population, funeral arrangements, etc.*

CONFIDENTIAL MEMORANDUM

To: High School Faculty
From: Dr. Mary Beth Johnson, Principal
Date: January 6, 1999

One of our seniors, Lawrence Fogel, died last night from a self-inflicted gunshot to his head. This is a tragedy for the Fogel family, our school and our community. I will be addressing the school this morning over the P.A. I have spoken with Mr. and Mrs. Fogel who have asked that I report the following information to our students and staff:

"Due to pressures beyond our understanding, Larry took his own life with a gun he supposedly obtained on the streets. He left a note indicating that he thought his life was hopeless.... We have been told that Larry died instantly from the gunshot. A funeral will be held on Friday, January 8th at 11:00 AM at Pine Hill Memorial Chapel on East Brook Drive."

—Mr. Ben Fogel

Our Crisis Response Team met this morning, before school hours, and is requesting that you direct students who need to speak with someone to the guidance lounge. Our psychologists, social workers and guidance counselors will be available. Students are asked to sign *out* of their assigned class and *in* at the lounge.

It will be important that we make every effort to maintain regular classroom instruction. However, I understand that for many of the students this will be difficult. Please feel free to read the statement from Mr. Fogel if you believe it is appropriate, and use it to facilitate discussion about this tragedy. You may wish to turn to the *Practical Guide for Crisis Response in Our Schools* for suggestions on how to best help the students. Copies have been disseminated in your department offices. Finally, tests scheduled for this Wednesday should be postponed due to funeral arrangements.

I understand that this may be a very difficult time for you and we need to be here for each other. If you feel the need to speak to someone, please contact our school psychologist, Dr. Mark Turner, at Ext. 250. Your contacts with him will remain strictly confidential.

F. Sample Letter to Parents

Note: *This sample is fictitious and is provided as an example to be utilized by the school principal, or his/her designee, in writing to parents. This letter will require modifications based upon confidentiality issues, wishes of the victim's family, nature of the crisis, age of student population, funeral arrangements, etc.*

Dear Parents,

On Tuesday afternoon, one of our 4th grade students, Reinaldo Garcia, was involved in an automobile accident with his mother. Mrs. Garcia is in stable condition in the intensive care unit of Central Hills Community Hospital. Reinaldo died as a result of his injuries. This is a tragedy for the Garcia family, our school and our community.

Reinaldo was a very bright and popular student at Berry Hill Elementary School. Our District Crisis Response Team has provided support for students and staff. Team members went into each of the classrooms and facilitated discussion with the children about this tragedy. For many, this was their first exposure to death. Some children have met individually with district psychologists, social workers and counselors. I have asked that the parents of these children be contacted.

Although classroom instruction will continue as always, I anticipate that the next few days will be particularly difficult for everyone. Please keep in mind that it is not uncommon for children to exhibit fears, poor concentration, nightmares, physical complaints, withdrawal, eating and sleep difficulties, regressive behaviors, crying and irritability.

Over the course of the days to come, please monitor your child and allow him/her to express feelings in a non-judgmental climate. If you wish to speak with someone concerning your child, please contact our school psychologists, Dr. Joseph Tepper or Dr. Veronica Keary at (516) 555-1234.

We need to be here for each other at this difficult time.

Sincerely,

Myra S. Reiss, Ed.D.
Principal, Berry Hill Elementary School

G. Traumatic Stress: An Overview

© 1999 by The American Academy of Experts in Traumatic Stress
Reprinted from *Trauma Response*®—Reproduced with Permission
The American Academy of Experts in Traumatic Stress, Inc.
368 Veterans Memorial Highway, Commack New York 11725
Tel. (516) 543-2217 • Fax (516) 543-6977 • http://www.aaets.org

Traumatic stress encompasses exposure to events or the witnessing of events that are extreme and/or life threatening. Traumatic exposure may be brief in duration (e.g., an automobile accident) or involve prolonged, repeated exposure (e.g., sexual abuse). The former type has been referred to as "Type I" trauma and the latter form, as "Type II" trauma (Terr, 1991). In North America, four out of ten people are exposed to at least one traumatic event in their lifetime (Meichenbaum, 1994). Approximately, 25% to 30% of individuals who witness a traumatic event may develop chronic Posttraumatic Stress Disorder (PTSD) and other forms of mental disorders (e.g., depression) (Yehuda, Resnick, Kahana, & Giller, 1993). Approximately 50% of individuals who develop PTSD continue to suffer from its effects decades later without treatment (Meichenbaum, 1994). Knowledge about traumatic stress—how it develops, how it manifests, and how it affects the lives of those who suffer with it—is the first step in its assessment and, ultimately, its treatment.

History of Traumatic Stress

Traumatic exposure and its aftermath are not new phenomena. Humans have experienced tragedies and disaster throughout history. Evidence for posttraumatic reactions date back as far as the sixth century B.C.; early documentation typically involved the reactions of soldiers in combat (Holmes, 1985). Beginning in the 17th century, anecdotal evidence of trauma exposure and subsequent responses were more frequently reported. In 1666, Samuel Pepys wrote about individual's responses to the Great Fire of London (Daly, 1983). It had been reported that the author Charles Dickens suffered from numerous traumatic symptoms after witnessing a tragic rail accident outside of London (Trimble, 1981).

Traumatic stress responses have been labeled in numerous ways over the years. Diagnostic terms applied to symptoms have included *Soldier's Heart, Battle Fatigue, War Neurosis, Da Costa's Syndrome, Tunnel Disease, Railway Spine Disorder, Shell Shock, Gross Stress Reaction, Adjustment Reaction of Adult Life, Transient Situational Disturbance, Traumatic Neurosis, Post-Vietnam Syndrome, Rape Trauma Syndrome, Child Abuse Syndrome, and Battered Wife Syndrome* (Everly, 1995). The *Diagnostic and Statistical Manual of Mental Disorders-Third Edition* (DSM-III) first recognized Posttraumatic Stress Disorder (PTSD) as a distinct diagnostic entity in 1980 (APA, 1980). It was categorized as an anxiety disorder because of the presence of persistent anxiety, hypervigilance, exaggerated startle response, and phobic-like avoidance behaviors (Meichenbaum, 1994). This recognition of stress-related reactions was a major step in the development of an empirical literature base investigating traumatic stress. In 1994,

The *Diagnostic and Statistical Manual of Mental Disorders-Fourth Edition* (DSM-IV) was published and the current diagnostic criteria reflect the findings of numerous empirical studies and field trials (APA, 1994).

Types of Traumatic Events

Traumatic events are typically unexpected and uncontrollable. They may overwhelm an individual's sense of safety and security and leave a person feeling vulnerable and insecure in their environment. Events that are abrupt, often lasting a few minutes and as long as a few hours can be referred to as short-term or Type I traumatic events (Terr, 1991). Included within this category are natural and accidental disasters as well as deliberately caused human-made disasters. Natural disasters include events such as hurricanes, floods, tornadoes, earthquakes, volcanic eruptions, and avalanches. Accidental disasters may include motor vehicle accidents (MVA), boat, train, or airplane accidents, fires, and explosions. Deliberately caused human-made disasters (i.e., intentional human design or IHD) involve bombings, rape, hostage situations, assault and battery, and robbery.

Sustained and repeated traumatic events (or Type II traumatic events) typically involve chronic, repeated, and ongoing exposure. Examples include natural and technological disasters such as chronic illness, nuclear accidents, and toxic spills. Events resulting from intentional human design include combat, child sexual abuse, battered syndrome (i.e., spousal abuse), domestic violence, being taken as political prisoner or prisoner of war (POW), and Holocaust victimization. It is important to consider that research indicates that despite the heterogeneity of traumatic events, individuals who directly or vicariously experience such events show similar profiles of psychopathology including chronic PTSD and commonly observed comorbid disorders such as depression, generalized anxiety disorder, and substance abuse (Solomon, Gerrity, & Muff, 1992).

Current Diagnostic Criteria and Other Considerations

The DSM-IV stipulates that for an individual to be diagnosed with Posttraumatic Stress Disorder, he or she must have experienced or witnessed a life-threatening event and reacted with intense fear, helplessness, or horror. The traumatic event is persistently reexperienced (e.g., distressing recollections), there is persistent avoidance of stimuli associated with the trauma, and the victim experiences some form of hyperarousal (e.g., exaggerated startle response). These symptoms persist for more than one month and cause clinically significant impairment in daily functioning. When the disturbance lasts a minimum of two days and as long as four weeks from the traumatic event, Acute Stress Disorder may be a more accurate diagnosis.

It has been suggested that responses to traumatic experience(s) can be divided into at least four categories (for a complete review, see Meichenbaum, 1994). *Emotional* responses include shock, terror, guilt, horror, irritability, anxiety, hostility, and depression. *Cognitive* responses are reflected in significant concentration impairment, confusion, self-blame, intrusive thoughts about the traumatic experience(s) (also referred to as flashbacks), lowered self-efficacy, fears of losing control, and fear of reoccurrence of the trauma. *Biologically-based* responses involve sleep disturbance (i.e., insomnia), nightmares, an exaggerated startle response, and psychosomatic symptoms. *Behavioral* responses include avoidance, social withdrawal, interpersonal stress (decreased intimacy and lowered trust in others), and substance abuse. The process through which the individual has coped prior to the trauma is arrested; consequently, a sense of helplessness is often maintained (Foy, 1992).

Posttraumatic symptoms often co-occur with other psychiatric conditions; this is referred to as comorbidity. For instance, substance abuse (especially, alcoholism), anxiety (e.g., panic disorder), depression, eating disorders, dissociative disorders, and personality disorders may all co-occur with PTSD. With regard to specific populations, Matsakis (1992) reported that between 40% to 60% of women in treatment for bulimia, anorexia, and obesity had described traumatic experiences at some point in their life. Kilpatrick et al. (1989) reported that, among crime victims with PTSD, 41% had sexual dysfunction, 82% had depression, 27% had obsessive-compulsive symptoms, and 18% had phobias. Sipprelle (1992) reported that personality disorders were especially widespread among Vietnam Veterans. Thus, it is important to assess for comorbid disorders when seeing a patient who presents with trauma-induced symptoms.

Assessment of Traumatic Stress

The clinician working with survivors of traumatic stress and Posttraumatic Stress Disorder must consider the multifaceted nature of these disorders. Meichenbaum (1994) recommends a multimodal approach which involves the collection of information from a number of sources, using several different methods over multiple contacts. For a complete review of assessment measures across victim and survivor populations, see Wilson and Keane (1997).

A comprehensive clinical interview is a primary assessment tool in the evaluation of traumatic stress. Careful questioning during an interview allows the survivor to tell his or her account of the event. Individuals need the opportunity to talk about their experience in a safe, non-judgmental setting. Survivors (and oftentimes, their significant others) need to feel understood and supported as they try to make sense of the traumatic event. Questioning also facilitates a working alliance with the person; the "connection" that the person feels with the treating clinician is often associated with continuation of treatment and psychotherapy treatment outcome (Safran & Segal, 1990; Wolfe, 1992).

Questioning allows for the gathering of details about the trauma, assessment of current and past levels of functioning, and the development of a treatment plan. Interviews with family members and significant others may provide further insight into the nature of the trauma and presenting symptoms. Commonly used structured interviews include the Clinician Administered PTSD Scale (CAPS; Blake et al., 1990) and the Anxiety Disorders Interview Schedule-IV (ADIS-IV; DiNardo, Brown, & Barlow, 1994). A number of paper-and-pencil assessment measures of PTSD have evolved over the past few years as well. Some of the more popular measures include the PTSD subscale of the Minnesota Multiphasic Personality Inventory (MMPI; Keane, Malloy, & Fairbank, 1984; Schlenger & Kulka, 1987), the Penn Inventory for PTSD (Hammarberg, 1992) and the Trauma Symptom Inventory (Briere, 1995). Some screening instruments for anxiety and depression that are also useful include the Beck Anxiety Inventory (BAI; Beck, 1993) and Beck Depression Inventory- Second Edition (BDI-II; Beck, Steer, & Brown, 1996). One performance-based measure that has been used successfully with combat, rape, and accident disaster patients is the Stroop Color Word Test (McNally, English, & Lipke, 1993). As indicated earlier, assessment for comorbid disorders must be part of the evaluative process.

Treatment of Traumatic Stress

Many techniques have been used to treat survivors after exposure to traumatic events. Presently, no one form of intervention has been shown to be superior for the treatment of traumatic stress and PTSD. Ochberg (1995) divides treatment methods into four categories. *Education* is the first method. This includes educating the survivor (and their families) about trauma and its effects on daily functioning. Cognitive, behavioral, and physical aspects of the stress response are explored with the individual. The clinician and patient may share books and articles relevant to the treatment of the traumatic symptoms (see Matsakis, 1996). This process helps give meaning to the symptoms that he or she experiences and may ultimately facilitate a sense of control or mastery over them.

The second category involves *holistic health*. This includes physical activity, nutrition, spirituality, and humor as they contribute to the healing of the individual. The clinician functions as both a teacher and a coach to his patient, offering support and encouragement as the individual attempts various ways to appropriately heal him or herself.

The third group of treatment techniques includes methods to enhance *social support* and *social integration*. Included within this category are family therapy and group psychotherapy. The former typically helps to improve communication and cohesion between family members. Group treatment allows individuals to reduce feelings of isolation, share difficult feelings and perceptions regarding the trauma, and learn more adaptive coping strategies.

Finally, there are clinical interventions best described as *therapy*. The goal to extinguish fear responses, and improve the quality of the individual's life. For example, cognitive-behavior therapy typically relies on exposure strategies to reduce intrusive memories, flashbacks, and nightmares related to the traumatic experience.

Exposure to fear-producing stimuli and cognitions in a safe and supportive environment, over time, often reduces the impact of these stimuli on the individual's reactivity (Foa & Kozak, 1986). Cognitive restructuring strategies are also utilized to address the meaning and, oftentimes, distortions in thought processes that accompany traumatic exposure (e.g., "Life is awful", "All people are cruel"). Problem-solving training (D'Zurilla, 1986) may help the individual combat indecisiveness and perceptions of helplessness. Other techniques include relaxation training and guided imagery-based interventions.

Pharmacological treatment of traumatic stress and PTSD indicates that different medications may affect the multifaceted symptoms of PTSD. For example, Clonidine has been shown to reduce hyperarousal symptoms. Propranolol, Clonazepam, and Alprazolam appear to regulate anxiety and panic symptoms. Fluoxetine may reduce avoidance and explosiveness, whereas reexperiencing of traumatic symptoms and depression may be treated with tricyclic antidepressants and selective serotonin reuptake inhibitors. It is important to note that pharmacotherapy as a sole source of intervention is rarely sufficient to provide complete remission of PTSD (Vargas & Davidson, 1993).

As indicated earlier traumatic stress, and particularly PTSD, are complex and multifaceted, and consequently a multimodal assessment is recommended. It is suggested that effective treatment will involve a number of the aforementioned techniques. Future research needs to address the outcomes of combining various treatment approaches and maintaining treatment gains over time.

Conclusion

It has been stated that posttraumatic stress may represent "one of the most severe and incapacitating forms of human stress known" (Everly, 1995, p. 7). Fortunately, traumatic stress and its consequences continue to gain recognition and investigation in the helping professions although, clearly, more research needs to be done. For example, motor-vehicle accidents (MVAs) are quite common and often precipitate traumatic stress and PTSD, yet there is a dearth of literature examining their impact as well as the treatment of survivors of motor vehicle accidents. There is also a need for greater investigation of secondary traumatic stress reactions. This involves the emotional, cognitive, and behavioral consequences for caregivers who work with traumatized people on a regular basis. That is, through their efforts to help a traumatized population, the helpers themselves become overwhelmed and are traumatized indirectly or secondarily. Moreover, the research examining the effects of traumatic stress in children is in its infancy. This area is especially crucial to study in light of the growing rates of domestic violence in our society.

Recognition of trauma-related stress is the first step in an individual's road to a healthier life. Medical and mental health providers as well as other workers (e.g., emergency care workers) are in an ideal position to offer information, support, and/or the appropriate referrals to victims of traumatic stress. Treatment with a clinician knowledgeable and experienced in working with anxiety and trauma-related difficulties can be a crucial factor in helping victims learn to cope and live life more fully.

Article References

American Psychiatric Association (1980). Diagnostic and statistical manual of mental disorders (3rd ed.). Washington, DC: Author.

American Psychiatric Association (1994). Diagnostic and statistical manual of mental disorders (4th ed.). Washington, DC: Author.

Beck, A.T., Steer, R.A., & Brown, G.K. (1996). Beck Depression Inventory (2nd ed.). San Antonio, TX: The Psychological Corporation.

Beck, A. T. (1993). Beck Anxiety Inventory. San Antonio, TX: The Psychological Corporation.

Blake, D., Weathers, F., Nagy, L., Kaloupek, D., Klauminzer, G., Charney, D., & Keane, T. (1990). Clinician Administered PTSD Scale (CAPS). Boston: National Center for Post-Traumatic Stress Disorder, Behavioral Science Division, Boston VA.

Briere, J. (1995). Trauma Symptom Inventory professional manual. Odessa, FL: Psychological Assessment Resources.

Cummings, N., & Vanden Bos, G.R. (1981). The twenty year Kaiser-Permanente experience with psychotherapy and medical utilization. Health Policy Quarterly, 1, 159-175.

Daly, R.J. (1983). Samuel Pepys and Posttraumatic Stress Disorder. British Journal of Psychiatry, 143, 64-68.

DiNardo, P.A., Brown, T.A., & Barlow, D.H. (1994). Anxiety Disorders Interview Schedule for DSM-IV: Clinician's Manual. New York: Graywind.

D'Zurilla, T.J. (1986). Problem solving therapy: A social competence approach to clinical intervention. New York: Springer.

Everly, G.S. (1995). Psychotraumatology. In G.S. Everly & J.M. Lating (Eds.), Psychotraumatology: Key papers and core concepts in posttraumatic stress (pp. 9-26). New York: Plenum.

Foa, E.B., & Kozak, M.J. (1986). Emotional processing of fear: Exposure to corrective information. Psychological Bulletin, 99, 20-35.

Foy, D.W. (1992). Introduction and description of the disorder. In D. W. Foy (Ed.), Treating PTSD: Cognitive-Behavioral strategies (pp 1-12). New York: Guilford.

Hammarberg, M. (1992). Penn Inventory for Posttraumatic Stress Disorder: Psychometric properties. Psychological Assessment, 4, 67-76.

Holmes, R. (1985). Acts of war. New York: Free Press.

Keane, T.M., Malloy, P.F., & Fairbank, J.A. (1984). Empirical development of an MMPI subscale for the assessment of combat-related Posttraumatic Stress Disorder. Journal of Consulting and Clinical Psychology, 52, 888-891.

Kilpatrick, D. G., Saunders, B.E., Amick-McMullen, A., Best, C.L., Veronen, L.J., & Resnick, H.S. (1989). Victim and crime factors associated with the development of crime-related Posttraumatic Stress Disorder. Behavior Therapy, 20, 199-214.

Matsakis, A. (1992). I can't get over it: A handbook for trauma survivors. Oakland, CA: New Harbinger Publications.

Matsakis, A. (1996). I can't get over it: A handbook for trauma survivors. (2nd ed.) Oakland, CA: New Harbinger Publications.

McNally, R.J., English, G.E., Lipke, H.J. (1993). Assessment of intrusive cognition in PTSD: Use of the modified Stroop paradigm. Journal of Traumatic Stress, 6, 33-42.

Meichenbaum, D. (1994). A clinical handbook/practical therapist manual for assessing and treating adults with Posttraumatic Stress Disorder. Ontario, Canada: Institute Press.

Ochberg, F.M. (1995). Posttraumatic therapy. In G.S. Everly & J.M. Lating (Eds.), Psychotraumatology: Key papers and core concepts in posttraumatic stress (pp. 245-264). New York: Plenum.

Safran, J.D., & Segal, Z.V. (1990). Interpersonal process in cognitive therapy. New York: Basic Books.

Schlenger, W.E., & Kulka, R.A. (1987). Performance of the Keane-Fairbank MMPI scale and other self- report measures in identifying Posttraumatic Stress Disorder. Paper presented at the 95th annual meeting of the American Psychological Association, New York.

Sipprelle, R.C. (1992). A vet center experience: Multievent trauma, delayed treatment type. In D.W. Foy (Ed.), Treating PTSD: Cognitive-Behavioral strategies (pp 13-38). New York: Guilford.

Solomon, S., Gerrity, E.T., & Muff, A.M. (1992). Efficacy of treatments for Posttraumatic Stress Disorder: An empirical review. Journal of the American Medical Association, 268, 633-638.

Terr, L. (1991). Childhood trauma: An outline and overview. American Journal of Psychiatry, 148, 10-20.

Trimble, M.R. (1981). Posttraumatic neurosis. Chicester: Wiley.

Vargas, M.A., & Davidson, J. (1993). Posttraumatic stress disorder. Psychopharmacology, 16, 737-748.

Wilson, J. P., & Keane, T.M. (Eds.). (1997). Assessing Psychological Trauma and PTSD. New York: Guilford.

Wolfe, B.E. (1992). Integrative psychotherapy of the anxiety disorders. In J.C. Norcross & M.R. Goldfried (Eds.), Handbook of Psychotherapy Integration. (pp 373-401). New York: Basic Books.

Yehuda, R., Resnick, H., Kahana, J., & Giller, E. (1993). Long-lasting hormonal alterations to extreme stress in humans: Normative or maladaptive'. Psychosomatic Medicine, 55, 287-297.

H. A Case Example (Fictitious)

Background

On Saturday, December 12, 1998, at approximately 1:30 AM, three students were killed on the Long Island Expressway on their way home from a party. The automobile in which they were driving struck a light pole and immediately became engulfed in fire. The students were seniors at Harperville Senior High School. One of the students was a well-known athlete, one was a class officer, and one, a popular cheerleader.

The Intervention

Sunday evening, the high school principal, Dr. Handley, was notified by the superintendent of the school district. Dr. Handley began exploring the details of the accident. He contacted the police in order to clarify the time, place, and manner in which the students were killed. Additionally, he spoke with the students' parents, and in one case, an aunt. There was discussion concerning what information would be disclosed to the school community. Dr. Handley called Mrs. Matthews, assistant principal. He then began calling the Crisis Response Team using the Emergency Contact List. Thus, Dr. Handley called Dr. Stone, the school psychologist, who called Mr. Tino, the social worker, and so on. It was agreed that the Crisis Response Team would meet at 6:00 AM, one and one half hours before the faculty and students would begin arriving at school on Monday morning.

Rooms for individual and small group counseling sessions were identified. Several signs were prepared in advance for posting in the hallways. The Crisis Response Team determined that given the popularity and high visibility of these students, additional support from all other schools in the district would be needed. Additionally, it was decided by the Crisis Response Team that a brief emergency staff meeting would take place upon the faculty's arrival at the school. It was discovered that one of the students killed in the accident had a younger sister in the elementary school. The psychologist in that building was informed of the situation. She was going to make a contact with this youngster and her teacher.

As expected, the faculty was shaken by the announcement. Several of the teachers began to sob as the principal reported what he knew at that point in time. The social worker, Mr. Tino, announced where the support staff would be located throughout the day for the students and faculty to receive help. Staff were strongly encouraged to seek assistance either by sending a student or using the intercom system if they felt a need for support from a Crisis Response Team member in the classroom. Members of the Crisis Response Team, namely the psychologist and school nurse, announced their availability beyond school hours for colleagues seeking support. Dr. Handley recommended that teachers postpone administration of tests on this day.

When the students arrived, Dr. Handley made an announcement to the school over the public address system. He stated that the death of these three students was a tragedy and that the school community would "miss them very much." He informed the students that support staff would be available all day if they felt a need to talk and where this staff would be located. Dr. Handley discouraged students and staff from speaking with the media and indicated that he would be addressing them. Signs were posted around the building indicating the location of support personnel. Finally, Dr. Handley asked that students who drove to school not leave the building during the school day.

A letter was prepared by the assistant principal to send home to the parents and guardians of the students. The letter stated the school community was currently facing a crisis, the types of reactions to expect from their children, and a recommendation that parents and guardians closely monitor the reactions of their children. A summary of the methods that the school was utilizing was provided as well as crisis line and emergency numbers in the event that their child was having difficulty coping with the tragedy. A memorandum was placed in faculty mailboxes.

Individual crisis intervention was provided by the psychologists. The social workers and guidance counselors were conducting small group counseling sessions. There was a flow of students into and out of the support groups. A list of all students seen in counseling was maintained. Students who were close to the individuals in the accident were closely monitored and in some cases, contact was made with their parents by guidance counselors. Students were only *encouraged* to talk and express themselves; the request for them to talk was *never* demanded. The parents and/or guardians of high risk students were contacted and referrals were provided for further intervention. Dr. Handley provided staff and students with juice and cookies.

In the classroom, teachers began their classes by addressing the loss with their students. Many of the students were visibly upset. Rather than lecturing, some of the teachers decided to conduct "group discussion" at the suggestion of the Crisis Response Team.

Two local news stations arrived at the school looking to interview faculty and students. A security guard advised them to speak directly with the principal, otherwise they would "have to leave school property." One reporter spoke with Dr. Handley.

At the end of the day, after the students and staff left the building, the Crisis Response Team reconvened. They shared their experiences with each other. A follow-up plan for students who seemed at high risk was developed that ensured that the parents/guardians of these students were called, and/or met with. Recommendations for close monitoring and/or outside counseling were made. Some of the team members elected to walk around the building for the remainder of the week and offer outreach where needed. Two members planned to continue conducting group counseling on a rotating basis. Several staff and faculty members planned to attend the funerals.

A follow-up faculty meeting was scheduled for the next morning. The purpose of this meeting was to give the latest information to the faculty regarding the tragedy, and to get their feedback regarding what had happened and relevant observations of their students. They were again reminded of the availability of support staff for themselves as well as their students. A meeting was held that evening for parents in the community to address their concerns.

It took approximately six weeks for the school community to adjust to the drastic changes that came about so suddenly and unexpectedly. The students established a memorial fund in the names of the deceased and a tree was planted on the side of the school building in memory of the three students.

I. Teacher Guidelines for Crisis Response

Reprinted from *A Practical Guide for Crisis Response in Our Schools*
© 1999 by The American Academy of Experts in Traumatic Stress—Reproduced with Permission
368 Veterans Memorial Highway, Commack New York 11725
Tel. (516) 543-2217 • Fax (516) 543-6977 • http://www.aaets.org

What is a crisis and what is crisis response?

A crisis is an event of limited duration that is typically unpredicted and overwhelming for those who experience it. This situation may be volatile in nature and, at times, may involve threat to the survival of an individual or groups of individuals. Moreover, a crisis state may result upon exposure to drastic and tragic change in an individual's environment which has become common and familiar to them. This alteration in the status quo is unwanted, frightening, and often renders a person with a sense of vulnerability and helplessness. Ultimately, with successful intervention, the equilibrium is restored between the environment and the individual's perception of their world as a safe and secure place. Examples of crises that can potentially have a large scale effect on the students, faculty and administrators in a school building or district include: an accident involving a student or faculty member, a suicide or death of a student or faculty member, severe violence (e.g., gang fight), hostage taking, fire at school or a natural disaster (e.g., hurricane).

Crisis response, as it pertains to the school environment, is a proactive, organized and well thought out plan to a crisis situation that has adversely affected many individuals in a school district, including students, faculty and administrators. The primary goals of crisis response are 1) to prevent a chaotic situation from escalating into a potentially catastrophic one, 2) to help those affected by the crisis to return, as quickly as possible, to pre-crisis functioning, and 3) to decrease the potential long-term effects of the crisis on functioning.

Why a Crisis Response Plan?

Research conducted over the past 10 years has revealed that schools are increasingly more prone to crisis situations that adversely affect large numbers of students and faculty. The rise in adolescent suicide, increased assaults on teachers, high levels of substance abuse among students and increased violence in the schools are some of the reasons cited. Research has also indicated that today's school districts need to contend with reactions to new types of trauma/disasters. For example, hostage taking, sniper attacks, murders, terrorist activities and bomb scares were almost nonexistent in the schools 30 years ago, but today occur with greater frequency.

Thus, it is strongly recommended that school districts need to be prepared for a crisis situation that can potentially affect the functioning of their students, faculty and administrators. Lerner (1997) comments:

"There are two kinds of beach front homeowners on the south shore of Long Island: those who have faced serious erosion, and those who will. Similarly, there are two kinds of schools: those that have faced a serious crisis situation, and those that will."

Research has emerged over the past ten years supporting a proactive approach to a crisis, as opposed to one that is reactive in nature. Such an approach is much better in dealing effectively with a large scale crisis situation. A reactive approach is spontaneous, and not fully thought out, planned, or practiced, and can result in the response that is less effective in meeting the immediate, and possibly the long-term needs of the students, faculty and administrators.

In summary, a proactive approach to a crisis is one that is organized, planned and practiced and more likely results in a response that can have a dramatic effect on reducing the short and long-term consequences of the crisis on the individuals in a school district.

What types of behaviors/reactions can teachers expect from their students after a crisis situation has occurred?

The manner in which people react to crisis situations is dependent upon a number of variables including personal history, personality variables, severity and proximity of the event, level of social support and the type and quality of intervention. While no two people respond to situations, including crisis situations, in exactly the same manner, the following are often seen as immediate reactions to a significant crisis:

- shock, numbness,
- denial or inability to acknowledge the situation has occurred,
- dissociative behavior—appearing dazed, apathetic, expressing feelings of unreality,
- confusion,
- disorganization,
- difficulty making decisions, and
- suggestibility.

It is important to note that most children will recover from the effects of a crisis with adequate support from family, friends and school personnel. Their response to a crisis can be viewed as "a normal response to an abnormal situation." While the emotional effects of the crisis can be significant and can potentially influence functioning for weeks to months, most children will evidence a full recovery.

Following are descriptions of responses likely to observed in children:

- **Regression in Behavior:** Children who have been exposed to a crisis often exhibit behaviors that are similar to children younger than themselves. This is especially true of toddlers, preschool and elementary school children. They may return to behavior that was abandoned long ago (e.g., thumb sucking, bed-wetting, fears of the dark). Traumatized children may also exhibit separation anxiety, clinging to parents and resistance to leaving the parents' side. They may resist going to bed alone. Bladder and bowel control may be temporarily lost in younger children.

- **Increase in Fears and Anxiety:** Children also exhibit an increase in their fears and worries. They may again become afraid of situations they mastered long ago. As mentioned above they may become fearful of the dark and refuse to go to bed alone. A school phobia may emerge where the child refuses to go to school for fear of something happening and/or fear of leaving his/her parents. They may openly verbalize their fear of the crisis occurring again in the school. It is important that parents do not allow the child to remain home as a means to deal with his/her anxiety. This will result in the anxiety increasing once the child needs to return to school. Due to the increase in fears, additional demands are made for parent attention and support. Adolescents may experience a more generalized anxiety and not the specific types of fears that are seen in younger children.

- **Decreased Academic Performance and Poor Concentration:** Given the increase in anxiety and the disruption a crisis can have on children's sense of safety and security, there is a decrease in the amount of mental energy and focus available to learn and complete academic assignments.

- **Increased Aggression and Oppositional Behavior, and Decreased Frustration Tolerance:** Children who have been exposed to a crisis can experience difficulty controlling their anger and frustration. Situations that would not have caused a heightened emotional response prior to the crisis, can post-crisis result in an aggressive response and/or expression of frustration. Adolescents may also exhibit an increase in oppositional behavior, refusing to live by the rules and regulations of school and home, and/or meet their responsibilities (e.g., chores, academic assignments). Some adolescents may resort to antisocial behavior (e.g., stealing).

- **Increased Irritability, Emotional Liability and Depressive Feelings:** Children can also exhibit stronger and more variable emotional responses to situations. There could be symptoms of depression that include general sense of sadness, difficulty falling and remaining asleep or sleeping more than normal, change in eating habits, loss of interest in activities once enjoyed, social withdrawal, mental and physical fatigue and/or suicidal ideation. In younger children there may be an increase in irritability and moodiness.

- **Denial:** In an effort to cope with the psychological and emotional ramifications of a crisis, certain children and adolescents will deny that a crisis has occurred and/or deny the significance of a crisis. A child whose mother has died

suddenly may demand that he can return home so that they can watch their favorite television program together. An adolescent whose favorite teacher was badly injured in a car accident may insist that he will recover fully, despite the medical evidence that indicates that this will not happen. Children who continue to utilize denial to cope may need to be confronted in a sensitive but straight forward manner. Anger and resentment may be expressed when confronting the child with the reality. In time, and with support, children do come to accept the reality of a situation.

Understanding the typical reactions of individuals exposed to a crisis situation is a critical step in identifying people who may be in need of further professional assistance. Several investigators (Greenstone & Levittown, 1993; Klingman, 1987; Weaver, 1995) have described **age-appropriate reactions** of individuals exposed to a traumatic event. Although there is heterogeneity in the reactions of individuals surrounding a crisis, most of these responses are expected reactions and subside in several weeks following the crisis.

Preschool Children (Ages 1 through 5)
- thumb sucking
- speech difficulties
- bed wetting
- decreases or increases in appetite
- fear of the dark
- clinging and whining
- loss of bladder control
- separation difficulties

Childhood (Ages 5 through 11)
- sadness & crying
- school avoidance
- physical complaints (e.g., headaches)
- poor concentration
- irritability
- fear of personal harm
- regressive behavior (clinging, whining)
- nightmares
- aggressive behavior at home or school
- bed wetting
- anxiety & fears
- confusion
- eating difficulty
- withdrawal/social isolation
- attention-seeking behavior

Early Adolescence (Ages 11 through 14)
- sleep disturbance
- withdrawal/isolation from peers
- increase or decrease in appetite
- loss of interest in activities
- rebelliousness

- generalized anxiety
- school difficulty, including fighting
- fear of personal harm
- physical ailments (e.g., bowel problems)
- poor school performance
- depression
- concentration difficulties

Adolescence (Ages 14 through 18)

- numbing
- intrusive recollections
- sleep disturbance
- anxiety and feelings of guilt
- eating disturbance
- poor concentration and distractibility
- psychosomatic symptoms (e.g., headaches)
- antisocial behavior (e.g., stealing)
- apathy
- aggressive behavior
- agitation or decrease in energy level
- poor school performance
- depression
- peer problems
- withdrawal
- increased substance abuse
- decreased interest in the opposite sex
- amenorrhea or dysmenorrhea

What types of personal reactions can teachers expect after a crisis situation has occurred?

As in the case of children, the answer to this question is dependent on a number of variables including personal history, personality variables, severity and proximity of the event, level of social support and type and quality of intervention. The fact that some of the possible immediate adult reactions to a crisis are confusion, disorganization and difficulty in decision making, underscores the need for a preplanned, practiced and organized response plan. Longer term reactions that are experienced by adults are:

Adulthood

- denial
- feelings of detachment
- unwanted, intrusive recollections
- depression
- concentration difficulty
- anxiety
- psychosomatic complaints
- hypervigilance
- withdrawal
- eating disturbance

- irritability and low frustration tolerance
- sleep difficulty
- poor work performance
- loss of interest in activities once enjoyed
- emotional and mental fatigue
- emotional lability
- marital discord

Since teachers are likely to be affected by the crisis situation, it is imperative that they receive the appropriate support and intervention. Without such intervention, they will be limited in their ability to meet the needs of their students. It is important that teachers have a forum to discuss their own feelings and reactions to the crisis and receive support. Teachers usually look to other teachers, and possibly school support personnel (e.g., psychologist, social worker, guidance counselor) to share their feelings. Family and friends outside the school environment can also serve as important sources of support. As with their students, most teachers will show a full recovery from the crisis situation. However, if the symptoms outlined above persist and continue to interfere with functioning, professional consultation may be beneficial.

What can classroom teachers do to address the reactions of their students during a crisis situation?

Teachers are on the "front lines" during and following a crisis situation. They have spent the most time with their students and often know them better than anyone in the school. Therefore, teachers are likely to be in a good position to provide early and ongoing intervention. However, they are also in a very difficult position because they need to remain composed and in control for their students at a time when they themselves may be experiencing a flood of emotions in response to the crisis. Classroom teachers can find this especially difficult if they are not trained in crisis response and/or are not familiar with how to address the needs of their students following a crisis. Following are interventions that teachers can provide to address the reactions of their students to a crisis situation:

- After obtaining the facts regarding the crisis, as well as permission from the principal to disclose them, classroom teachers should accurately and honestly explain what has happened to their students. Their students should be told the information in a manner that they can understand, taking such variables as age and functioning levels into consideration.

- Teachers can, and most of the time should, consult with school personnel who are trained in crisis response and crisis intervention (e.g., school psychologist, school social worker, guidance counselors) on how to most effectively address their students' reactions to the crisis.

- It is often helpful when teachers model appropriate expression of feelings for their students and let them know that they have permission to verbalize what they are experiencing. It is important that teachers remain in control of their own emotions while dealing with their students, a task that may be difficult given that teachers themselves may have been significantly affected by the crisis. Children tend to look toward adults to assess how to react to a situation. A teacher who is experiencing difficulty may not model the optimal ways of coping and expressing feelings.

- If a teacher is unable to function adequately and meet the immediate needs of his/her students, another school official may need to replace the teacher temporarily or help him/her deal with the students. Every attempt should be made to keep the classroom teacher with his/her students.

- Education of students regarding likely responses to the crisis is essential. Students should not feel they are "abnormal" or that they are "going crazy." Explaining to students that they will likely have a "normal reaction to an abnormal situation" can be helpful for them. Teachers may wish to share the age appropriate reactions described in this document.

- Students need to be warned that they may experience waves of strong emotions and coached on how to effectively deal with them (e.g., by talking to others, looking to others for support).

- The strong emotional reactions to a crisis situation are usually overcome in one to six weeks following the crisis. The long-term effects outlined above, however, could take weeks to months to dissipate.

- Classroom teachers should be vigilant for students who are experiencing significant difficulty in comparison to peers, and who may require additional and more individualized crisis intervention. Criteria for determining which students require additional intervention is outlined below.

- It is imperative that students, as a group, be given the opportunity to discuss their feelings and reactions to the crisis situation. The world as they know it has been threatened, their security undermined. They need to be able to discuss these feelings and know that their fears and reactions are shared by others.

- When students are discussing their feelings, teachers need to listen in a noncritical and non-judgmental manner, with empathy and support. It is important that teachers communicate to the students that they understand the students' feelings and as previously indicated, that their feelings are normal reactions to an abnormal situation. Students who are hesitant to verbalize their feelings should be encouraged to do so but demands to verbalize should be avoided.

- The students should be given the opportunity to express themselves through other modes of communication (e.g., writing, and perhaps drawing for younger children), especially those students who are hesitant to verbalize their feelings.

- Teachers can develop classroom activities and assignments, and homework assignments that address students' feelings regarding the crisis. Assignments that are a catalyst for group discussion are best and may facilitate empowerment at a time when many individuals feel a sense of hopelessness and vulnerability.

- Crisis intervention is ongoing. Therefore, future discussions may need to ensue and address residual feelings regarding the crisis. Some students may not experience a reaction to the crisis until days or weeks later. Teachers need to remain sensitive to this fact and remain vigilant to reactions for some time after the crisis. Some students may even try to convince others that they were not affected, and then suddenly show a strong emotional reaction.

When should teachers refer students for more individualized assessment and intervention?

With support from school personnel and their families, and the passage of time, most students will be able to recover from the effects of a crisis and return to pre-crisis functioning. They will be able to meet the demands of their environment, most particularly the school environment. However, there are those students, due to their own psychological makeup (including history and ability to obtain and respond to support), and the severity and proximity of the precipitating event, who will continue to experience difficulties which interfere with functioning. These students are in need of further, and probably more individualized intervention.

The following are guidelines for determining which students should be referred to counselors for additional intervention:

- students who can not engage adequately in classroom assignments and activities after a sufficient amount of time has passed since the crisis and after a majority of their peers are able to do so,

- students that continue to exhibit high levels of emotional responsiveness (e.g., crying, tearfulness) after a majority of their peers have discontinued to do so,

- students who appear depressed, withdrawn and non-communicative,

- students who continue to exhibit poorer academic performance and decreased concentration,

- students who express suicidal or homicidal ideation, or students who are intentionally hurting themselves (e.g., cutting themselves),

- students who exhibit an apparent increased usage of alcohol or drugs,

- students who gain or lose a significant amount of weight in a short period of time,

- students who exhibit significant behavioral changes, and

- students who discontinue attending to their hygienic needs.

Conclusion

The immediacy and unpredictability of crisis situations often leave individuals with a sense of worry, vulnerability and distrust. A school system is unique in that it brings together individuals of all ages and professionals from numerous disciplines. Effective response to a crisis capitalizes on the resources within the school environment. *A Crisis Response Team that identifies and responds to a crisis in a unified and collaborative manner can alter the aftermath of a crisis.*

J. Parent Guidelines for Crisis Response

Reprinted from *A Practical Guide for Crisis Response in Our Schools*
© 1999 by The American Academy of Experts in Traumatic Stress—Reproduced with Permission
368 Veterans Memorial Highway, Commack New York 11725
Tel. (516) 543-2217 • Fax (516) 543-6977 • http://www.aaets.org

In an effort to help you to understand and deal effectively with your child's reactions to a crisis situation, our district is providing you with this information. This literature is part of a larger district-wide Crisis Response Plan intended to help our school community deal more effectively with a crisis by providing appropriate support and intervention.

What is a crisis and what is crisis response?

A crisis is an event of limited duration that is typically unpredicted and overwhelming for those who experience it. This situation may be volatile in nature and, at times, may involve threat to the survival of an individual or groups of individuals. Moreover, a crisis state may result upon exposure to drastic and tragic change in an individual's environment which has become common and familiar to them. This alteration in the status quo is unwanted, frightening, and often renders a person with a sense of vulnerability and helplessness. Ultimately, with successful intervention, the equilibrium is restored between the environment and the individual's perception of their world as a safe and secure place. Examples of crises that can potentially have a large scale effect on the students, faculty and administrators in a school building or district include: an accident involving a student or faculty member, a suicide or death of a student or faculty member, severe violence (e.g., gang fight), hostage taking, fire at school or a natural disaster (e.g., hurricane).

Crisis response, as it pertains to the school environment, is a proactive, organized and well thought out plan to a crisis situation that has adversely affected many individuals in a school district, including students, faculty and administrators. The primary goals of crisis response are 1) to prevent a chaotic situation from escalating into a potentially catastrophic one, 2) to help those affected by the crisis to return, as quickly as possible, to pre-crisis functioning, and 3) to decrease the potential long-term effects of the crisis on functioning.

Why a Crisis Response Plan?

Research conducted over the past 10 years has revealed that schools are increasingly more prone to crisis situations that adversely affect large numbers of students and faculty. The rise in adolescent suicide, increased assaults on teachers, high levels of substance abuse among students and increased violence in the schools are some of the reasons cited. Research has also indicated that today's school districts need to contend with reactions to new types of trauma. For example, hostage taking, sniper attacks, murders, terrorist activities and bomb scares were almost nonexistent in the schools 30 years ago, but today occur with greater frequency.

Thus, it is strongly suggested that school districts need to be prepared for a crisis situation that can potentially affect the functioning of their students, faculty and administrators. Lerner (1997) comments:

"There are two kinds of beach front homeowners on the south shore of Long Island: those who have faced serious erosion, and those who will. Similarly, there are two kinds of schools: those that have faced a serious crisis situation, and those that will."

Research has emerged over the past ten years supporting a proactive approach to a crisis, as opposed to one that is reactive in nature, is much better in dealing effectively with a large scale crisis situation. A reactive approach is spontaneous, and not fully thought out, planned, or practiced, and can result in a response that is less effective in meeting the immediate, and possibly the long-term needs of the students, faculty and administrators.

In summary, a proactive approach to a crisis is one that is organized, planned and practiced and more likely results in a response that can have a dramatic effect on reducing the short and long-term consequences of the crisis on the individuals in a school district.

What types of behaviors/reactions can parents expect from their child after a crisis situation has occurred?

The manner in which people react to crisis situations is dependent on a number of variables including personal history, personality variables, severity and proximity of the event, level of social support and the type and quality of intervention. While no two people respond to situations, including crisis situations, in exactly the same manner, the following are often seen as immediate reactions to a significant crisis:

- shock, numbness,
- denial or inability to acknowledge the situation has occurred,
- dissociative behavior—appearing dazed, apathetic, expressing feelings of unreality,
- confusion,
- disorganization,
- difficulty making decisions, and
- suggestibility.

It is important to note that most children will recover from the effects of a crisis with adequate support from family, friends and school personnel. Their response to a crisis can be viewed as "a normal response to an abnormal situation." While the emotional effects of the crisis can be significant and can potentially influence functioning for weeks to months, most children will evidence a full recovery.

Following are descriptions of responses likely to observed in children:

- **Regression in Behavior**: Children who have been exposed to a crisis often exhibit behaviors that are similar to children younger than themselves. This is especially true of toddlers, preschool and elementary school children. They may return to behavior that was abandoned long ago (e.g., thumb sucking, bed-wetting, fears of the dark). Traumatized children may also exhibit separation anxiety, clinging to parents and resistance to leaving the parents' side. They may resist going to bed alone. Bladder and bowel control may be temporarily lost in younger children.

- **Increase in Fears and Anxiety**: Children also exhibit an increase in their fears and worries. They may again become afraid of situations they mastered long ago. As mentioned above they may become fearful of the dark and refuse to go to bed alone. A school phobia may emerge where the child refuses to go to school for fear of something happening and/or fear of leaving his/her parents. They may openly verbalize their fear of the crisis occurring again in the school. It is important that parents do not allow the child to remain home as a means to deal with his/her anxiety. This will result in the anxiety increasing once the child needs to return to school. Due to the increase in fears, additional demands are made for parent attention and support. Adolescents may experience a more generalized anxiety and not the specific types of fears that are seen in younger children.

- **Decreased Academic Performance and Poor Concentration**: Given the increase in anxiety and the disruption a crisis can have on children's sense of safety and security, there is a decrease in the amount of mental energy and focus available to learn and complete academic assignments.

- **Increased Aggression and Oppositional Behavior, and Decreased Frustration Tolerance**: Children who have been exposed to a crisis can experience difficulty controlling their anger and frustration. Situations that would not have caused a heightened emotional response prior to the crisis, can post-crisis result in an aggressive response and/or expression of frustration. Adolescents may also exhibit an increase in oppositional behavior, refusing to live by the rules and regulationsof school and home, and/or meet their responsibilities (e.g., chores, academic assignments). Some adolescents may resort to antisocial behavior (e.g., stealing).

- **Increased Irritability, Emotional Liability and Depressive Feelings**: Children can also exhibit stronger and more variable emotional responses to situations. There could be symptoms of depression that include general sense of sadness, difficulty falling and remaining asleep or sleeping more than normal, change in eating habits, loss of interest in activities once enjoyed, social withdrawal, mental and physical fatigue and/or suicidal ideation. In younger children there may be an increase in irritability and moodiness.

- **Denial**: In an effort to cope with the psychological and emotional ramifications of a crisis, certain children and adolescents will deny that a crisis has occurred and/or deny the significance of a crisis. A child whose mother has died suddenly may demand that he can return home so that they can watch their favorite television program together. An adolescent whose favorite teacher was badly injured in a car accident may insist that he will recover fully, despite the medical evidence that indicates that this will not happen. Children who continue to utilize denial to cope may need to be confronted in a sensitive but straight forward manner. Anger and resentment may be expressed when confronting the child with the reality. In time, and with support, children do come to accept the reality of a situation.

What types of reactions may <u>parents</u> experience after a crisis situation has occurred that involves themselves and/or their child?

As in the case of children, the answer to this question is dependent on a number of variables including personal history, personality variables, severity and proximity of the event, level of social support and type and quality of intervention. The fact that some of the possible immediate adult reactions to a crisis are confusion, disorganization and difficulty in decision making, underscores the need for a preplanned, practiced and organized response plan. Longer term reactions that are experienced by adults are:

Adulthood
- denial
- feelings of detachment
- unwanted, intrusive recollections
- depression
- concentration difficulty
- anxiety
- psychosomatic complaints
- hypervigilance
- withdrawal
- eating disturbance
- irritability and low frustration tolerance
- sleep difficulty
- poor work performance
- loss of interest in activities once enjoyed
- emotional and mental fatigue
- emotional lability
- marital discord

Since you are likely to be affected by the crisis situation, either directly through exposure to the crisis or indirectly through your child's exposure, it is imperative that you receive the appropriate support and intervention. Without such intervention, you will be limited in your ability to meet the needs of your child. It is important that you have a forum to discuss your own feelings and reactions to the crisis and receive support. You should look to family members, other parents in the district, friends, and/or school support personnel (e.g., psychologist, social worker, guidance counselor) to share your feelings. It is likely that the school will have a meeting for parents to discuss the crisis, and offer them support and education. You are encouraged to attend. As with your child, you will most likely not experience long-term effects because of the crisis. However, if the symptoms outlined above persist and continue to interfere with your ability to function, professional consultation may be beneficial.

What can parents do to address the reactions of their child to a crisis situation?

As parents you are probably the most influential factor in the recovery of your child from the emotional consequences of a crisis. Since you are the most emotionally involved with your child, your support, encouragement and reassurance is of utmost importance in your child's recovery. While you may be frequently frustrated that you can't do more to alleviate your child's suffering, you need to realize that your efforts can not be replaced by anyone else.

As a parent of a child exposed to a crisis, you face several challenges in your effort to help your him/her. First, you may experience guilt because you were unable to protect your child from the wrath of the crisis. Even though this guilt may have no foundation in reality, it is real to you, and needs to be kept under control so that it doesn't disable you from focusing on your child's needs. Second, you need to keep yourself under control in a situation that may have been very emotional and traumatizing to you. This is especially true if you were also exposed to the crisis situation. You need to realize that you can suffer secondary traumatization due to your child's exposure to a crisis. As discussed above, you need to attend to your own emotional responses and seek intervention. While you need to be fully involved in your child's recovery, time for yourself will do more to help your child. Following are interventions that you can provide to address the reactions of your child to a crisis situation.

- Speak to your child regarding the crisis and provide him/her with accurate information regarding the crisis in a language that he/she can understand.
- Your child needs to feel that he/she is allowed to express his/her thoughts and feelings regarding the crisis without the fear that he/she will be judged negatively. It is important for you to listen carefully to your child and show him/her that you understand what he/she is feeling and thinking.
- Your child needs constant reassurance that things will get better and that in the long-term things will improve. This should only be stated if it is indeed true. No false statements regarding the future should be made in an effort to help your child feel better in the present. This will only lead to false hopes and distrust in the future.
- Reassure your child that you will continue to "be there" for him/her, and that you will see them through the aftermath of the crisis.
- Your child may need additional affection in the form of hugs and other physical contact.
- You will most likely need to keep in touch with your child's teacher to monitor his/her academic performance.

- You will need to spend additional individualized time with your child. Try to structure your time with him/her by playing games, having discussions and going places. During your time together, focus a majority of your attention on your child.
- You will need to monitor the adjustment of your adolescent from somewhat of a distance since his/her primary support group may be his/her peers. Don't be hesitant to ask your adolescent child how he/she is coping even though you may expect an answer of "fine." The fact that you ask will most likely be important to your adolescent child, even though he/she may not show this.
- Monitor your adolescent child for increased use of alcohol or drugs. There may be an attempt to "self-medicate" by using these substances. Also monitor your adolescent child for increased symptoms of depression.
- Regardless of your adolescent child's response to you, reassure him/her that you are there if he/she needs help and/or assistance. You may want to outline just how you can help him/her (e.g., by talking, by getting him/her professional help).

When should your child receive additional help in the form professional intervention?

With support and reassurance from you and others in your family, intervention from school personnel, and the passage of time, your child should be able to recover from the effects of a crisis and return to pre-crisis functioning. He/she should be able to meet the demands of his/her environment, most particularly his/her home and school environments. However, there is a chance that your child, due to the nature of the crisis itself and due to his/her psychological makeup, history and ability to respond to support, will continue to experience difficulties which interfere with his/her functioning. If the symptoms outlined above persist, your child is probably in need of further, and probably more individualized, intervention. The following are guidelines for determining if your child requires additional intervention from professionals trained in addressing traumatic stress:

- your child can not engage adequately in home-based responsibilities and in school-based assignments and activities after a sufficient amount of time has passed since the crisis and after a majority of his/her peers are able to do so,
- your child continues to exhibit high levels of emotional responsiveness (e.g., crying, tearfulness) after a majority of his/her peers have discontinued to do so,
- your child appears depressed, withdrawn and non-communicative,
- your child continues to exhibit poorer academic performance and a decreased capacity for concentration,
- your child expresses suicidal or homicidal ideation, or your child is intentionally hurting him/herself (e.g., cutting him/herself),
- your child exhibits an apparent increase usage of alcohol or drugs,
- your child gains or loses a significant amount of weight in a short period of time,

- your child evidences significant changes in behavior, and
- your child discontinues attending to his/her hygienic needs.

What can school personnel provide in the form of support and intervention for your child?

The Crisis Response Plan discussed earlier incorporates support and intervention to help your child return to pre-crisis functioning and cope effectively with the crisis. Teachers have been made aware through similar literature as this, disseminated by the district, on how to address their students' needs. The building psychologist, social worker and/or guidance counselors can consult with teachers to help them deal effectively with their students' reaction to the crisis. Discussions led by support staff and/or the classroom teacher regarding the crisis can be implemented if deemed necessary. These discussions hopefully will afford your child a forum in order to express his/her feelings regarding the crisis and understand how his/her classmates are coping. Specialized work may be assigned that can help your child to deal with the emotional aftermath of the crisis.

The classroom teachers can also assess their students' functioning and recovery from the crisis. They should be sensitive to the effects of the crisis on their students and can adjust the classroom demands accordingly. They can also monitor their students for signs that additional, and more individualized intervention is needed. If your child is experiencing difficulty in class and/or is referred to support staff for assessment and/or intervention, you will be notified as soon as possible.

Conclusion

The immediacy and unpredictability of crisis situations often leave individuals with a sense of worry, vulnerability and distrust. A school system is unique in that it brings together individuals of all ages and professionals from numerous disciplines. Effective response to a crisis capitalizes on the resources within the school environment. *A Crisis Response Team that identifies and responds to a crisis in a unified and collaborative manner can alter the aftermath of a crisis.*

K. Preventing Violent Tragedies in Our Schools

Reprinted from *A Practical Guide for Crisis Response in Our Schools*
© 1999 by The American Academy of Experts in Traumatic Stress—Reproduced with Permission
368 Veterans Memorial Highway, Commack New York 11725
Tel. (516) 543-2217 • Fax (516) 543-6977 • http://www.aaets.org

During the last several years, there has been a dramatic increase in the frequency of violence in our schools including assaults on teachers and administrators, gang activity, substance abuse, sexual assaults, child molestation, abandonment of newborns, homicide and adolescent suicide. And today, we are also contending with new types of trauma including hostage-taking, sniper attacks and bombings.

In response to this disturbing trend, The American Academy of Experts in Traumatic Stress published *A Practical Guide for Crisis Response in Our Schools*. Today, the fourth edition of this guide is being utilized as a "Crisis Response Plan" by school districts across the country. The importance of having an organized and preconceived strategy for responding effectively in the wake of a school-based tragedy cannot be underscored enough.

Notwithstanding, in the face of a rapidly changing zeitgeist, we must address means of *preventing* violent tragedies in our schools. Specifically, we need to assist children in developing their communication, coping and problem-solving skills. The following are practical strategies.

We must help our children to:

- develop and enhance their communication and problem-solving skills,

- understand the importance of articulating their feelings about themselves and for others,

- know that it is okay to err on the side of caution when expressing their concerns about others,

- regularly remind them that they can turn to school support personnel who will take the time to listen and respond to them,

- identify physiological changes in their bodies which may precede or coincide with feelings of frustration and anger,

- understand which behaviors/actions cause others to become frustrated and angry,

- become aware of and identify negative self-statements that generate feelings of frustration and anger,

- learn to replace self-defeating statements with positive coping statements, and

- learn to make more adaptive goal-directed decisions when faced with feelings of frustration (e.g., deciding to walk-away from altercations... to take a few moments to "cool down"... to express oneself assertively... to implement relaxation techniques, or to utilize conflict resolution skills).

L. Identifying Students "At-Risk" for Violent Behavior: A Checklist of "Early Warning Signs"

Reprinted from *A Practical Guide for Crisis Response in Our Schools*
© 1999 by The American Academy of Experts in Traumatic Stress—Reproduced with Permission
368 Veterans Memorial Highway, Commack New York 11725
Tel. (516) 543-2217 • Fax (516) 543-6977 • http://www.aaets.org

There has been a dramatic increase in the frequency of violence in our schools and, in a sense, we should consider all of our students "at-risk." The purpose of this Infosheet is to assist parents and school personnel in identifying children and adolescents who are at greater risk for engaging in violent behavior.

The following checklist of "early warning signs" will facilitate identification of students who may be in need of intervention. The greater the number of items that are checked, the greater the potential for violent acting-out behavior. For help, turn to individuals who regularly work with at-risk children and adolescents—professionals in the fields of education, law enforcement, social services, medicine, mental heath, etc.

Children and adolescents at-risk may:

- ❏ express self-destructive or homicidal ideation
- ❏ have a history of self-destructive behavior
- ❏ articulate specific plans to harm self and/or others
- ❏ engage in "bullying" other children
- ❏ have difficulty with impulse control
- ❏ evidence significant changes in behavior
- ❏ engage in substance abuse
- ❏ become involved with gangs
- ❏ evidence a preoccupation with fighting
- ❏ have a history of antisocial behavior
- ❏ evidence a low tolerance for frustration
- ❏ externalize blame for their difficulties
- ❏ have harmed small animals
- ❏ have engaged in fire setting
- ❏ evidence persistent bed wetting
- ❏ appear/acknowledge feeling depressed
- ❏ talk about not being around

- ❏ express feelings of hopelessness
- ❏ give away possessions
- ❏ appear withdrawn
- ❏ evidence significant changes in mood
- ❏ experience sleep and eating disturbances
- ❏ have experienced prior trauma/tragedy
- ❏ have been/are victims of child abuse
- ❏ have experienced a significant loss
- ❏ evidence a preoccupation with television programs/movies with violent themes
- ❏ evidence a preoccupation with games with violent themes
- ❏ evidence a preoccupation with guns and other weapons
- ❏ have access to a firearm
- ❏ have brought a weapon to school
- ❏ evidence frequent disciplinary problems
- ❏ exhibit poor academic performance
- ❏ have been frequently truant from school

M. About the Academy

The American Academy of Experts in Traumatic Stress is a multidisciplinary network of professionals who are committed to the advancement of intervention for survivors of trauma. Our international membership includes individuals from over 200 professions in the health-related fields, emergency services, criminal justice, forensics, law, business and education. The Academy is presently represented by professionals in every state of the United States and over 40 foreign countries.

Society is becoming increasingly aware of the emotional, cognitive and behavioral experience of individuals facing a serious illness or who are exposed to other significant traumatic events. The Academy recognized a need to identify expertise among professionals, across disciplines, and to provide standards for those who regularly work with survivors. Our association is now the largest organization of its kind in the world.

The mission of the Academy is to increase awareness of the effects of trauma and, ultimately, to improve the quality of intervention with survivors. It is in this spirit that we offer:

- membership/associate membership in a prestigious professional association,
- Board Certification Programs,
- Diplomate and Fellow Credentials,
- continuing education credits,
- *Trauma Response®*, *The Academy Update*™ and *Trauma Response® Infosheets*™, the official publications of the Academy,
- listing in *The National Registry of The American Academy of Experts in Traumatic Stress*™,
- an award winning "guest quarters" on the Internet at http://www.aaets.org,
- an Automated Fax Back System (516) 771-8103, and
- a Code of Ethical & Professional Standards.

Membership

Membership with The American Academy of Experts in Traumatic Stress demonstrates a commitment to the field. It is the first step in a sequential process aimed at identifying expertise among professionals across disciplines. There are four levels of membership in the Academy:

- **Member**

  Members must hold a Doctorate in their field of expertise or hold a Masters Degree and have a minimum of three (3) years experience working with survivors of traumatic events. The Executive Officers reserve the right to grant membership to an individual who does not meet the aforementioned criteria, but who has made important contributions to the field or to the Academy.

- **Associate Member**

  This non-doctoral level of membership is reserved for individuals who have at least two (2) years experience working with survivors of traumatic events. Associate Members are afforded all benefits of membership with the exception of qualifying for the Diplomate credential. However, qualified Associate Members may apply for other Academy certifications.

- **Diplomate**

  Members of the Academy may apply for the designation Board Certified Expert in Traumatic Stress—Diplomate, American Academy of Experts in Traumatic Stress.

  To achieve this credential, a comprehensive application and examination, along with supporting documentation, are utilized in concert to validate a member's experience working with survivors of traumatic events, knowledge of the literature and level of education. The Diplomate credential establishes a much needed standard for professionals, across disciplines, who regularly work with survivors of traumatic events. It is the aim of the Academy to have all of our qualified members achieve Diplomate status.

- **Fellow**

  Fellowship is the highest honor the Academy can bestow upon a member. This designation is awarded to Diplomates who have made significant contributions to the field and to the Academy.

Continuing Education Credits

The Academy awards eight (8) continuing education credits to those members who successfully complete the application/examination process leading to Board Certification and the Diplomate Credential. Additionally, six (6) credits are also awarded to those credentialed experts who complete the evaluative process leading to Fellowship with the Academy.

Publications

Trauma Response®, *The Academy Update*™ and *Trauma Response® Infosheets*™ are the official publications of the Academy. *Trauma Response®* and *Trauma Response® Infosheets*™ offer members, from diverse specialties, the opportunity to have articles peer reviewed and published. *The Academy Update*™ aims to keep members informed of organizational developments.

Certification Programs in Traumatic Stress Specialties

All qualified Members and Associate Members of the Academy will have the opportunity to pursue the following credentials:

 Board Certification in Forensic Traumatology™
 Board Certification in Emergency Crisis Response™
 Board Certification in Motor Vehicle Trauma™
 Board Certification in Disability Trauma™
 Board Certification in Pain Management™
 Board Certification in Illness Trauma™
 Board Certification in Bereavement Trauma™
 Board Certification in Domestic Violence™
 Board Certification in Sexual Abuse™
 Board Certification in Rape Trauma™
 Board Certification in Stress Management™
 Board Certification in School Crisis Response™

These programs require candidates to demonstrate extensive knowledge, experience and education specific to each certification area.

The National Registry

All members in good standing are listed in *The National Registry of The American Academy of Experts in Traumatic Stress*™, the association's official directory and referral network. Members who have achieved Board Certification are listed as credentialed experts in the field. The registry is available in bound copy and can also be accessed directly through the Academy's award winning "guest quarters" on the Internet at **http://www.aaets.org**.

Credentials

The following are examples of the correct use of The American Academy of Experts in Traumatic Stress' credentials:

- A Member may present his/her status as:
  Robert J. Miller, M.D.
  Member, American Academy of Experts in Traumatic Stress
  Listed in The National Registry of The American Academy of Experts in Traumatic Stress

- A Board Certified Expert — Diplomate may use the following credentials:
  Robert J. Miller, M.D., B.C.E.T.S.
  Board Certified Expert in Traumatic Stress
  Diplomate, American Academy of Experts in Traumatic Stress
  Listed in The National Registry of The American Academy of Experts in Traumatic Stress

- A Fellow (who has achieved Board Certification) may use the following credentials:
  Robert J. Miller, M.D., B.C.E.T.S., F.A.A.E.T.S.
  Board Certified Expert in Traumatic Stress
  Fellow, American Academy of Experts in Traumatic Stress
  Listed in The National Registry of The American Academy of Experts in Traumatic Stress

Members, Associate Members, Diplomates and Fellows who have achieved additional certifications with the Academy in a specialty area may identify themselves with the appropriate credential (e.g., Board Certified in Forensic Traumatology, Board Certified in Emergency Crisis Response, etc.). These professionals may additionally use the respective Academy Credentials, after their educational degree (e.g., Ph.D., B.C.F.T.) or other primary certification (e.g., E.M.T., B.C.E.C.R.), denoting their achievement of specific Academy certifications.

Code of Ethical & Professional Standards

As a multidisciplinary group of professionals, the Academy established a Code of Ethical & Professional Standards for practice across disciplines. All members must adhere to the code.

As a member of The American Academy of Experts in Traumatic Stress, I pledge:

- To be committed to the advancement of intervention for survivors of trauma.
- To maintain the highest standards of competence and professional practice in my work with trauma victims.
- To provide only those services for which I am qualified by virtue of my knowledge, experience and education.
- To maintain my knowledge of the research literature directly related to the services I render.
- To respect the rights of individuals to privacy and confidentiality.
- To never misrepresent my credentials, education or membership status.
- To refrain from conduct that would be adverse to the interest and purpose of the Academy.
- To work toward increasing awareness of traumatic stress and improving intervention with survivors.

Excerpts from *Trauma Response*® Profiles

"The American Academy of Experts in Traumatic Stress fosters awareness. As Sir Francis Bacon said, 'Information is Power.' If we are aware that there is a problem, then there will be people motivated to address the problem. The Academy additionally fosters discovery, innovation, creativity and advancement. And I think that an organization like the Academy helps us strive for raising, to some degree shall I say, the level of quality assurance in the field while promoting creativity and innovation—all with the ultimate goal of being able to better serve people in need."

George S. Everly, Jr., Ph.D., B.C.E.T.S., F.A.A.E.T.S.
Founder & Senior Representative to the United Nations for
the International Critical Incident Stress Foundation

"Being an eclectic group is a very great strength because it allows for a cross-pollination of strategies that have been effective in different disciplines.... The Academy has brought together the best and the brightest to work on better understanding of what it is that occurs during traumatic stress and how to advance clinical applications."

Francine Shapiro, Ph.D., B.C.E.T.S.
Originator & Developer of EMDR

"The Academy is a good forum for a variety of professionals to show people (i.e., survivors of traumatic events) that they can cope with the worst kind of adversity or trauma and not upset themselves about it. Now, people in the field who have some "know-how" in working with trauma can be located in the Academy's National Registry—I think that is a good idea."

Albert Ellis, Ph.D., B.C.E.T.S., B.C.B.T.
Founder, Albert Ellis Institute

"The American Academy of Experts in Traumatic Stress serves a unique and vital purpose. We have to take traumatic stress out of the exclusive domain of psychology and psychiatry. We have to do this! Traumatic stress and its aftermath belong to all of us—medical doctors, lawyers, police departments, psychologists, psychiatrists, teachers, insurance companies, legislators, etc. Education is a crucial step and the issues must be addressed in a public forum."

Beverly J. Anderson, Ph.D., B.C.E.T.S.
President, American Academy of Police Psychology

"Providing an umbrella organization that facilitates dialogue is a valuable service. What the physician, the emergency worker and the psychotherapist have in common and how interventions can be coordinated across disciplines is important. Such a dialogue should result in better treatments for survivors and for those who provide such services."

Donald Meichenbaum, Ph.D.
Clinical Psychologist

"The Academy is multidisciplinary and facilitates different professions coming together under one umbrella. I think that's a great virtue. The cross-pollination that comes from that kind of interaction can only begin to generate a deeper understanding of the phenomenon of traumatic stress as it affects victims and survivors of trauma from all kinds of experience. The Academy provides the opportunity to bring together efforts which allow us to define a mission that transcends ourselves. And in that sense, the Academy, with its diverse and international membership, provides a forum for education, training, publication, and consultation. This not only becomes a national priority or national opportunity, it becomes a potentially global priority of internetting experts in traumatic stress. And I can't think of many things more exciting from my perspective than trying to actualize those objectives which are readily achievable given our technological capacities."

John P. Wilson, Ph.D., B.C.E.T.S., F.A.A.E.T.S.
Founding Member and Past
President of the International
Society for Traumatic Stress Studies

"One of the Academy's major contributions has to do with the fact that this field is so much bigger than any of the individuals in it. To achieve great things, we need to join resources together and have a multidisciplinary approach. Instead of competing, we need to cooperate. Working together, I think we have greater potential to make a larger impact. No one will listen to a small organization with a few members, but when you have a large organization that cuts across the boundaries of many, many professions, then politicians will listen, governments will listen, the citizens will listen, perhaps a serious difference can be made rather than trying to do this all by one's self. I just don't think it's a good idea to work alone in this field—we need to be allied with one another and assist one another in making progress to do something to mitigate the impact of traumatic stress in people's lives."

Jeffrey T. Mitchell, Ph.D.
President, International Critical Incident Stress Foundation

Committed to the Advancement of Intervention for Survivors of Trauma

The American Academy of Experts in Traumatic Stress®
368 Veterans Memorial Hwy., Commack, NY 11725 • Tel. (516) 543-2217 • Fax (516) 543-6977 • Automated Fax Back System (516) 771-8103 • http://www.aaets.org

REFERENCES

Acklin, M.W. (1998). Divorce your spouse, not the kids. http://www.divorcesource.com.

Adolescent Pregnancy Prevention, Inc. (1998). Statistics and facts about teen pregnancy. http://www.appifw.org.

American Academy of Pediatrics (1994). Divorce and children. Elk Grove Village, IL: American Academy of Pediatrics

American Foundation for Suicide Prevention (1996). Suicide Facts: Child and Adolescent Suicide.

American Foundation for Suicide Prevention (1998). Youth Suicide. http://www.afsp.org.

American Psychiatric Association (1994). Diagnostic and statistical manual of mental disorders (4th ed.) Washington, DC: Author.

American Psychological Association (1999). Warning signs. http://helping.apa.org.

Anderson, K. (1998). Drug abuse. Probe Ministries, http://www.leaderu.com.

Baker, J.E., Sedney, M., & Gross, E. (1992). Psychological tasks for bereaved children. American Journal of Orthopsychiatry, 62, 105-116.

Baker, J.E., & Sedney, M. (1996). How bereaved children cope with loss: An overview. In C.A. Corr & D.M. Corr (Eds.), Handbook of childhood death and bereavement (pp. 109-129). New York: Springer.

Baum, A., Fleming, R., & Davidson, L.M. (1983). Natural disaster and technological catastrophe. Environment and Behavior, 15, 333-354.

Blanchard, E.B., & Hickling, E.J. (1997). After the crash: Assessment and treatment of motor vehicle accident survivors. Washington, DC: American Psychological Association.

Bowlby, J. (1980). Attachment and loss, Vol. 3 - Sadness and depression. New York: Basic Books.

Center for Disease Control and Prevention (1994). CDC, adolescent and HIV/AIDS. Health Information: Adolescents & HIV/AIDS. CDC National AIDS Clearinghouse.

Center for Disease Control and Prevention (1998). National Center for HIV, STD, and TB Prevention.

Child Welfare Partnership (1995). Domestic violence summary: The intersection of child abuse and domestic violence. Published by Portland State University.

Davidson, L.E. (1989). Suicide cluster and youth. In C.R. Pfeffer (Ed.), Suicide among youth (pp. 83-99). Washington, DC: American Psychiatric Press.

Dutton, M.A. (1992). Women's response to battering: Assessment and intervention. New York: Springer.

Dutton, M.A. (1994). Post-traumatic therapy with domestic violence survivors. In M.B. Williams & J.F. Sommer (Eds.), Handbook of post-traumatic therapy (pp. 146-161). Westport, CT: Greenwood Press.

Figley, C.R. (1995). Compassion fatigue: Coping with secondary traumatic stress disorder in those who treat the traumatized. New York: Brunner/Mazel.

Forman, S.G. (1993). Coping skills interventions for children and adolescents. San Francisco, CA: Jossey-Bass.

Foy, D.W. (1992). Introduction and description of the disorder. In D. W. Foy (Ed.), Treating PTSD: Cognitive-Behavioral strategies (pp 1-12). New York: Guilford.

Fremouw, W.J., de Perczel, M., & Ellis, T.E. (1990). Suicide risk: Assessment and response guidelines. New York: Pergamon.

Ganley, A. (1989). Integrating feminist and social learning analyses of aggression: Creating multiple models for intervention with men who battered. In P. Caesar & L. Hamberger (Eds.), Treating men who batter (pp. 196-235). New York: Springer.

Gonet, M. (1994). Counseling the adolescent substance abuser: School-based intervention and prevention. Thousand Oaks, CA: Sage.

Graham-Bermann, S. (1994). Preventing domestic violence. University of Michigan research information index. UM-Research-WEB@umich.edu.

Greenstone, J.L., & Levittown, S.C. (1993). Elements of crisis intervention: Crises & how to respond to them. California: Brooks/Cole.

Harmon, M. (1993). Reducing the risk of drug involvement among early adolescents: An evaluation of drug abuse resistance education (DARE), Institute of Criminal Justice and Criminology, University of Maryland.

Hill, D.C., & Foster, Y.M. (1996). Postvention with early and middle adolescents. In C.A. Corr & D.E. Balk (Eds.), Handbook of adolescent death and bereavement (pp. 250-272). New York: Springer.

Klingman, A. (1987). A school-based emergency crisis intervention in a mass school disaster. Professional Psychology: Research and Practice, 18, 604-612.

Kovacs, M., & Beck, A.T. (1977). An empirical approach toward a definition of childhood depression. In J. G. Shchulterbrandt & A. Raskin (Eds.), Depression in childhood: Diagnosis, treatment and conceptual models (pp. 43-57). New York: Raven Press.

Kovacs, M., Goldston, D., & Gatsonis, C. (1993). Suicidal behavior and childhood-onset depressive disorders: A longitudinal investigation. Journal of the American Academy of Child and Adolescent Psychiatry, 32, 8-20.

Kubler-Ross, E. (1969). On death and dying, New York: MacMillan.

Lerner, M. (1988). Perceptions of Desirable Characteristics of Psychotherapists. Doctoral Dissertation. Hofstra University.

Lerner, M. (1997). Early Intervention—A Multidisciplinary Effort. Trauma Response. The American Academy of Experts in Traumatic Stress, Winter, 1997.

Lerner, M. (1998). From the President's Desk. Trauma Response. The American Academy of Experts in Traumatic Stress.

Matsakis, A. (1996). I can't get over it: A handbook for trauma survivors (2nd ed.). Oakland, CA: New Harbinger Publications.

McKay, M. (1994). The link between domestic violence and child abuse: Assessment and treatment considerations. Child Welfare League of America, 73, 29-39.

McKee, P.W., Jones, R.W., & Richardson, J.A. (1991, November). Student suicide: Educational, psychological issues, and legal issues for schools. Paper presented at the LRP Publications Conference, San Francisco, CA.

Meichenbaum, D. (1994). A clinical handbook/practical therapist manual for assessing and treating adults with post-traumatic stress disorder. Ontario, Canada: Institute Press.

Meyers, A.W., & Craighead, W.D. (1984) (Eds.). Cognitive behavior therapy with children. New York: Plenum Press.

National Highway Traffic Safety Administration (1998). Young drivers: Traffic safety facts, 1997. U.S. Department of Transportation.

National Institute on Drug Abuse (1994). Monitoring the future study, 1975-1994; National high school senior drug abuse survey. NIDA Capsules. Rockville, MD: National Institute on Drug Abuse.

National Institute of Mental Health (1992). Suicide facts. Mental Health Fax4U.

Noppe, L.D., & Noppe, I.C., (1996). Ambiguity in adolescent understandings of death. In C.A. Corr & D.E. Balk (Eds.), Handbook of adolescent death and bereavement (pp. 25-41). New York: Springer.

Oltjenbruns, K.A. (1996). Death of a friend during adolescence: Issues and impacts. In C.A. Corr & D.E. Balk (Eds.), Handbook of adolescent death and bereavement (pp. 196-215). New York: Springer.

Olweus, D. (1984). Development of stable aggressive reaction: Patterns on males. In R.J. Blanchard & D.C. Blanchard (Eds.), Advances in the study of aggression (pp. 103-137). New York: Academic Press.

Petersen, S. & Straub, R.L. (1992). School crisis survival guide. West Nyack, NY: The Center for Applied Research in Education.

Pitcher, G.D. & Poland, S. (1992). Crisis intervention in the schools. New York: The Guilford Press.

Planned Parenthood (1998). Fact sheets: Reducing teenage pregnancy. http://www.plannedparenthood.org.

Princeton Survey Research Associates (1996). The 1996 Kaiser family foundation survey on teens and sex: What they say teens today need to know and who they listen to. Menlo Park, CA: The Henry J. Kaiser Family Foundation.

Range, L. (1996). Suicide and life-threatening behavior in childhood. In C.A. Corr & D.E. Balk (Eds.), Handbook of adolescent death and bereavement (pp. 71-88). New York: Springer.

Regier, D.A., & Cowdry, R.W. (1995). Research on violence and traumatic stress (program announcement, PA 95-068). National Institute of Mental Health.

Reynolds, W. (1987). Suicide ideation questionnaire. Odessa, FL: Psychological Assessment Resources.

Sandoval, J., & Brock, S.E. (1996). The school psychologist's role in suicide prevention. School Psychology Quarterly, 11, 169-185.

Sexual Assault Survivor Services (1996). Facts about domestic violence. http://www.portup.com.

Sexuality Information and Education Council of the U.S. (1995). Fact sheet: Sexuality education in the schools - issues and answers. New York: Sexuality Information and Education Council of the U.S.

Solomon, S., Gerrity, E.T., & Muff, A.M. (1992). Efficacy of treatments for Posttraumatic Stress Disorder: An empirical review. Journal of the American Medical Association, 268, 633-638.

Straus, M.A., & Gelles, R.J. (1990). Physical violence in American families. New Brunswick, NJ: Transaction Publishers.

Substance Abuse and Mental Health Services Administration (1994). National household survey on drug abuse: Population estimates, 1993. Rockville, MD: Department of Health and Human Services, Substance Abuse and Mental Health Services Administration (DHHS Publication no. (SMA) 94-3017).

Terr, L. (1991). Childhood trauma: An outline and overview. American Journal of Psychiatry, 148, 10-20.

The Center for the Study and Prevention of Violence (1999). http://www.colorado.edu/cspv.

United States Department of Justice (1994). Violent crime. Doc. NCJ-147486.

United States Department of Justice (1998). Bureau of Justice Statistics.

Ursano, R.J., McCaughey, B.GF., & Fullerton, C.S. (1994). Individual and community responses to trauma and disaster: The structure of human chaos. New York: Cambridge.

Weaver, J.D. (1995). Disasters: Mental health interventions. Sarasota, FL: Professional Resource Press.

Weinberg, R.B. (1990). Serving large numbers of adolescent victim-survivors: Group interventions at school. Professional Psychology: Research and Practice, 21, 271-278.

Yehuda, R., Resnick, H., Kahana, J., & Giller, E. (1993). Long-lasting hormonal alterations to extreme stress in humans: Normative or maladaptive? Psychosomatic Medicine, 5, 287-297.

The American Academy of Experts in Traumatic Stress®

MEMBERSHIP APPLICATION

Last Name   First Name   M.I.   Title (Dr., Mr., Mrs., Ms.)

Street Address   City   State   Zip Code

Home Telephone (non-published)   Office Telephone(s)   Fax Number

E-mail Address   Highest Educational Degree   Years of Experience in Field

The following list reflects the **professions** of the membership of the Academy at the time of printing. Carefully fill in the boxes corresponding to as many as three (3) of your **primary** professions.

- acupuncture
- addiction medicine
- addictionology
- aerospace psychology
- applied psychology
- anesthesiology
- aviation medicine
- bariatric medicine
- behavioral medicine
- bereavement counseling
- biofeedback
- biomedical engineering
- cardiac rehabilitation
- cardiology
- cardiovascular surgery
- career couns./develop.
- child abuse management
- child psychology
- child psychiatry
- chiropractic
- Christian counseling
- clergy
- clinical psychology
- clinical social work
- colon & rectal surgery
- community health
- community psychology
- community trauma intervention
- coroner
- corrections officer
- counseling
- counseling psychology
- court interpreter
- criminal justice
- crisis intervention
- critical incident debrief.
- critical care
- cross cultural psychiatry
- dentistry
- disability evaluation

- disability management
- disability medicine
- disaster relief
- disaster response
- diving medicine
- divorce mediation
- economist
- education
- EMDR
- emergency med. services
- emergency medicine
- emergency psychiatry
- emergency services
- employee assistance
- endocrinology
- family medicine
- female psychology
- fire service
- flight nursing
- flight surgery
- forensic dentistry
- forensic medicine
- forensic odontology
- forensic pathology
- forensic psychiatry
- forensic psychology
- forensic science
- forensic traumatology
- gastroenterology
- general medicine
- geriatric medicine
- gerontology
- geropsychology
- gynecology
- hand surgery
- health education
- health law & policy
- health psychology
- holistic healing
- holistic medicine

- homeopathic med.
- hostage negotiation
- human factors engineering
- hypnosis
- injury prevention
- insurance medicine
- integrative medicine
- intensive care med.
- internal medicine
- journalism
- law
- legal medicine
- liability management
- marriage & family ther.
- massage therapy
- media psychology
- mediation
- medical oncology
- medical psychology
- medical psychother.
- medical writer
- motor vehicle trauma
- military chaplaincy
- military medicine
- military psychology
- mind-body integration
- mind-body medicine
- mind-body therapy
- ministry
- muscle therapy
- music therapy
- natural disaster trauma
- NLP
- neonatology
- nephrology
- neurobehavioral toxicology
- neurologic surgery
- neurological rehab.
- neurology
- neuropsychology

- neurosurgery
- nuclear medicine
- nursing
- nursing administration
- nursing education
- nutrition
- obstetrics
- occupational medicine
- ophthalmology
- oral & maxillo-facial surg.
- orthopedic surgery
- osteopathic & holistic med.
- pain management
- pain medicine
- parapsychology
- pastoral counseling
- pathology
- peace psychology
- pediatrics
- penologic medicine
- pharmacology
- pharmacy
- physiatry
- physical medicine
- physical therapy
- physical trainer
- physician assistant
- plastic & recon. surgery
- podiatric medicine
- police officer
- police psychology
- preventative medicine
- professor
- psychiatric nursing
- psychiatry
- psychoanalysis
- psychobiology
- psychodramatist
- psychohistory
- psycho-oncology

- psychopharmacology
- psychotherapy
- public health administra.
- pulmonary medicine
- pulmonary rehabilitation
- rehabilitation
- rehabilitation medicine
- rehabilitation psychology
- respiratory therapy
- school counseling
- school psychology
- sex therapy
- social work
- spiritual psychotherapy
- speech-language pathol.
- sports medicine
- sports psychology
- substance abuse testing
- suicideology
- surgery
- surgical critical care
- surgical pathology
- thoracic surgery
- toxicology
- transpersonal hypnotherapy
- transpersonal psychology
- trauma surgery
- trauma therapy
- traumatology
- trial advocacy
- trial attorney
- trigger point myotherapy
- veterinary medicine
- vocational counseling
- war surgery
- **other:**

All members will have the opportunity to provide additional information (e.g., areas of specialization) for *The National Registry*, the Academy's official membership directory and referral network. I wish to apply for:

❑ Membership

Membership with The American Academy of Experts in Traumatic Stress demonstrates a commitment to the advancement of intervention for survivors of trauma. Members must hold a Doctorate in their field of expertise or hold a Masters Degree and have a minimum of three (3) years experience working with survivors of traumatic events. All members of the Academy will receive a copy of the Academy's *Application & Examination for Board Certification and the Diplomate Credential*. Qualified Members may additionally apply for other Academy certifications. Annual dues payment for membership is **$ 125**.

❑ Associate Membership

Associate Membership with The American Academy of Experts in Traumatic Stress demonstrates a commitment to the advancement of intervention for survivors of trauma. This non-doctoral level of membership is reserved for individuals who have at least two (2) years experience working with survivors of traumatic events. Associate Members are afforded all benefits of membership with the exception of qualifying for the Diplomate Credential. However, qualified Associate Members may apply for other Academy certifications. Annual dues payment for associate membership is **$ 80**.

Please send me information about the Academy's other certification programs:

- ❑ BOARD CERTIFICATION IN FORENSIC TRAUMATOLOGY™
- ❑ BOARD CERTIFICATION IN EMERGENCY CRISIS RESPONSE™
- ❑ BOARD CERTIFICATION IN MOTOR VEHICLE TRAUMA™
- ❑ BOARD CERTIFICATION IN DISABILITY TRAUMA™
- ❑ BOARD CERTIFICATION IN PAIN MANAGEMENT™
- ❑ BOARD CERTIFICATION IN ILLNESS TRAUMA™
- ❑ BOARD CERTIFICATION IN BEREAVEMENT TRAUMA™
- ❑ BOARD CERTIFICATION IN DOMESTIC VIOLENCE™
- ❑ BOARD CERTIFICATION IN SEXUAL ABUSE™
- ❑ BOARD CERTIFICATION IN RAPE TRAUMA™
- ❑ BOARD CERTIFICATION IN STRESS MANAGEMENT™
- ❑ BOARD CERTIFICATION IN SCHOOL CRISIS RESPONSE™

Membership dues payment **must** accompany this application. Please make personal/company check (from an American Bank only) payable to **The American Academy of Experts in Traumatic Stress, Inc.** Upon approval of the Executive Officers, an elegant membership/associate membership certificate, suitable for framing, will be forwarded to you and you will begin receiving *Trauma Response*® and *The Academy Update*™, the Academy's official publications.

I certify that the information provided on this application is accurate and complete:

Signature   Date

Enclosed is my check for $_____ or please charge $_____ to my ❑ VISA   ❑ American Express   ❑ MasterCard   ❑ Discover Card

Account No.   Expiration Date   Signature   Date

The American Academy of Experts in Traumatic Stress®

368 Veterans Memorial Highway, Commack, New York 11725 • Telephone (516) 543-2217 • Fax (516) 543-6977 • http://www.aaets.org

MEMBERSHIP APPLICATION & WAIVER OF EXAMINATION FORM FOR BOARD CERTIFICATION IN SCHOOL CRISIS RESPONSE™

Last Name	First Name	M.I.	Title (Dr., Mr., Mrs., Ms.)

Street Address	City	State	Zip Code

Home Telephone (non-published)	Office Telephone(s)	Fax Number

E-mail Address	Highest Educational Degree	Years of Experience in Field

Membership with The American Academy of Experts in Traumatic Stress® demonstrates a commitment to the advancement of intervention for survivors of trauma. The designation, **Board Certified in School Crisis Response**™ is awarded by the Academy to professionals who demonstrate *expertise* in the field by virtue of their extensive knowledge, experience and education. This waiver of examination is offered to qualified professionals as part of a time-limited Grandfather Period. Candidates must achieve or exceed a total score of 100 points. Certified professionals are identified in the Academy's National Registry, the association's official directory and referral network. The registry is available in bound copy and can also be accessed directly on the Internet at **http://www.aaets.org**.

Applicants who fail to demonstrate that they have met the requisite criteria for Certification will be informed as to the reason for denial. The applicant will be given a second opportunity to provide additional supportive documentation. If an applicant continues to provide insufficient data, the Academy will refund the full fee required for certification.

Please place a check in the appropriate boxes:

EDUCATION (Check box representing your highest level of education/training)

❐ Doctoral level education/training with relevant course work concerning school counseling and/or school crisis response (60 pts.)
❐ Masters level education/training with relevant course work concerning school counseling and/or school crisis response (50 pts.)
❐ Bachelor level education/training with relevant course work concerning school counseling and/or school crisis response (30 pts.)

KNOWLEDGE

❐ Author/Co-author/Editor of a book related to school counseling and/or school crisis response (40 pts.)
❐ Author/Co-author of an article, paper and/or presentation related to school counseling and/or school crisis response (30 pts.)
❐ Have attended presentations, seminars and/or workshops related to school counseling and/or school crisis response (25 pts.)
❐ Hold a state license and/or certification in the mental health field independent of school certification (25 pts.)
❐ Hold an Administrative/supervisory certificate (20 pts.)

EXPERIENCE

❐ Twenty (20) or more years working in the schools (35 pts.)
❐ Ten (10) to nineteen (19) years working in the schools (30 pts.)
❐ Five (5) to nine (9) years working in the schools (25 pts.)
❐ Three (3) to four (4) years working in the schools (20 pts.)

TOTAL SCORE: _____

Please type or print your name and title as you would like it to appear on your certificates: _____

I hereby certify that all information provided on this Membership Application & Waiver of Examination Form is accurate and complete. I understand that **Board Certification in School Crisis Response**™ aims to establish a *standard* among professionals who regularly respond to school-based crises. I agree to abide by the Academy's Code of Ethical & Professional Standards and agree to hold harmless The American Academy of Experts in Traumatic Stress, Inc. its officers, consultants and employees for any misrepresentation of my credentials and for any malpractice on my part either willful or through negligent conduct, recklessness, and gross misconduct and for all claims, loss, damage, judgment or expense. I understand that The American Academy of Experts in Traumatic Stress does not practice medicine or psychology or provide direct or indirect patient/client care. Furthermore, I understand that Membership and/or Certification do not attest to my ability to treat survivors of traumatic events.

I understand that as a Member of the Academy I will be listed in the National Registry and that I will receive a copy of the Academy's *Application & Examination for Board Certification and the Diplomate Credential* as well as *Trauma Response*® and *The Academy Update*™, the Academy's official publications.

Signature	Date

Finally, in order for The American Academy of Experts in Traumatic Stress® to consider you for **Board Certification in School Crisis Response**™, you must:

- provide a copy of your resume/vita,
- provide copies of your State License and/or Certification(s), and
- enclose one time payment of **$350**.

Enclosed is my check for **$350** or please charge $350 to my ❐ VISA ❐ American Express ❐ MasterCard ❐ Discover Card

Account No.	Expiration Date	Signature	Date

Mail to:

The American Academy of Experts in Traumatic Stress
368 Veterans Memorial Highway, Commack, New York 11725

Quick Fax back to:

If paying by credit card, you may Fax back your Waiver Form <u>and</u> supporting documentation to: (516) 543-6977

IMPORTANT NOTICE:
PROFESSIONALS WHO ELECT TO APPLY DIRECTLY FOR THIS WAIVER OF EXAMINATION FOR BOARD CERTIFICATION IN SCHOOL CRISIS RESPONSE™ WILL HAVE THEIR FIRST YEAR MEMBERSHIP DUES PAYMENT WITH THE ACADEMY ($125) WAIVED.

The American Academy of Experts in Traumatic Stress®

Administrative Offices, 368 Veterans Memorial Highway, Commack, New York 11725
Tel. (516) 543-2217 • Fax (516) 543-6977 • Automated Fax Back System (516) 771-8103
http://www.aaets.org
FEDERAL IDENTIFICATION NO. 11-3285203

ORDER FORM

A PRACTICAL GUIDE FOR CRISIS RESPONSE IN OUR SCHOOLS
Fourth Edition

Name (Including Title): _____

Position: _____

School District: _____

Street Address: _____

City: _____

State & Zip Code: _____

Tel. No.: _____

Fax. No.: _____

PLEASE ASSIST THE ACADEMY IN KNOWING OTHER EDUCATORS
WHO MAY BE INTERESTED IN PURCHASING THIS GUIDE.

Name (Including Title): _____

Position: _____

School District: _____

Street Address: _____

City: _____

State & Zip Code: _____

Paperback 8 ½ x 11, 64 pages
ISBN 0-9674762-0-8
$19.95 US + S&H

Shipping & Handling
All orders are processed and shipped within 24 hours.
United States
Priority Mail: $5.00 first book, $1.00 for each additional book
For orders over 50, call the Academy at (516) 543-2217.
Canada & Foreign
Air Mail: $6.00 first book, $1.50 for each additional book

Purchase Orders
Purchase orders are accepted from school districts and
governmental agencies. The Academy's Fed. I.D. No. is 11-3285203.

Credit Card Orders
American Express, VISA, MasterCard or Discover Card are accepted.
Please telephone the Academy at (516) 543-2217.

Checks
Please make checks payable to:
The American Academy of Experts in Traumatic Stress.

Orders from Libraries & the Book Trade
Libraries, bookstores and other resellers, please contact the Academy at
(516) 543-2217 for pricing and discount information.

	Quantity	Price
$19.95 U.S. Funds	_____	_____
Shipping & Handling		_____
TOTAL AMOUNT		_____

For Credit Card Orders:

Please charge $_____ to my ❏ VISA ❏ American Express ❏ MasterCard ❏ Discover Card

_____   _____   _____   _____
Account No.   Expiration Date   Signature   Date

Please send this order form and your check or money order (i.e., Payable in U.S. Funds) to:
The American Academy of Experts in Traumatic Stress
Administrative Offices
368 Veterans Memorial Highway
Commack, New York 11725

THIS FORM MAY BE FAXED DIRECTLY TO THE ACADEMY'S ADMINISTRATIVE OFFICES FOR IMMEDIATE PROCESSING.
FAX: (516) 543-6977

dk online

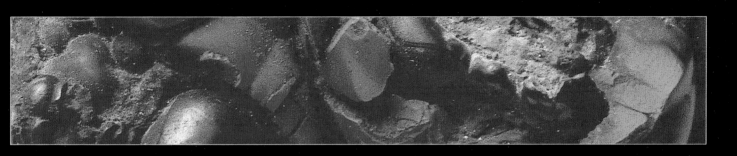

rock & mineral

LONDON, NEW YORK, MELBOURNE,
MUNICH, and DELHI

Senior Editor Clare Lister   **Project Art Editor** Steve Woosnam-Savage
Project Editor Nigel Ritchie   **Illustrator** Kuo Kang Chen
Weblink Editors Niki Foreman, Roger Brownlie

Managing Editor Linda Esposito   **Managing Art Editor** Diane Thistlethwaite

Digital Development Manager Fergus Day   **Picture Research** Cynthia Frazer
DTP Co-ordinator Tony Cutting   **Picture Librarians** Kate Ledwith, Sarah Mills, Karl Stange

Jacket Copywriter Adam Powley   **Production** Erica Rosen
Jacket Editor Mariza O'Keeffe   **Jacket Designer** Neal Cobourne

Publishing Managers Andrew Macintyre, Caroline Buckingham   **Art Director** Simon Webb

Consultant Steve Laurie, Sedgwick Museum, Department of Earth Sciences, University of Cambridge   **Produced for DK by Toucan Books Ltd.**
Managing Director Ellen Dupont

First American hardback edition 2005
This paperback edition first published in 2007
Published in the United States by DK Publishing, Inc.
375 Hudson Street, New York, New York 10014

05 06 07 08 09 10 9 8 7 6 5 4 3 2 1

A Cataloging-in-Publication record for this book is available from the
Library of Congress.

ISBN 978-0-75663-136-9

Color reproduction by Colourscan, Singapore
Printed in China by Toppan Printing Co. (Shenzen) Ltd.

Discover more at
www.dk.com

dk online

rock & mineral

Written by John Farndon

Google

CONTENTS

How to use the Web site

DK online Rock and Mineral has its own Web site, created by DK and Google™. When you look up a subject in the book, the article gives you key facts and displays a keyword that links you to extra information online. Just follow these easy steps.

http://www.rockandmineral.dkonline.com

 Enter this Web site address...

Address : http://www.rockandmineral.dkonline.com

 Enter the keyword...

Find the keyword in the book...

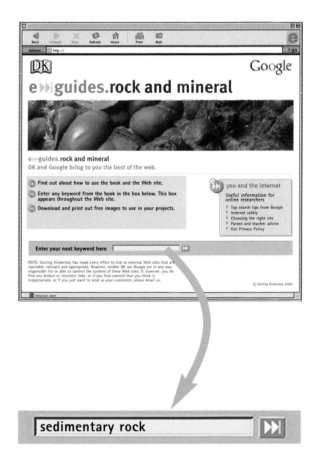

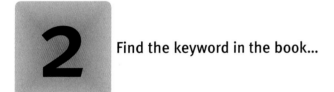
sedimentary rock

You can use only the keywords from the book to search on our Web site for the specially selected DK/Google links.

Be safe while you are online:

- Always get permission from an adult before connecting to the internet.

- Never give out personal information about yourself.

- Never arrange to meet someone you have talked to online.

- If a site asks you to log in with your name or email address, ask permission from an adult first.

- Do not reply to emails from strangers—tell an adult.

Parents: Dorling Kindersley actively and regularly reviews and updates the links. However, content may change. Dorling Kindersley is not responsible for any site but its own. We recommend that children are supervised while online, that they do not use chat rooms, and that filtering software is used to block unsuitable material.

 Click on your chosen link...

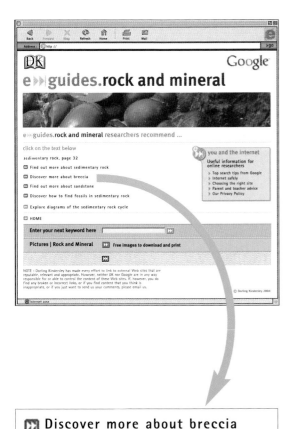

 Download fantastic pictures...

Pictures | Rock and Mineral

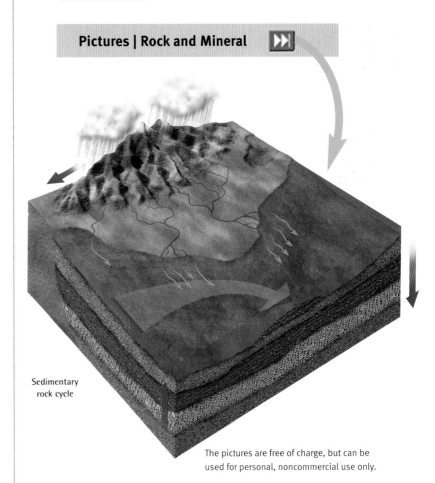

Sedimentary rock cycle

The pictures are free of charge, but can be used for personal, noncommercial use only.

▶▶ Discover more about breccia

Links include animations, videos, sound buttons, virtual tours, interactive quizzes, databases, timelines, and realtime reports.

Go back to the book for your next subject...

UNDERSTANDING THE LANDSCAPE ▲
By studying landscapes, geologists (Earth scientists) can understand the processes that have shaped them over billions of years. The magnificent Grand Canyon (shown above) in Arizona, which is 320 miles (515 km) long, was carved out of the desert by river erosion. This has revealed layers of ancient sandstone, resting on top of granite and gneiss.

ROCKY EARTH

Many millions of years ago humans used rocks as the first tools. This stage of humankind's development is known as the Stone Age. Later, people learned to use clay (rock particles) to make pottery, and since then vast numbers of ways of using rocks have been found. Almost every kind of rock can be cut or broken to provide building materials for our homes and cities. A huge range of minerals can be taken from the ground and processed to make particular materials. All our metals, such as iron and steel, come from minerals found in the rock. So too do most of our fuels, such as oil and coal, as well as the salt we put on food, the fertilizers we use to help grow our food, and much more.

Pole for taking lava samples

◄ VULCANOLOGIST AT WORK
The study of the Earth is such a huge subject that geology is divided into many specialties. Mineralogists study minerals, petrologists study rock, and vulcanologists study volcanoes. Because of the extreme temperatures, vulcanologists often wear special protective clothing, that reflects the heat away from them. Taking lava samples (shown here) for analysis of their mineral content is one method used to monitor volcanic eruptions.

rocks and minerals

MINING AND QUARRYING ►
Rocks and minerals are usually mined or quarried from the ground. Shown here is the Super Pit, Australia's largest opencast goldmine, which is 2 miles (3 km) long. Strip mining is used when the ore (rocks or minerals from which metal can be extracted for a profit) deposits are close to the surface. It is cheaper and easier than underground mining. Quarries are deep pits dug into the ground to allow the excavation of large quantities of building materials, such as large stone blocks or sand and gravel.

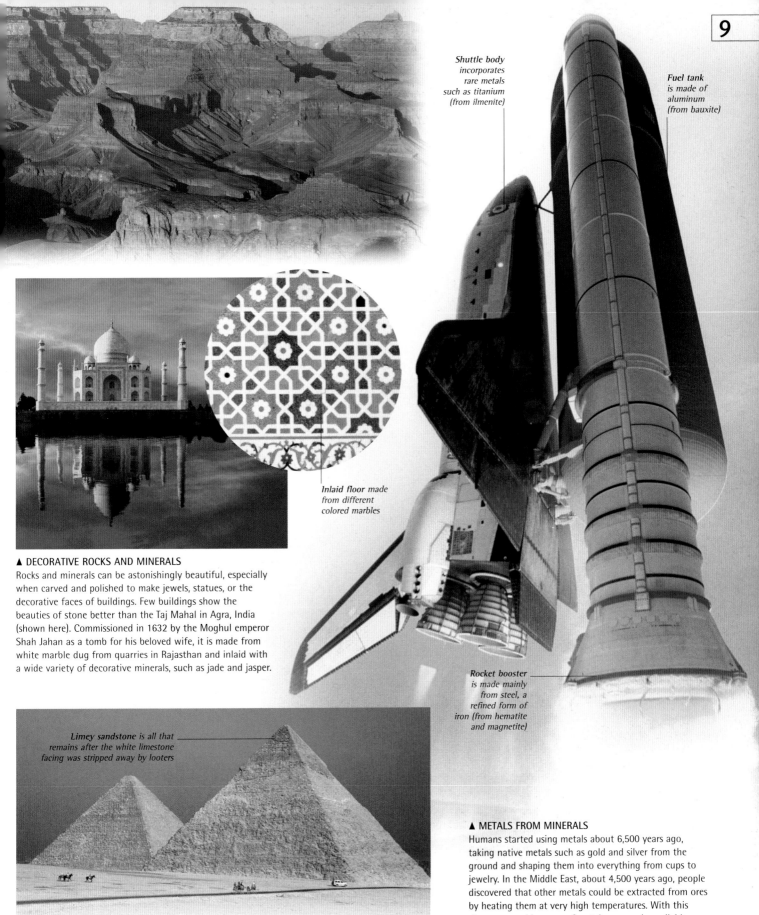

Shuttle body incorporates rare metals such as titanium (from ilmenite)

Fuel tank is made of aluminum (from bauxite)

Inlaid floor made from different colored marbles

Rocket booster is made mainly from steel, a refined form of iron (from hematite and magnetite)

Limey sandstone is all that remains after the white limestone facing was stripped away by looters

▲ DECORATIVE ROCKS AND MINERALS

Rocks and minerals can be astonishingly beautiful, especially when carved and polished to make jewels, statues, or the decorative faces of buildings. Few buildings show the beauties of stone better than the Taj Mahal in Agra, India (shown here). Commissioned in 1632 by the Moghul emperor Shah Jahan as a tomb for his beloved wife, it is made from white marble dug from quarries in Rajasthan and inlaid with a wide variety of decorative minerals, such as jade and jasper.

▲ BUILT TO LAST

When people want buildings to last, they build from stone because it is so durable. Few buildings have lasted longer than the Great Pyramids, erected by the Ancient Egyptians more than 3,500 years ago. The Egyptians were experts at using different kinds of rocks, and the pyramids are masterpieces of masonry. The cores of the three Great Pyramids of Giza—two of which are shown here—were made from millions of huge blocks of limey sandstone. These were then covered in brilliant white limestone and finished off with a granite capstone on the summit.

▲ METALS FROM MINERALS

Humans started using metals about 6,500 years ago, taking native metals such as gold and silver from the ground and shaping them into everything from cups to jewelry. In the Middle East, about 4,500 years ago, people discovered that other metals could be extracted from ores by heating them at very high temperatures. With this discovery, a wide range of metals was made available. These provided the raw materials for making nearly all our tools and machinery. Without these metals, technological developments such as the space shuttle (shown here) would never have been possible. All the metals used in the shuttle—from steel and aluminum to rarer light metals such as titanium—come from the Earth's mineral ores.

ROCKS AND MINERALS

Rocks and minerals are the raw materials of the Earth's surface. Rocks are made of countless grains of minerals—some large, some visible only under a microscope. A few rocks are made of a single mineral; others contain half a dozen or more. Minerals are natural, solid chemicals. They are classified according to their chemistry and structure. Rocks are put in three groups according to how they formed: igneous (from molten rock), metamorphic (altered by extreme heat and pressure), and sedimentary (created from layers of sediment—loose material that has settled).

COPPER COMPOUND ▲
Most minerals are compounds (combinations) of at least two chemical elements. Carbonate minerals, for example, form when metals and semimetals combine with a carbonate, which is a compound of carbon and oxygen. Malachite (shown here) is carbonate formed with copper, which gives it a bright green color.

Sulfur deposits brought to surface by hot spring activity

Sulfur minerals transported away by river

◄ ELEMENTAL SULFUR
Only a few minerals are native elements—minerals made entirely from a single chemical element. Even fewer are nonmetal native elements. Sulfur is one of these. At the hot springs in Yellowstone Park (shown left), sulfur deposits have been left behind by very hot, mineral-rich water emerging from the Earth's crust.

rocks and minerals

THREE MAIN MINERAL TYPES

NATIVE ELEMENT: METALS
Native metals such as gold (shown here), silver, copper, platinum, and lead are metal elements found in pure form and can be taken straight from a rock or riverbed. But most metals, such as iron, aluminum, and tin, occur in combination with other chemicals. These ores must be processed to extract the metal.

NATIVE ELEMENT: NONMETALS
Sulfur (shown here), graphite, and diamond are the only nonmetals found in pure form. Many more nonmetal elements are found in combination in minerals. Native sulfur tends to crystallize around hot springs and volcanic craters. However, it is more commonly found in compound sulfide and sulfate minerals.

COMPOSITE MINERALS
Most minerals occur in composite form as compounds of elements, usually when one or more metals combine with a nonmetal. These composite minerals are split into nine groups according to which nonmetallic combination they contain. Gypsum (shown here) is a sulfate made from calcium, sulfur, and oxygen.

Scree (loose particles)
created by weathering
of rock on steep
mountain slopes

GRANITE MOUNTAIN RANGE ▶
Granite rock forms the backbone of the Sierra Nevada range in California.
Granite forms underground when molten magma welling up from the
Earth's interior cools and solidifies. It is so tough that it is often exposed at
the surface long after softer overlying rock has been weathered away.

Quartz
is the main
component
in granite

Mica biotite
comes in a black,
platelike form

Feldspar
gives
granite a
pinkish tint

Soil created by
further weathering
of rock particles

Granite blocks
turned into
smooth
boulders after
prolonged
weathering

▲ PHOTOMICROGRAPH OF THIN SLICE OF GRANITE
Most rocks are aggregates—mixtures of minerals. To the naked eye,
granite is a light-colored rock, speckled with black spots.
Photographs taken by a polarizing microscope help to distinguish
the different minerals present, but the colors appear different from
those seen under natural light. Granite is made from three main
minerals: black mica, pink or white feldspar, and sandy-gray
quartz. Quartz and feldspar minerals form the bulk of many rocks.

THE THREE TYPES OF ROCK

IGNEOUS
Igneous rock begins as magma—
rock heated in Earth's interior
until it is molten. When magma
rises through Earth's crust, it cools
and crystallizes into new rock. It
can either solidify underground to
form intrusive igneous rock such
as granite, or erupt on the surface
as lava to form extrusive igneous
rock, like the basalt shown here.

METAMORPHIC
Metamorphic rock forms when
other rocks are transformed by
extreme heat or pressure, such as
deep volcanic heat or the stresses
of mountain building. Sometimes
these changes occur locally;
sometimes they occur on a vast
scale. Some metamorphic rocks,
such as gneiss (shown here), take
on a banded appearance.

SEDIMENTARY
Sedimentary rock, such as
claystone (shown here), forms
from sediments—tiny fragments of
rock or living matter deposited in
layers by wind and water. Older,
deeper layers are squeezed under
the weight above them and
become compacted into solid rock
over millions of years in a process
known as lithification.

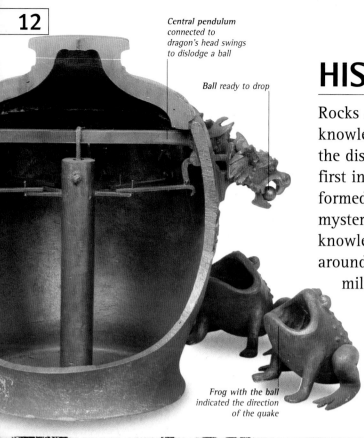

Central pendulum connected to dragon's head swings to dislodge a ball

Ball ready to drop

Frog with the ball indicated the direction of the quake

HISTORY OF GEOLOGY

Rocks and minerals have formed since time began, but our knowledge about them is relatively recent. It was probably the discovery of metals and the search for their ores that first inspired people to find out more about how rocks formed. Yet rocks and minerals remained enough of a mystery to attract many myths. Dramatic advances in our knowledge of the processes that formed the Earth began around 200 years ago with the idea that rocks take millions of years to form.

◀ EARLY EARTHQUAKE DETECTOR
This early geological instrument is a reconstruction of an earthquake detector designed by Chinese scholar Chang Heng about AD 130. It was a heavy urn surrounded by eight dragon heads, each of which held a ball in its mouth. When the ground shook, a ball dropped into the mouth of one of eight frogs around the base, indicating the direction of the quake.

history

▲ MINERALS AND MINING
Much early geological knowledge came from dealing with metal ores. The first great geology book, *De Re Metallica* (*On Metals*), was published in the 16th century by German mining engineer Georgius Agricola. This illustration from it shows miners sifting and washing the mineral ores on a raised channel.

▲ CYCLES OF EROSION
Historians say that modern geology began in the 18th century with the Scottish geologist James Hutton. Hutton argued that the Earth's landscapes were formed and destroyed over millions of years by repeated cycles of erosion, sedimentation, and uplift. The heavily eroded appearance of the mountains of Scotland (shown here) convinced him that these processes were still continuing.

▲ GEOLOGICAL MAPS
Geological maps show where different rock formations occur. The first map (shown here) was made in 1815 by Englishman William Smith as he surveyed routes for canals. He noticed that each rock layer contained its own fossil types. He realized that rocks that formed long distances apart, but which contained the same types of fossils, must be the same age.

220 MILLION YEARS AGO

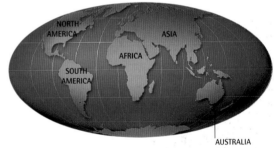

100 MILLION YEARS AGO

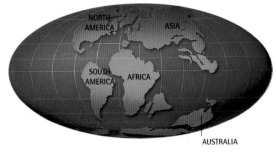

TODAY

▲ THE PILLARS OF SERAPIS
The influential 19th-century geologist Charles Lyell supported Hutton's theory of continuous geological processes. Crucial to this theory is the idea that whole blocks of land can move up and down over time. On the inside cover of his landmark *Principles of Geology*, Lyell illustrated this with a picture of the 1,600-year-old Temple of Serapis from Pozzuoli on the Italian coast (shown here). Holes, made by shellfish, on the temple columns show that they were once submerged under water before being raised up again.

Markings on the pillars suggest the fall and rise of the land caused by local volcanic and earthquake activity

▲ CONTINENTAL DRIFT
The idea that the Earth's continents moved was first proposed in the 1920s by German meteorologist Alfred Wegener. Wegener pointed to the remarkable match between the east coast of South America and the west coast of Africa and suggested that they had once been joined together. At the time he was ridiculed, but further evidence has proved that the continents are indeed drifting fragments of a former supercontinent.

MINERAL MYTHS

PELE'S HAIR
Volcanoes have inspired many myths. According to Hawaiian legend, the fire goddess Pele is responsible for their eruptions. Hawaiian lava is very runny. Lava spray flying through the air can stretch into fine, golden-brown fibers of basalt glass. These collect together into the wiry rock known as "Pele's hair" (shown above).

QUARTZ CRYSTAL BALL
Quartz has been valued by many cultures throughout history for its mystical properties. For centuries, people thought that quartz (rock crystal) was ice that had frozen so hard it could not melt. Tibetan monks, Celtic druids, and gypsy psychics have all gazed into "crystal" balls, hoping to see the future.

PROTECTIVE GEMSTONES
The Bible describes a gem-encrusted breastplate (shown here) worn by Aaron, the first High Priest of Israel. Each stone represents one of the 12 Tribes of Israel. The symbolic association of gemstones with people continues today with birthstones. Different gems represent different months of the year.

COPPER SHIELD
Copper was one of the first metals to be used because it is found in the ground in its pure form. Its rarity gave it a high value for trading. These engraved, shield-shaped plaques, known as "coppers," were highly prized as symbols of wealth and prosperity by Native American Northwest Coast tribes.

AMULET
Ancient Egyptians used jeweled amulets (charms) to protect them from harm. Some precious and semiprecious stones, such as turquoise, were believed to possess magical powers. This scarab (sacred dung beetle) was used as a chest amulet. It is shown supporting a red carnelian, which symbolizes the Sun.

Atmosphere of gases

Thin crust
of solid rock

Upper mantle
of warm, mobile rock

Lower mantle of dense rock
formed under pressure

Core of
iron and
nickel

◀ INSIDE THE EARTH
This wedge cross-section shows the Earth's main layers, right down to the core. These layers developed early in Earth's history. Denser materials, such as iron, sunk to the center to form the core, and lighter materials, such as silicates, rose to the surface. Since no one has actually seen Earth's interior, our knowledge of what goes on in each layer is mainly informed guesswork.

LAYERS OF THE EARTH

CRUST
The crust (0–25 miles, 0–40 km) is Earth's thin, upper layer. It is made up of mostly silicate-rich rocks, such as basalt (shown here). It is attached in giant slabs to the hard part of the upper mantle to form the lithosphere. These slabs drift on the mantle below causing continental drift, volcanoes, and earthquakes.

UPPER MANTLE
The rigid lithosphere floats on a layer of the upper mantle (10–420 miles, 16–670 km) known as the asthenosphere. Rock here is so hot that it melts in places to form magma that sometimes erupts on the surface through volcanoes. Upper mantle rock, such as peridotite (shown here), is denser than crustal rock.

LOWER MANTLE
In the lower mantle (420–1,800 miles, 670–2,900 km), huge pressures turn the lighter, silicate minerals of the upper mantle into very dense pyroxene (shown here) and perovskite minerals. Perovskite is the most abundant mineral in the mantle and therefore the Earth, since the mantle makes up 80 percent of the Earth's volume.

CORE
The Earth's core (1,800–3,960 miles, 2,900–6,370 km) is a dense ball of mostly iron with some nickel. The outer core is so hot, reaching temperatures of more than 6,000°F (3,300°C) that the metal is molten. The inner core is even hotter, reaching 12,600°F (7,000°C), but enormous pressures prevent the iron from melting.

STRUCTURE OF THE EARTH

The deepest boreholes dug by geologists only penetrate 9 miles (15 km) into the Earth. But geologists have found out about the different layers of the Earth's interior by analyzing earthquake waves. The surface is a thin, rocky crust, barely 4 miles (6 km) thick in places. Below this, a very thick mantle of rock flows like sticky syrup. A farther 1,800 miles (2,900 km) down is a core of iron and nickel—with a center under so much pressure it cannot melt, despite temperatures of 12,600°F (7,000°C).

EXPOSED PERIDOTITE FROM THE UPPER MANTLE

Geologists can only study directly rocks that are on the Earth's surface. However, rocks from deep in the mantle are occasionally brought to the surface by tectonic plate movement and volcanic activity. This photograph shows a massive slab of weathered peridotite from the Tablelands of Gros Morne in Newfoundland, Canada. In this case, immense forces have shoved a slab of oceanic plate (combining the crust with the upper layer of the upper mantle) onto the continental plate, exposing dense peridotite rock from the mantle.

▼ CUTTING THROUGH THE CRUST
This diagram shows a cross-section of the Earth's crust and lithosphere with some of the main features of the landscape—and how these surface features relate to what is going on below them in Earth's interior. Notice how ridges on the ocean floor align with cracks in the crust where hot material from the mantle rises up. Notice too how volcanoes erupt over weak points in the crust or plate boundaries. Changes in pressure created by the movement of plates help to melt the mantle material and cause it to erupt.

Lithosphere extends about 60 miles (100 km) below the surface

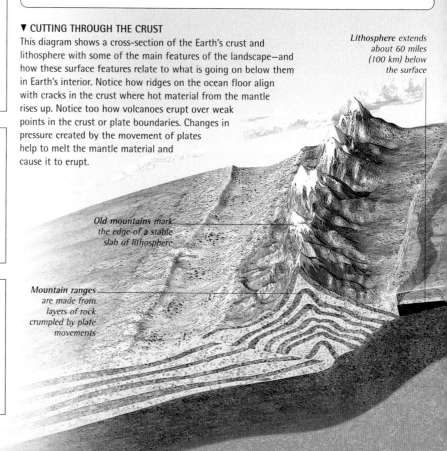

Old mountains mark the edge of a stable slab of lithosphere

Mountain ranges are made from layers of rock crumpled by plate movements

AURORA BOREALIS (NORTHERN LIGHTS) ►
This spectacular light show, seen in the sky above the North Pole, is known as the aurora borealis. A similar phenomenon above the South Pole is known as the aurora australis. Both are caused when electrically charged particles pouring from the Sun are drawn into the atmosphere by Earth's magnetic field and flung toward the Earth. These then collide with air particles, making the upper air glow around the poles. Scientists believe the Earth's magnetic field or magnetosphere, which extends far out into space, is generated deep inside our planet by the rotating liquid outer core.

▲ **MAGNETIC ROCK**
Some minerals found on Earth, such as magnetite (shown here) and pyrrhotite, are naturally magnetic. When these minerals move freely in molten magma, they line up with the Earth's magnetic field. The alignment of such minerals in old rocks can reveal a great deal about the movement of the continents.

Earth's structure

MINERALS THAT MAKE UP THE EARTH

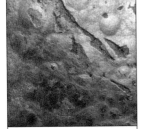

IRON
Most of the Earth's minerals are made from four chemical elements—iron (35%), oxygen (28%), magnesium (17%), and silicon (13%). Although iron makes up a third of the Earth's weight and most of the core, it is rarely found in the crust as a pure element. It is usually joined with other elements in compounds.

SILICON
Much of Earth's crust is made from combinations of two elements—oxygen and silicon—called silicates. These materials are so light that they rose to form the crust early in the Earth's history. Silicon is rarely found on its own, but is almost always found joined to oxygen as a silicate. Quartz is a typical silicate mineral.

MAGNESIUM
Magnesium is the third most common element in the Earth. Silicates containing iron and magnesium are the most common minerals found in the upper mantle. Lower mantle minerals are mostly magnesium compounds attached to iron and oxygen. Magnesium is also found in many silicates in the crust.

NICKEL
Nickel is quite a rare element in Earth's crust, appearing as nickel-iron or in compounds. Much of the Earth's core is made from nickel-iron. Iron meteorites falling to Earth are rich in nickel-iron, showing that nickel was a key element in the early solar system. Nickel for industry is extracted from the ore pentlandite.

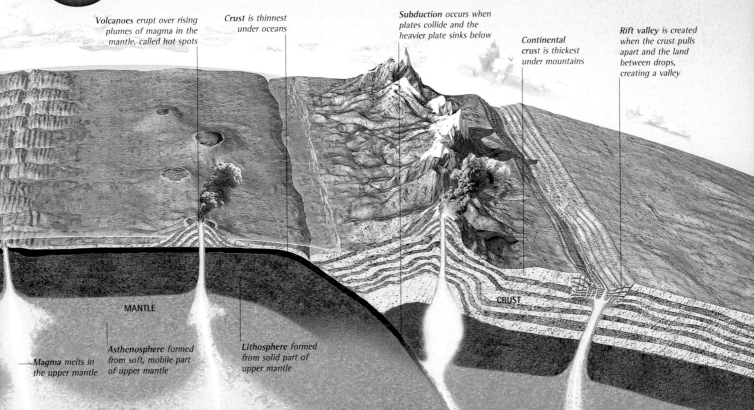

Volcanoes erupt over rising plumes of magma in the mantle, called hot spots

Crust is thinnest under oceans

Subduction occurs when plates collide and the heavier plate sinks below

Continental crust is thickest under mountains

Rift valley is created when the crust pulls apart and the land between drops, creating a valley

MANTLE

CRUST

Magma melts in the upper mantle

Asthenosphere formed from soft, mobile part of upper mantle

Lithosphere formed from solid part of upper mantle

PLATE TECTONICS

The Earth's continents have not always been where they are now. In fact, they are moving around very slowly beneath our feet all the time. It is not just the continents that are moving—so is the ocean floor. Earth's rigid outer shell of rock (made up of the crust and the hard, upper part of the mantle) is split into 20 or so giant slabs known as tectonic plates—seven huge ones and about a dozen smaller ones—which are jostling one another all the time. The continents are embedded in these plates and so move with them.

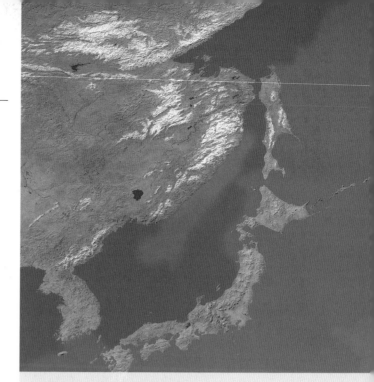

▲ CONVERGING: OCEAN TO OCEAN

In some places, tectonic plates are converging (colliding). The denser plate (usually oceanic) sinks, while the lighter one rides over it, forcing it down into the mantle. This is called subduction. Melted material from the subducted plate forces its way up through the weakened edge of the overlying plate to create a string of volcanoes. When the overlying plate is oceanic, the effect creates an arc of volcanic islands. The islands of Japan were created in this way—the Pacific and Philippine plates were subducted beneath the North American and Eurasian plates.

PLATE BOUNDARIES

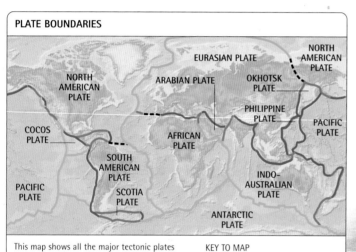

NORTH AMERICAN PLATE

EURASIAN PLATE

ARABIAN PLATE

OKHOTSK PLATE

NORTH AMERICAN PLATE

PHILIPPINE PLATE

PACIFIC PLATE

COCOS PLATE

AFRICAN PLATE

SOUTH AMERICAN PLATE

PACIFIC PLATE

SCOTIA PLATE

INDO-AUSTRALIAN PLATE

ANTARCTIC PLATE

This map shows all the major tectonic plates and some of the smaller ones. The plates move together in three ways: pushing together (convergent), moving apart (divergent), or sliding past (transform). Of the seven large plates—the Pacific, African, North and South American, Eurasian, Indo-Australian, and Antarctic—only the Pacific does not carry a continent. Plates under oceans are the newest, since they are always forming at divergent boundaries.

KEY TO MAP

———— *convergent boundary*

———— *divergent boundary*

———— *transform fault*

- - - - *uncertain boundary*

Eurasian plate is pulling eastward away from the North American plate

DIVERGING BOUNDARY ▶

In some places—usually midocean—tectonic plates are slowly diverging (moving apart). As they separate, molten magma from the Earth's interior wells up through the gap and solidifies creating new crust. In this way, the seabed spreads wider and wider. The Atlantic Ocean is growing by about 8 in (20 cm) every year. The upwelling of hot magma from the Earth's mantle along the crack where the plates are pulling apart, creates a long, raised ridge along the ocean floor. This is known as the midocean ridge. Thingvellir in Iceland is one of the few places where this ridge can be seen on the land.

plate tectonics

Andes mountain range

Pacific Ocean

Indo-Australian plate | Himalayan foothills | Eurasian plate

▲ CONVERGING: CONTINENT TO CONTINENT

Sometimes two plates carrying continental landmasses collide. This is what is happening in southern Asia where the Indo-Australian plate is driving northward into the Eurasian plate. The tremendous power of this collision has distorted the rocks of both continents. Here, the Himalayas—the world's highest mountains—have been thrown up like a great wave as India plows into Asia. India is still moving northward by nearly 2 in (5 cm) every year. The mountains spread out far and wide from the line of impact.

▲ CONVERGING: OCEAN TO CONTINENT

Where an oceanic plate is subducted beneath another plate, there is often a very deep trench in the ocean floor. All around the Pacific, plates are being subducted. Some of the world's deepest trenches, such as the Mariana trench, which is 35,830 ft (10,920 m) deep, mark the point where these plates descend into the mantle. The collision of the Nazca plate with the South American plate has not only created a deep ocean trench, but has also crumpled up the western edge of the continent to create the world's longest mountain range, the Andes.

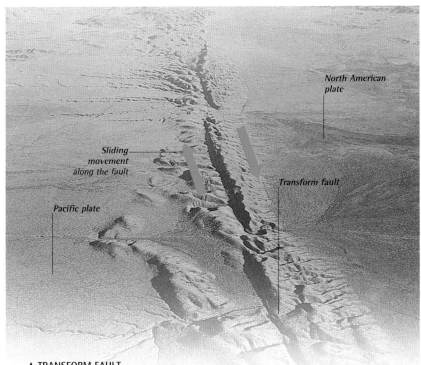

North American plate

Sliding movement along the fault

Transform fault

Pacific plate

▲ TRANSFORM FAULT

The relentless movement of the Earth's tectonic plates can put the rock under so much strain that it fractures. This creates a crack in the Earth called a fault. Where this fault marks a boundary between two tectonic plates, it is known as a transform fault. The San Andreas fault (shown here) in California, is the world's most famous transform fault. East of the fault lies the North American plate. To its west lies the Pacific plate, which is slowly rotating counterclockwise. As it rotates, the Pacific plate slides along the fault—generating the earthquakes that are common in the region.

TYPES OF FAULT

NORMAL FAULT
Areas or zones of fault activity tend to be near plate margins. A normal fault occurs where two tectonic plates are diverging. The resulting tension pulls blocks of rock apart, allowing one block to slip down. The surface that it slips down is called the fault plane. Huge cliffs, known as fault scarps, can be created this way.

REVERSE OR THRUST
Where tectonic plates coverge, the force of collision can compress (squeeze) the rocks so much that it creates reverse faults. This is where one block of rock is pushed up and over another. If the fault is very shallow—so that it is almost horizontal—it is called a thrust fault. Landslides are often associated with these faults.

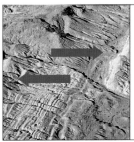

STRIKE-SLIP
Sometimes, plates neither converge nor diverge. Instead they slide past each other horizontally. In this case, they tear blocks of rock apart sideways, creating a strike-slip fault like this one in Nevada. Transform faults between plates, such as the San Andreas fault, are gigantic strike-slip faults.

FORCES OF EROSION

Mountains, hills, valleys, and plains look as if they have been in place forever. But all Earth's landscapes are being worn away slowly by the weather, by running water, moving ice, waves, wind, and natural chemicals. Occasionally, the effect is sudden and dramatic—as when an entire hillside is washed away in a heavy rainstorm. But most of the time the weathering is so slow that you barely notice it. Over tens of thousands of years, mountains crumble, hills are worn flat, and valleys are broadened into plains. The process of breaking up rock and carrying off the fragments is called erosion. Deposition happens when material picked up by water, wind, or ice, is dropped again.

erosion

Avalanches feed the glacier with ice and rock debris

Arches created by wind erosion

◄ WEATHERING
Wherever rock is exposed to air, wind, sun, and rain, it starts to break down in a process called weathering. Over time, weathering can break up the hardest granite, eventually turning it to sand. Sometimes rock can be broken by changes in the weather, such as extreme heat and cold. For example, water freezing in cracks can expand with such force that it shatters solid rock. Repeated cycles of freezing and thawing help to erode exposed mountain peaks.

◄ CORROSION
Sometimes rocks are attacked by chemicals in the air or dissolved in rainwater. In limestone country, the effects of chemical corrosion are very visible. Carbon dioxide in the air dissolves in rainwater to form carbonic acid. The acid is weak, but as the rainwater trickles down through cracks in the rock, it eats away the limestone very quickly. Cracks in a limestone plateau are often etched into deep grooves called grykes, like those shown here.

◄ WATER EROSION

Water is a powerful agent of erosion. Inland rivers carve out deep valleys as they run down to the sea. Coastal waves, packed full of energy by wind blowing over huge expanses of ocean, batter the shore relentlessly. As well as pounding the coastal rock with wave-borne shingle, they also split the rock apart by ramming air into the cracks. Sometimes the constant battering of the waves undercuts coastal slopes to create cliffs. These cliffs may then be further undermined, making them collapse. This can leave lonely stacks like the Twelve Apostles (shown here) on Australia's Victoria coast.

▲ TRANSPORTATION

As rock is worn away, the fragments are transported or carried away by water, ice, or—if the debris is fine and dry—blown away by the wind. The material carried along by a river is called its load. It varies according to the speed and volume of water in the river and the kind of terrain it is flowing through. Some rivers, like China's Huang He and the Amazon in South America (shown here), carry so much silt at certain times of the year that they turn brown or yellow.

◄ GLACIAL EROSION

Glacier moves slowly along the valley floor

Stripes on the glacier show the debris being carried along

On some mountains it is so cold that snow never melts and over the years slowly compacts into a mass of ice. Eventually, this mass becomes so heavy that it starts to flow slowly downhill, forming a river of ice called a glacier. Today, glaciers such as the Batura Glacier in Gojal, Pakistan (shown here), form only in the highest mountains and in the polar regions. But in the past, during the long, cold periods called Ice Ages, vast areas of North America and Europe were buried under ice. The sheer weight of glaciers gives them the power to shape the landscape. They gouge out huge, U-shaped valleys, scoop deep bowls called cirques, remove entire hills, and push frost-shattered rock debris into massive piles known as moraines.

TYPES OF DEPOSITION

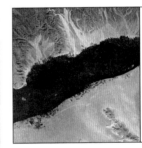

DELTA

As a river flows into the sea or a lake, it slows down and can no longer carry its load of silt. Often, the silt is dumped over a fan-shaped area called a delta, where the river splits into smaller branches called distributaries. This aerial view shows mud being deposited in a delta off the east coast of New Caledonia.

FLOODPLAIN

As a river nears the sea, it becomes shallower and meanders across broad valleys. When the river floods, it leaves behind a wide floodplain of fine sand and mud. This view of the Nile River in Egypt clearly shows the extent of these deposits. Annual flooding has created a rich, fertile corridor of land in the midst of the desert.

◄ WIND EROSION

In damp regions the power of the wind plays little part in shaping the land. But in dry landscapes, such as deserts, the wind can blast suspended dust and sand at rocks with devastating effect. Sometimes the abrasive action of the sand (which acts like very rough sandpaper) can sculpt the rock into fantastic shapes, like this sandstone Turret Arch from the Arches National Park in Utah. Wind can also roll loose rocks and sand along the desert floor, scooping out shallow bowls called blowouts. Geologists once thought that deserts were shaped mostly by the wind, but the effect of floods in the past may be even more important.

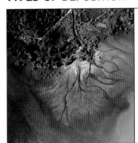

DESERT DUNES

In some deserts, the wind piles up vast seas of sand into giant dunes. In the Sahara Desert of northern Africa, these dunes can grow up to 60 miles (100 km) long and rise up to 650 ft (200 m) high. They form a dramatic, ever-changing landscape depending on the amount of sand and the strength and direction of the wind.

LOESS

Wind action is not just important in deserts, but wherever there is light, loose material—such as on a beach and at a glacier's edge. These eroded peaks in Iowa were formed by wind-blown silt, called loess, left behind by retreating glaciers during the last Ice Age. Vast areas of Central Asia are also covered by loess deposits.

THE ROCK CYCLE

Erosion relentlessly destroys rock wherever it is exposed on the Earth's surface, but new rocks are always being made from the remants of the old ones. This recycling is called the rock cycle. Some parts are quick and obvious—cliffs crumble and volcanoes bring up lava. Much of the cycle, however is hidden deep in the Earth and happens over millions of years. Plate movements turn sedimentary and igneous rocks into metamorphic rocks, or turn metamorphic rocks into igneous rocks.

A ROCK JOURNEY

EROSION
Even these tough-looking basalt cliffs will be broken down in the perpetual rock cycle. In time, they will be worn to sand by pounding waves. The sand may form new sediments, or it may be subducted into the mantle along with the seabed and mix with rising magma to form new igneous rock.

FROST-SHATTERING
The rock cycle can happen anywhere. These igneous rocks scattered across a Welsh hillside in the UK have been shattered by water seeping into cracks and expanding as it freezes. When further erosion has made the fragments small enough, they will be carried away down the hillside by water, wind, or ice.

▲ DUST CLOUD OVER JAPAN
Even the wind can play its part in the rock cycle. In this photograph, fine dust blown off the plains of Central Asia is carried eastward over the Sea of Japan. Eventually, the dust will settle and sink to the seabed where it may form new sedimentary rock or be carried back into the mantle by subduction (the downward movement of one plate beneath another).

Sulfur and carbon gases from volcanoes contribute to chemical weathering

Rock broken down by weathering

Glacier transports rock debris

Sediments deposited in layers eventually turn to rock

SEDIMENTARY ROCK

Molten lava cools on the surface to form extrusive igneous rock such as basalt

CONTINENTAL CRUST

Magma cools underground to form intrusive igneous rock such as granite

METAMORPHIC ROCK

Rising magma fills chamber in the crust

Sediments and oceanic crust are subducted beneath another plate

THE ROCK CYCLE ▶
This diagram shows how the Earth's rocks are continually being made, destroyed, and remade in the rock cycle. Material brought to the crust as magma (molten rock) in intrusions and volcanoes forms igneous rock. Exposed on the Earth's surface, the rocks are eroded, and the fragments may be washed into the sea where they solidify into new sedimentary rock. This rock may then be uplifted to form mountains or tranformed by heat and pressure into metamorphic rock. Sedimentary and metamorphic rock can also be exposed and eroded. The fragments may be washed into the sea to form new sedimentary rock, or be carried down into the mantle by subduction to eventually rise again as magma or be transformed into metamorphic rock.

IGNEOUS ROCK

IGNEOUS ROCK

Sediments and crust on subducting plate melts, creating magma

TRANSPORTATION
To form new rock, weathered fragments must be carried to places where they can accumulate. Here a river can be seen depositing sediment (the lighter patches) on its bed on every twist and turn of its course. When these sediments turn to rock, the ripple marks of the river may be clearly visible.

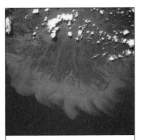

DEPOSITION
Some sediments are washed all the way down a river to the sea where they are deposited in a delta, such as this one off southeast Borneo, Indonesia. Heavier grains are dropped first and tend to compact into sandstone. Lighter sediments are carried farther out and settle to form shale and mudstone.

SEDIMENTARY ROCK
Once sediments have lithified (turned to rock), the beds may be raised to the surface by the movement of tectonic plates. There exposed rocks, like the shale beds shown here, can be eroded by water and weather to provide raw material for new rock. Unexposed sedimentary rock may be metamorphosed into new rock.

METAMORPHIC ROCK
All kinds of rock—igneous, metamorphic, or sedimentary—can be altered by heat and pressure to form new metamorphic rock. For example, shale changes into slate when subjected to tectonic pressure. Slate can then be altered by more extreme heat and pressures to form schist (shown here) and gneiss.

IGNEOUS ROCK
Lava erupting on the surface or magma solidifying underground constantly refill the Earth's crust with new rock. Yet even this material is recycled. The lava erupting here off the coast of Hawaii may contain material that was subducted millions of years ago, and which has since circulated through the mantle.

Sediments washed out to sea, deposited in layers, and lithified

◄ ERRATIC BOULDER
These giant boulders, known as erratics, are rolled over the landscape by glaciers. Some have been carried up to 500 miles (800 km) before the glacier melts and leaves them behind. They may look too large to be part of the rock cycle, but even the biggest boulders are eventually reduced to sedimentary rock-forming sand and clay by prolonged weathering.

rock cycle

MIDOCEAN RIDGE

Magma forms midocean ridge, where plates are pulling apart

Sediments carried out to the deep ocean floor

OCEANIC CRUST

LITHOSPHERE

Magma wells up between diverging plates

THE PROCESSES IN THE ROCK CYCLE

- Diverging and converging tectonic plates create new igneous rock. Subduction often triggers volcanic activity and upwelling of magma
- Weathering by wind, rain, and chemicals, such as sulfuric acid from volcanic eruptions, breaks down exposed rock
- Rock fragments are transported by water (rain, rivers, sea), wind, and ice (glaciers)
- Rock fragments are deposited as sediments on the land and seabed where they are compressed and compacted into rock
- Rock is uplifted and exposed at the surface by plate movements
- Exposure to pressure (from mountain building) and heat (from magma) alters existing rock to create new metamorphic rock

MAGMA

ASTHENOSPHERE

▲ PILLOW LAVA ON THE MID-ATLANTIC RIDGE
Running right down the middle of the Atlantic Ocean is a crack between two major tectonic plates. These plates are slowly moving apart, allowing lava to ooze up through the gap and cool on the receding edges, forming a raised midocean ridge. The hot lava solidifies in pillow-shaped lumps, called pillow lava, as it rapidly cools in the cold seawater.

VOLCANOES

At certain places on the Earth, hot magma emerges onto the surface from deep underground, flowing out over the ground as red-hot lava. These places are known as volcanoes. Sometimes, a volcano can become clogged up with a thick plug of magma—then it suddenly erupts in a gigantic explosion, throwing out jets of steam and fiery fragments high into the air. Successive eruptions can build up such a huge cone of ash and lava around the volcano that it becomes a mountain.

◄ STROMBOLIAN ERUPTION
In places where the magma is acidic and sticky—typically along converging plate margins—volcanic eruptions are often quite dramatic, as on Mount Etna, Sicily, Italy (shown here). When Etna erupts, it repeatedly spits out blobs of lava. This is called a Strombolian eruption, after Stromboli, an island off Sicily.

Blobs of molten magma

Huge clouds of ash and steam

GLOBAL VOLCANIC ACTIVITY

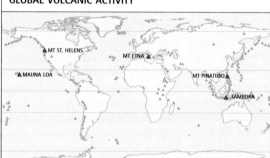

▲ MT ST. HELENS ▲ MT ETNA ▲ MAUNA LOA ▲ MT PINATUBO ▲ TAMBORA

Volcanoes are places where magma (molten rock) breaks through to the surface and are not randomly located. All but a few of the world's active volcanoes lie close to the margins of tectonic plates, especially in a ring around the Pacific Ocean known as the "Ring of Fire." The exceptions are hot-spot volcanoes, such as Mauna Loa, Hawaii, which was formed as the Pacific plate moved over a fixed hot spot. It is a shield volcano with frequent but gentle eruptions.

TYPES OF VOLCANO

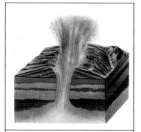

STRATOVOLCANO
When sticky magma erupts explosively from a single vent, successive eruptions build up a distinctive cone-shaped mountain from layers of lava and ash. The characteristic steep shape is due to the sticky lava cooling and hardening before it can spread very far. Stratovolcanoes are also known as composite volcanoes.

SHIELD
Where tectonic plates are pulling apart, magma reaches the surface easily, so it is less acidic and less sticky. Runny basalt lava floods out steadily to form broad, gently sloping volcanoes—often more than 6 miles (10 km) wide—known as shield volcanoes. Mauna Loa on Hawaii is the world's largest shield volcano.

FISSURE
Not all eruptions come from a single hole; fissure eruptions occur where lava floods up to the surface through a long crack. Large-scale fissures mainly occur along midocean ridges, where tectonic plates are pulling apart. Small fissures occur on the flanks of large volcanoes, creating a "curtain of fire" as the lava spurts up.

volcanoes

TYPES OF EFFUSIVE LAVA

PAHOEHOE
Effusive volcanoes produce two very distinctive kinds of lava, known by their Hawaiian names of pahoehoe and a'a. Pahoehoe is common in Hawaiian eruptions. This very fluid lava flows rapidly over large areas. As its surface cools, it wrinkles into ropelike coils, while molten lava continues to flow beneath it.

A'A
Hawaiian volcanoes are famous for their spectacular jetlike sprays of lava called fire fountains. This lava cools and clots as it falls, creating a lumpy lava called a'a (pronounced "ah-ah"), which is slower flowing than pahoehoe. As a'a piles up on the ground, a thick skin forms, which crumbles as it oozes forward.

▲ RIVER OF LAVA FROM MOUNT ETNA, SICILY
Lava is the name given to molten magma after it has emerged onto the surface. Explosive volcanoes tend to produce lava and other debris in short spurts during eruptions. By contrast, effusive (flowing) volcanoes ooze lava almost continuously. Mount Etna, which displays a complex mixture of stratovolcano and shield volcano characteristics, is a continuously active volcano that produces mainly effusive lava, but also mild explosive eruptions.

Ash and steam blasted high into the air

▲ PLINIAN ERUPTION
Plinian eruptions, such as this one seen on Mount St. Helens, Washington, in 1980, are the most explosive of all. They are named after Pliny the Younger. He witnessed the devastating eruption of Mount Vesuvius, which buried the Roman city of Pompeii in AD 79. In eruptions such as these, an explosion of steam and carbon dioxide gas blasts clouds of burning ash and volcanic fragments high into the stratosphere.

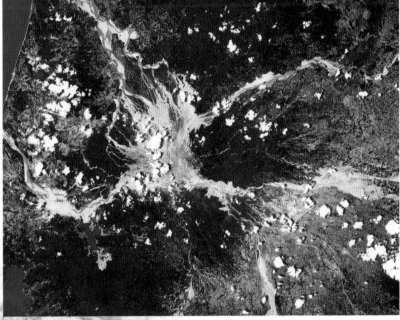

Pyroclastic cloud of ash and magma moves very fast

▲ MUDFLOWS ON MOUNT PINATUBO
The eruption of Mount Pinatubo in the Philippines in June 1991 was one of the largest of the 20th century. However, the main devastation came not from the initial explosion, nor from hot lava, but from deadly mudflows of rain mixed with ash and rock debris that covered the land (as seen on this satellite photo), destroying crops and causing thousands of buildings to collapse.

◄ PYROCLASTIC FLOW, MOUNT PINATUBO
Often the most devastating effects of an eruption like that of Mount Pinatubo come from pyroclastic flows, or *nuées ardentes* (glowing clouds). These are scorching avalanches of ash and pyroclasts—chunks of solid magma shattered by the explosion—that roar down the side of a volcano. These flows can reach speeds of 300 mph (500 kmh) and temperatures of up to 1,500°F (800°C), incinerating everything in their path.

IGNEOUS ROCK

Although often covered by a thin layer of sedimentary rock, igneous rock forms most of the Earth's crust. There are more than 600 different kinds, but all form from magma—molten rock from Earth's hot interior. This cools and crystallizes as it nears the surface into solid masses of hard rock. Sometimes the magma erupts from volcanoes before it turns to rock. Rock like this is described as volcanic or extrusive igneous rock. Sometimes the rock forms intrusively, when magma solidifies underground to form structures, such as batholiths, dykes, and sills.

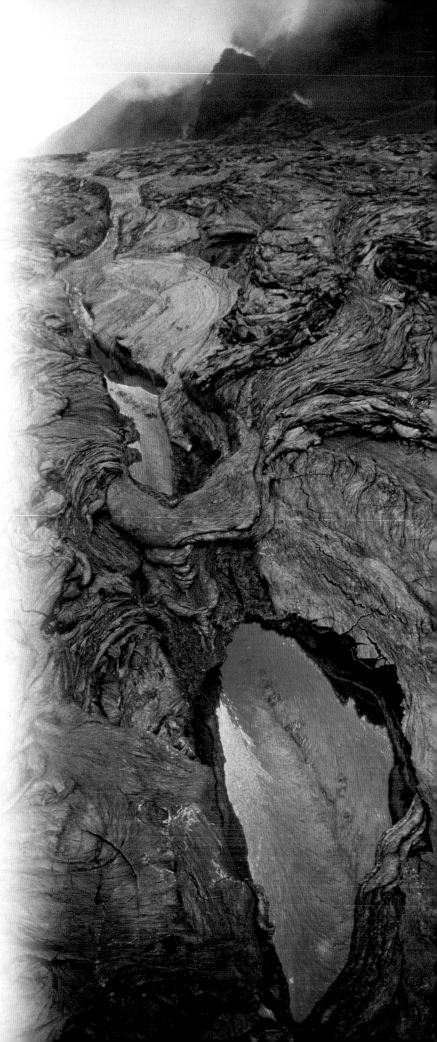

ROCK FORMATION IN ACTION ▶
At some volcanoes, like these in Hawaii, it is possible to see igneous rock actually being formed. The hot magma oozes onto the surface as lava and flows out across the landscape. The lava's surface cools so quickly that it forms a crust of rock, while red-hot lava flows on below. Lava cools so quickly that there is no time for crystals to grow. This results in very fine-grained volcanic rocks such as basalt.

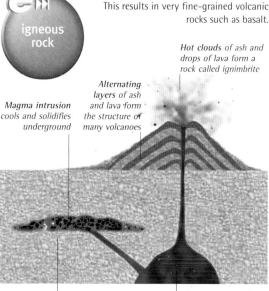

igneous rock

Hot clouds of ash and drops of lava form a rock called ignimbrite

Alternating layers of ash and lava form the structure of many volcanoes

Magma intrusion cools and solidifies underground

Sedimentary rock near an intrusion may melt

Magma chamber supplies huge volumes of hot magma

▲ MAGMA INTO ROCK
Magma can form igneous rock either by erupting on the surface through volcanoes, or by solidifying in masses underground. Volcanoes spew out magma in many different forms—as molten rock (lava), as ash, as cinders, or even as froth—all of which can cool and turn to rock. Volcanic ash, for example, forms a rock called tuff. The froth on top of molten lava forms pumice, a rock so light and full of holes that it can float.

COOLED LAVA FLOW ►

The Giant's Causeway on the north coast of Northern Ireland is a remarkable formation of hexagonal columns of basalt rock. These columns are so regular that they inspired a legend about a giant called Finn MacCool who built them as a road out to sea, joining Ireland to Scotland. In fact, the causeway is an ancient lava flow that spilled out over the landscape about 60 million years ago. The columns formed as the lava cooled, shrank, and cracked.

Basalt pillar forms a natural paving stone

INTRUSIVE STRUCTURES

BATHOLITH
Immense bubbles of hot magma can force their way up toward the Earth's surface, pushing other rock aside, or melting it. Some bubbles harden below the surface, creating giant masses of hard rock called batholiths. Over millions of years, the soft rock surrounding them erodes, turning the exposed batholiths into mountains.

DYKE
A dyke on the landscape shows where upwelling magma split the overlying rock and forced itself up through the crack. As the softer overlying rock is worn away, the wall or dyke is left standing proud above the landscape. Dykes and other intrusions that cut across existing rock structures are called discordant intrusions.

SILL
The dark band of rock visible here is a sill, a thin band of igneous rock that forms when hot magma oozes its way into a crack between two layers of rock. This can sometimes leave a thin strip of igneous rock across a wide area. Sills and other intrusions that follow existing rock structures are called concordant intrusions.

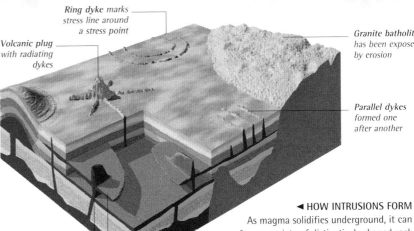

Ring dyke marks stress line around a stress point

Volcanic plug with radiating dykes

Granite batholith has been exposed by erosion

Parallel dykes formed one after another

Vertical dyke follows stress lines through strata

Horizontal sill intrudes between layers of rock

◄ HOW INTRUSIONS FORM
As magma solidifies underground, it can form a variety of distinctively shaped rock formations. Typically, it forms large domes (batholiths) as the magma bubbles up through the ground, or thin sheets in cracks called dykes and sills. But magma intrusions can also take on other shapes, depending on the pressure of the magma and the existing rock structure.

COARSE-GRAINED PEGMATITE ►
The crystals in this pegmatite rock are so large that they are easy to see without a microscope. Large crystals indicate that the rock cooled slowly in an intrusion deep underground. Pegmatites typically form in fissures (cracks) that open up when granite batholiths cool and solidify. They are basically granite but can contain giant crystals of gems such as topaz and beryl. The dark crystals seen here are tourmaline.

Tourmaline crystal took time to grow this large

FINE-GRAINED ANDESITE ►
Andesites are the most common volcanic rocks after basalt. They get their name from the Andes mountains in South America. Andesite is formed from a sticky lava that tends to clog up volcanoes before bursting through in a mighty explosion. Like most volcanic rocks, andesite is fine-grained because it cools rapidly on the Earth's surface. However, this sample includes larger crystals that formed in the magma before it reached the surface.

IDENTIFYING IGNEOUS ROCK

All igneous rocks are crystalline (made of crystals joined together). It is usually easy to recognize them by their shiny, grainy appearance. A few, such as obsidian, have a glassy (no grain) appearance. The chemical composition of the magma, where it formed (above or below the ground), and how quickly it cooled, all contribute to the formation of different igneous rocks. Acid magmas form pale rocks like rhyolite; less acid magmas form darker rocks like basalt. Rocks that form deep down, such as granite, are coarse-grained because they cool slowly. Rocks that form near the surface, such as basalt, are fine-grained because they cool quickly.

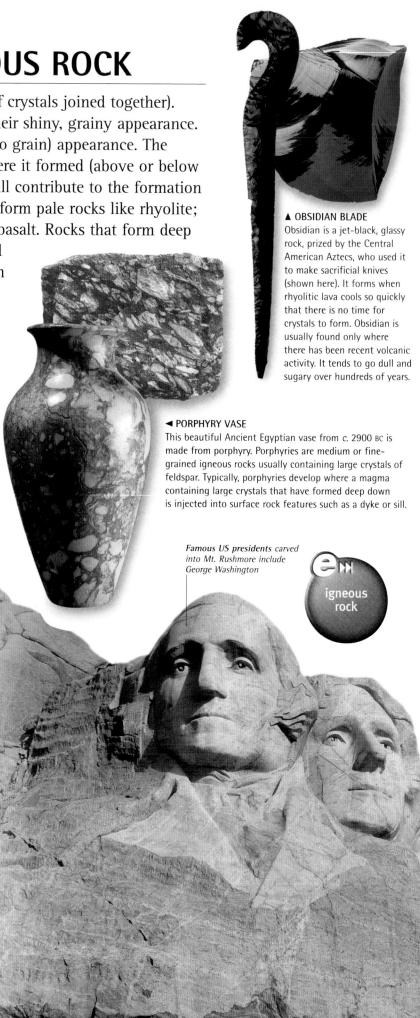

▲ OBSIDIAN BLADE
Obsidian is a jet-black, glassy rock, prized by the Central American Aztecs, who used it to make sacrificial knives (shown here). It forms when rhyolitic lava cools so quickly that there is no time for crystals to form. Obsidian is usually found only where there has been recent volcanic activity. It tends to go dull and sugary over hundreds of years.

◄ PORPHYRY VASE
This beautiful Ancient Egyptian vase from c. 2900 BC is made from porphyry. Porphyries are medium or fine-grained igneous rocks usually containing large crystals of feldspar. Typically, porphyries develop where a magma containing large crystals that have formed deep down is injected into surface rock features such as a dyke or sill.

Famous US presidents carved into Mt. Rushmore include George Washington

igneous rock

GRAIN SIZE (RATE OF COOLING)

FINE-GRAIN (FAST)
Lava tends to cool too quickly for large crystals to grow much and so produces rocks that are fine-grained. The crystals are too small to identify with the naked eye, but they can be seen twinkling if the rock is turned in the light. The three most common fine-grained rocks are basalt, andesite, and rhyolite (shown here).

MEDIUM-GRAIN (MEDIUM)
Magma that cools more slowly in underground dykes and sills forms medium-sized grains. These are large enough to see, but not to identify with the naked eye. Dolerite (shown here) is the most common form of medium-grained rock, forming both the Palisades Sill in New Jersey and the Great Whin Sill in England.

COARSE-GRAIN (SLOW)
Magma that crystallizes in large masses deep down cools very slowly. This gives plenty of time for crystals – such as the dark tourmaline and pink feldspar shown in this pegmatite – to grow large enough to see with the naked eye. The most common coarse-grained igneous rocks are granite and gabbro.

GRANITE-FACED PRESIDENTS ▶
Igneous rock is so tough that anything made from it—whether a building or carving—tends to be very long-lasting. The four US presidents' heads (Washington, Jefferson, Theodore Roosevelt, and Lincoln) on Mount Rushmore in the Black Hills of South Dakota were carved out of 1.7-billion-year-old granite. The work took 14 years. The presidents will probably keep their features for tens of thousands of years. The white streaks on the foreheads of Washington and Lincoln are pegmatite dykes.

CLASSIFICATION BY CHEMICAL COMPOSITION

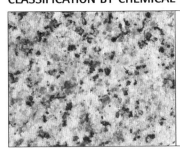

ACID
Magma containing more than 65 percent silica is said to be acid. Acid rock also has a high content of quartz (more than 10 percent) and feldspar. When it crystallizes, the glassy quartz and beige-colored feldspar make the rock very pale. Acid intrusive rock includes granite (shown here). Its extrusive equivalent is rhyolite.

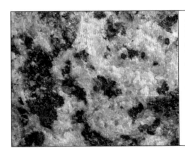

INTERMEDIATE
Magma containing 55–65 percent silica forms rock called intermediate rock. It is darker than acid rock because it has less pale-colored quartz and more darker-colored minerals, such as hornblende. Intermediate intrusive rock includes diorite (shown here). The surface equivalent of diorite is andesite.

BASIC
Magma with 45–55 percent silica, forms basic rock, which is dark or even black. At the surface, basic lava typically forms fine-grained basalt, the most common igneous rock. In sills and dykes just below the surface, basic magma forms medium-grained dolerite, while deeper down it forms coarse-grained gabbro (shown here).

ULTRABASIC
Igneous rocks that contain less than 45 percent silica and no feldspar minerals are known as ultrabasic. Rocks such as peridotite (shown here) and pyroxenite are composed mostly of pyroxene and olivine. Peridotite is a relatively rare rock, which is brought up from the mantle during continental collisions.

HALF DOME, YOSEMITE ▲
Yosemite's Half Dome, in California's Sierra Nevada range, is a dramatic example of an exposed batholith (*see* p.25). A large mass of magma solidified underground about 50 million years ago and was gradually exposed over millions of years as the softer (nonigneous) overlying rock weathered away. The much harder granodiorite (a mixture of granite and diorite) Dome was eventually left behind and then carved in half by a glacier.

AMYGDALES IN BASALT

Some igneous rock, such as basalt and andesite, can contain pockets of other minerals known as amygdales. Amygdales form from gas bubbles in the magma. The word "amygdale" comes from the Latin for "almond." Typically, the mineral-rich liquid trapped in the bubbles forms minerals called zeolites.

Zeolite

Granite rock ensures sculptures will last a long time

METAMORPHIC ROCK

Metamorphic rock is rock that has been changed beyond recognition by exposure to intense heat or pressure or both. Contact metamorphism happens when rock comes into contact with the searing heat of the red-hot magma found in an igneous intrusion. The extreme temperatures can realign the crystals within the rock so much that it can change into a new rock, such as marble or hornfels, depending on the intensity of the heat.

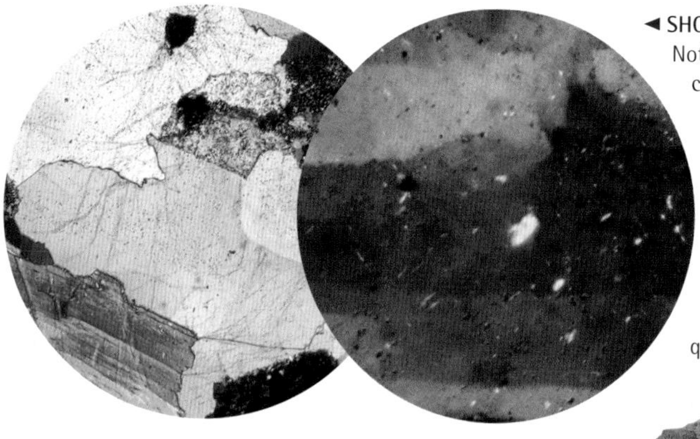

QUARTZ: BEFORE

QUARTZ: AFTER

◄ SHOCK METAMORPHISM
Not all contact metamorphism is caused by volcanic activity. When a meteorite hurtles into the Earth, the impact sends tremendous shockwaves through the ground, squeezing the rock to two or three times its original density. This micrograph shows the changes to the quartz's crystal structure.

Contact aureole is the region of heat-altered rock around a batholith

Mudstone changed to hornfels

HORNFELS: CHANGED FROM MUDSTONE

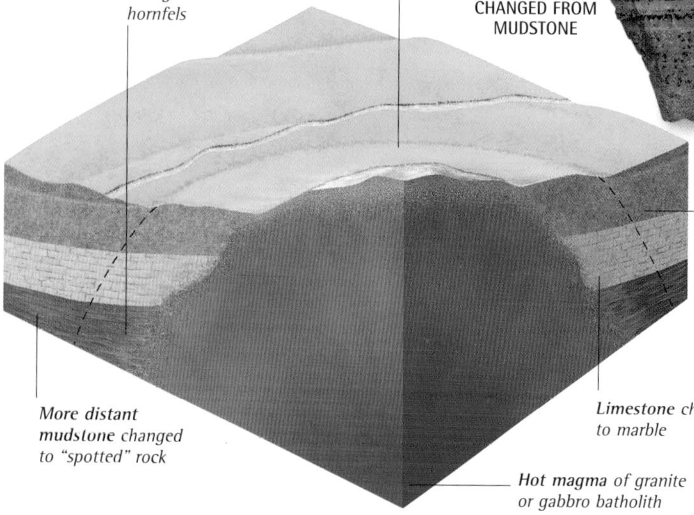

Sandstone changed to metaquartzite

More distant mudstone changed to "spotted" rock

Limestone changed to marble

Hot magma of granite or gabbro batholith

▲ CONTACT METAMORPHISM
The scorching heat of a large magma batholith transforms the rocks around it. The closer the rocks are to the batholith, and the larger the batholith, the more they are altered by the heat. Sandstone changes to hard quartzite. Limestone turns to brilliant white or banded marble. Closer to the edges of the batholith, mudstone turns to dark, splintery hornfels. Farther away some minerals are left unaltered, and some new ones grow, creating "spotted" rock.

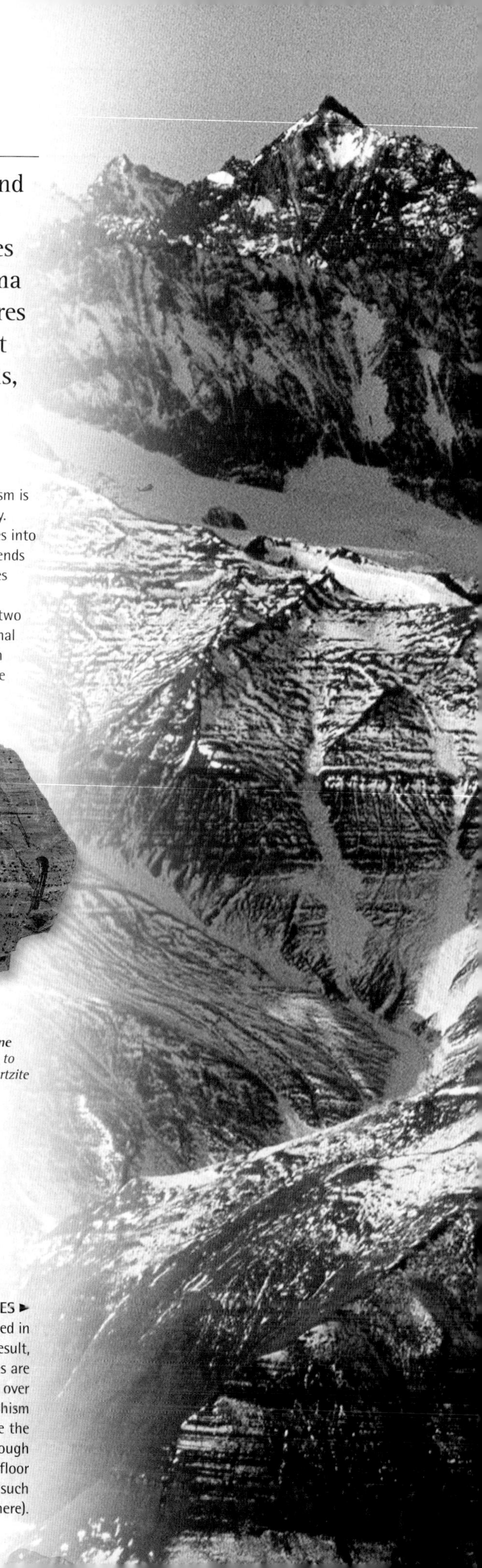

HUGE FORCES ►
The temperatures and pressures involved in metamorphism are enormous. As a result, the rocks produced by these forces are very tough and can withstand erosion over millions of years. Some metamorphism takes place deep underground. Here the Earth's tectonic plates move with enough force to open abysses in the ocean floor or throw up giant mountain ranges, such as Greenland's Stauning Alps (shown here).

Garnet crystals

e▸▸
metamorphic rock

Schist created from mudstone

▲ NEW CRYSTALS

Molten magma is so hot that it can virtually melt the surrounding country rock—rock that existed before metamorphism occurred—allowing entirely new crystals to form. Minerals such as andalusite, kyanite, and sillimanite are clear signs of metamorphic rock, because they only form at high temperatures and pressures. Some beautiful gem crystals are formed this way, such as the almandine garnets embedded in this schist rock—a form of highly metamorphosed mudstone.

◄ SANDSTONE TO QUARTZITE

The quartz grains in sandstone are so tough that the heat of metamorphism has little effect—simply forging sandstone (shown left) into a much tougher rock called quartzite (show right). Quartzite can look a little like hard brown sugar. It is so hard that quartzites in Western Australia are among the oldest rocks on Earth, dating from around 3.5 billion years ago.

◄ LIMESTONE TO MARBLE

Limestone (shown left) and dolomite are transformed into marble (shown right) by exposure to intense heat and pressure. Limestone is rich in calcite (calcium carbonate), which comes from living matter. Limestones are dull and powdery, but contact metamorphism transforms them into tough, white marble.

Carrara's bright white marble is highly prized for its purity

Checking the marble to ensure it has no faults or coloring minerals

MARBLE QUARRY IN CARRARA ▲

In mountain-building regions, contact and regional metamorphism (where enormous pressure is felt over a large area) can recrystallize the calcite in limestone, transforming it into marble. The purer the limestone is, the whiter the marble. The brilliant white marble from Carrara in Italy's Apennine mountain region is considered the most perfect marble of all and was cherished by Renaissance sculptors, such as Michelangelo. Impurities in the original limestone (such as silica and iron) give marble its distinctive colored streaks.

Michelangelo's David is carved from a single, carefully selected block of Carrara marble

REGIONAL METAMORPHISM

The tremendous forces involved when continents collide can crush and bake rocks over a large region, metamorphosing rocks over a wide area. Sometimes, regional metamorphism can create similar rocks to those produced by contact metamorphism. But at other times the metamorphism is much more intense creating entirely new kinds of rock. The most extreme metamorphism creates its own unique banding structures.

GRADES OF METAMORPHISM

SLATE (LOW)
Mudstone is transformed into flaky, gray slate by low-grade regional metamorphism. High pressure and low temperatures realign minerals found in clay, such as mica and chlorite, into flat layers.

PHYLLITE (LOW)
Like slate, phyllite is created by mild regional metamorphism of mudstone or shale. But the effect is more intense—the mica flakes are larger and more visible and develop a silky, mirrorlike sheen.

SCHIST (MEDIUM)
Medium-grade metamorphism creates the rock schist by realigning crystals of chlorite and mica into bands sandwiched between bands of quartz and feldspar. The banding is called schistosity.

GNEISS (HIGH)
Gneiss is formed by the highest grade of metamorphism. Extreme heat and pressure create a glittering rock in which entirely new crystals form in alternating wavelike dark and light bands.

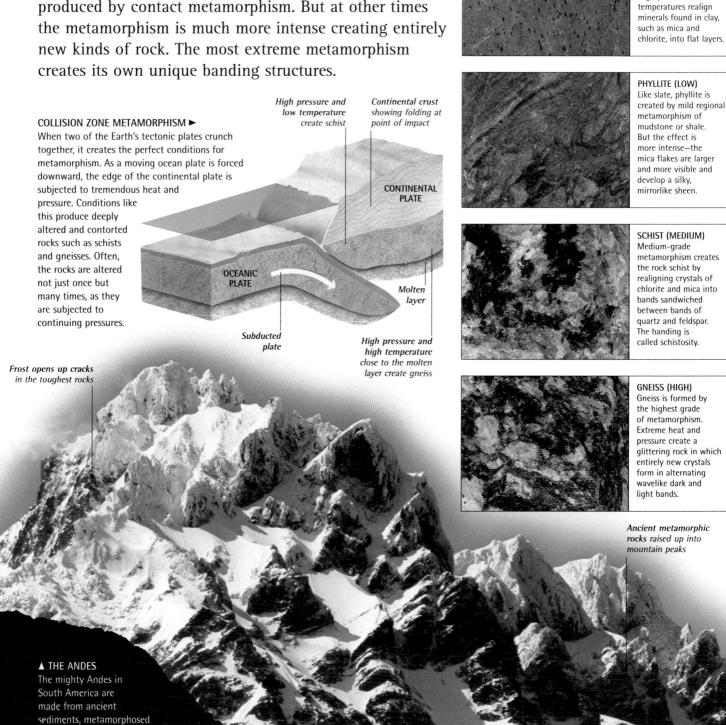

COLLISION ZONE METAMORPHISM ▶
When two of the Earth's tectonic plates crunch together, it creates the perfect conditions for metamorphism. As a moving ocean plate is forced downward, the edge of the continental plate is subjected to tremendous heat and pressure. Conditions like this produce deeply altered and contorted rocks such as schists and gneisses. Often, the rocks are altered not just once but many times, as they are subjected to continuing pressures.

High pressure and low temperature create schist

Continental crust showing folding at point of impact

CONTINENTAL PLATE

OCEANIC PLATE

Molten layer

Subducted plate

High pressure and high temperature close to the molten layer create gneiss

Frost opens up cracks in the toughest rocks

Ancient metamorphic rocks raised up into mountain peaks

▲ THE ANDES
The mighty Andes in South America are made from ancient sediments, metamorphosed into tough quartzite and slate tens of millions of years ago. These rocks were then thrown up by colliding plates to create the world's longest mountain range. The huge forces involved are also creating new metamorphic rock deep underground in the mountain's roots. One day, these too will be exposed on the surface.

Close-up of gneiss showing dark biotite mica

FOLIATION ►
Rocks metamorphosed from mudstone and shale are often marked by flat or wavy lines called foliation. The dark lines are created when bands of sheetlike minerals, such as mica, are squeezed flat by the pressure. Slate, phyllite, schist, and gneiss all have foliations like this. Rocks metamorphosed from limestone (marble), sandstone (quartzite), and coal (anthracite) have none of these foliations, and the interlocking crystal grains show no specific pattern. This is called a granular texture.

Gneiss in cliff face shows bands of quartz and feldspar

Flat cleavage planes, where slate is easily broken

◄ SLATE QUARRY IN WALES
In slate, all the minerals are dark gray and fine-grained. Foliation of slate does not create alternate dark and light bands. Instead, pressure realigns the mica and chlorite minerals into layers. This creates a rock that cleaves (splits) easily into smooth, flat sheets, some of which can be huge. This slate quarry is in Wales, a country that was once world-famous for its slate industry.

SPLITTING SLATE

Slate is brittle and flakes easily, but it is also very weather resistant. The combination of weather resistance and the ease with which it can be broken into flat sheets made slate the perfect roofing material. During the 19th and 20th centuries, it was used for roofing vast numbers of new houses in Europe and the US. Slatemakers were highly skilled craftsmen who were able to split blocks of stone into smooth, thin rectangular tiles using just a hammer and chisel.

Dramatic folding of layers of mudstone and sandstone

FOLDED GNEISS

Separate bands of pale and dark minerals

e►►
metamorphic rock

FOLDING ►
In folded gneiss, the separated bands of dark hornblende and mica and pale quartz and feldspar minerals can be clearly seen. Folding is when rock layers are contorted by plate movements, which are not powerful enough to alter the actual composition of the rock, shown here in these folded cliffs from South Wales, UK.

SEDIMENTARY ROCK

Sedimentary rock, formed from the debris of other rocks and living matter, is the third basic rock type. Although it only makes up 5 percent of the Earth's crust by volume it covers about 75 percent of the Earth's land surface. Sedimentary rock can be divided into three categories: detrital (from rock particles), chemical or inorganic (from particles that can dissolve in water), and organic (from plant remains). Some sedimentary rock contains fossils, which provide vital clues to understanding Earth's geological history.

◄ LAYERS OF SEDIMENT

When rock is exposed to the elements—wind, rain, and repeated cycles of freezing and thawing—it slowly erodes. The debris is carried away by water, wind, and ice and deposited in layers. Over time these layers are buried by more sediments and eventually harden into sedimentary rock. When sedimentary rock is exposed in cross-section as here, you can see the layers in which the sediments have been deposited, one on top of the other.

sedimentary rock

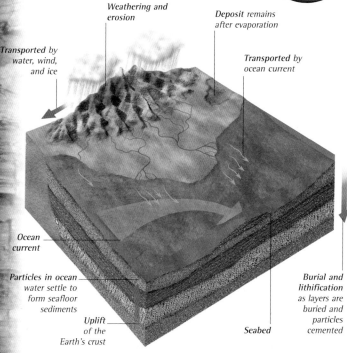

Weathering and erosion

Deposit remains after evaporation

Transported by water, wind, and ice

Transported by ocean current

Ocean current

Particles in ocean water settle to form seafloor sediments

Uplift of the Earth's crust

Seabed

Burial and lithification as layers are buried and particles cemented

▲ SEDIMENTARY (DETRITAL) ROCK CYCLE

In this phase of the rock cycle, detrital sedimentary rock forms from millions of rock particles. These particles are transported by wind, water, and ice, before being deposited as sediments on the beds of oceans, lakes, and rivers. Layer is buried by layer, until the particles are cemented together by a combination of the weight of the layers above and minerals deposited from water moving through the sediments. Over millions of years, the layers form sedimentary rock.

PARTICLE SIZE FOR DETRITAL ROCKS

BOULDERS
Detrital rocks are composed of many particle sizes, ranging from microscopic (clay) to huge (boulders). Boulders rocks more than 10 in (25 cm) across—tend to be moved only by glaciers. When smaller boulders combine with finer particles they form a "mixture" called conglomerate.

COBBLES
Cobbles range in size from 2½–10 in (6 cm to 25 cm) across. Strong forces sort particles by size, so they are often found in high-energy environments such as fast-flowing rivers and landslides. Cobbles can combine to form conglomerate or breccia—see opposite.

PEBBLES
Pebbles, the typical particles found in conglomerates, range in size from ⅙–2½ in (4 mm to 60 mm). Any sharp edges are gradually smoothed away as the pebbles are continuously rolled and bounced along rivers and seashores, suggesting a long period of transportation.

SAND
Below pebble come gravel and then sand particles. Sand particles can be up to 1/12 in (2 mm) and can still be seen by the naked eye. Sand particles are found in a number of environments, ranging from mountain lakes to the ocean floor. They combine to form sandstone.

SILT
Silt particles are smaller than sand and can no longer be seen with the naked eye. The result of prolonged weathering, silt particles usually settle in quiet riverbeds with little or no current. They combine with clay to form fine-grained rocks such as mudstone and shale.

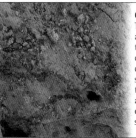

CLAY
The smallest particles of all are clay. Little energy is needed to transport clay particles, so clay settles very slowly and is carried out farthest from the shore. Accumulation of these tiny particles is usually associated with quiet environments such as lakes, swamps, or lagoons.

▲ BEDDING WITH UNCONFORMITY

Sedimentary rocks form when layers of sediment are laid down in beds. This layering is one of the most characteristic features of sedimentary rock. Each layer is unique, with variations in composition and thickness reflecting the different conditions under which it was deposited. A bedding plane—the boundary between two layers of sedimentary rock—is usually visible as a line across the rock. Unconformities are breaks in the regular pattern of beds, which show where a new phase of rock-building has begun on top of older rock.

▲ CROSS BEDDING

Most layers are deposited horizontally since sediments usually accumulate as particles from a fluid. Sometimes sediments do not settle in horizontal layers. If sloping beds form across and within the main bed, the result is known as cross bedding. This is a characteristic feature of sand-dune, river-delta, and stream-channel environments. The distinctive pattern in this eroded Navajo sandstone from Colorado, is caused by the currents moving in different directions at different times.

◄ MUDSTONE
The fine-grained group of rocks that includes mudstone, shale, and siltstone are the most common sedimentary rocks. Mudstone breaks into chunks or blocks, while shale splits in layers.

◄ CONGLOMERATE
Conglomerates are formed when rounded particles of pebble size and larger become cemented together in a fine-silt matrix. They are very hard. Pebbly-sized conglomerates were once used for grinding grain.

Fine matrix of sediments binds rock fragments together

Angular fragments of granite and other rock

LOESS ►
Loess is dust and silt that probably originated on the margins of retreating ice sheets. It can be blown by the wind over great distances, forming extremely fertile soils. Estimates suggest that 10 percent of Earth's surface is covered by large loess deposits, such as those found in northern China.

◄ SANDSTONE
Quartz is the predominant mineral in most sandstone. Sandstones that contain feldspar are called arkose, while those formed from a mixture of particles are called graywacke. Sandstone carves easily and resists weathering.

BRECCIA ►
When the large particles in the rock mixture are angular rather than rounded, the rock is called breccia. Most breccias form in mountain regions, where the freeze-thaw cycle breaks the rocks into coarse, sharp-edged pieces. These can gather in cone-shaped deposits at the foot of steep slopes.

CHEMICAL SEDIMENTS

Detrital sedimentary rocks are formed from fragments of rock, and you can often see the original mineral grains or even entire pebbles in them. But sedimentary rocks made through the action of chemicals in the earth have a powdery texture with no trace of the original fragments. These rocks are formed from minerals like calcite that dissolve in water. These dissolved minerals may create solid deposits, or precipitates. Some precipitates simply fill in the spaces in other sediments; some form entirely new rocks, such as limestone.

OOLITH FORMATION ▲
Ooliths form in shallow, carbonate-rich tropical waters like these in the Bahamas. Wherever oolitic limestone appears, it is evidence that conditions were like this millions of years ago. The famous oolitic limestones of Kansas and Dorset, England, formed in conditions like these.

OOLITIC LIMESTONE ►
Oolitic limestone is made from tiny balls of calcite called ooliths. Ooliths are made when calcite precipitates out of lime-saturated water and sticks to tiny grains of silt that roll around in underwater currents. Oolith comes from the Greek word for "egg." This rock is also known as roe limestone after its resemblance to fish roe (eggs).

Saw-edged ridges caused by chemical weathering

Oolitic "balls" formed by calcite deposits

Compact carbonate rock

▲ DOLOMITIC LIMESTONE
In shallow tropical seas with plenty of evaporation, carbonate minerals may be precipitated on the seabed. These deposits eventually turn into limestone. When the predominant carbonate is calcium, it forms limestone. When it is magnesium (common in seawater), it forms dolomitic limestone.

THE DOLOMITES ►
The term dolomitic comes from the Dolomite range in northern Italy, at the eastern end of the Alps. Like all Alpine sediments, the limestone in the Dolomites formed on the bed of the sea that once lay between northern Europe and Africa. But over millions of years, the pressure of the north-moving African plate pushed it upward to create the dramatic mountains seen today.

Tufa formations

▲ TUFA TOWERS IN MONO LAKE, CALIFORNIA
Tufas are white, knobbly rocks formed from deposits of calcite (calcium carbonate). They typically form around springs, or in caves, on stalagmites and stalactites. Where springs rich in calcium bubble into lakes rich in carbonate, towers of tufa may form as the calcium combines with the carbonate. The towers grow underwater, but in California's Mono Lake they have become visible as water levels have dropped. The Trona Pinnacles area of California's Mojave Desert has tufa towers up to 140 ft (43 m) high, left behind by the evaporation of ancient lakes.

MINERAL FORMATIONS IN SEDIMENTARY ROCK

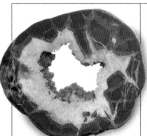

SEPTARIAN NODULE
Nodules are tough balls of mineral that form in sedimentary rock. Septarian nodules began as mudballs that formed around decomposing sea life. When they dried out, they filled with minerals, such as dolomite. These minerals in turn cracked, and the cracks filled with veins of calcite (shown here in white).

FLINT
Flint nodules appear in chalk and other limestones. They form when bubbles of silica-rich fluid—from the remains of sea sponges—solidified. On the outside they are nobbly, white pebbles, but inside they look like brown glass. They fracture with such a sharp edge that they were used as knives in the Stone Age.

PYRITE NODULE
Pyrite nodules are frequently mistaken for meteorites because of their shape. They are often found in mudstone and shale, where long, radiating, needlelike crystals of iron pyrite form around a mineral fragment. Pyrite makes sparks when struck on stone, and pyrite nodules were probably humankind's earliest firelighters.

Crude salt starting to crystallize at lake edge

▲ EVAPORITES IN QINGHAI SALT LAKE, CHINA
Evaporites are salts that were once dissolved in water. When the water in which they were dissolved evaporates, they are left behind as deposits. Typically, the minerals in evaporites are halite (rock salt) and gypsum. They are common where seawater evaporates in lagoons and around the salty lakes of desert regions, such as the Great Salt Lake in Utah and the Qinghai Salt Lake in China.

sedimentary rock

Dramatic, jagged landscape caused by chemical erosion of limestone

KARST LANDSCAPE ▶
The Stone Forest of Yunnan Province, China, is a striking example of karst scenery. Karst gets its name from the distinctive limestone formations found in the Karst region of Slovenia. The limestone is easily dissolved by acid rainwater seeping down through cracks in the rock. These fantastic shapes are the result of tens of thousands of years of chemical corrosion.

CAVES

Many mountains, hills, and cliffs contain natural holes or caves. The largest and most common caves are those that form when rock is dissolved by chemicals in water trickling through it. These are called solution caves. They are typical of limestone regions, where the rock is often hollowed out into spectacular caverns. But caves can also form in other ways. Sea caves, for instance, are hollowed out of sea cliffs where pounding waves have opened up cracks. Ice caves are formed by ice melting under glaciers. Lava caves are tunnels left behind by hot lava in lava flows.

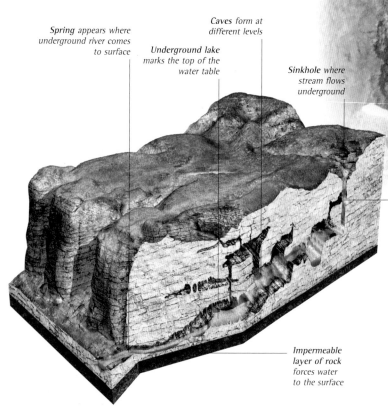

Spring appears where underground river comes to surface

Caves form at different levels

Underground lake marks the top of the water table

Sinkhole where stream flows underground

Pothole where water plunges down a vertical shaft

Gallery full of unusual calcite mineral formations such as this arch

Stalactites hang from the cavern roof

Impermeable layer of rock forces water to the surface

▲ CAVE SYSTEM

There is little surface water in limestone country because the water seeps away so easily through joints (cracks) in limestone. Streams mostly plunge down through potholes, and as the water flows downward, so acid in it dissolves the rocks and widens pipelike channels into tunnels and caves. At a certain point, the water meets the water table—the level up to which the rock is permanently soaked with groundwater. This is where the largest caves occur. The water table fluctuates with changing weather, so new caves form at different levels. Over thousands of years, complex, multilevel cave systems can develop, such as the famous Mammoth Caves in Kentucky.

caves

CAVE PAINTING FROM LASCAUX

In prehistoric times, people often took shelter in caves. Evidence of this comes from the artifacts and cave art they left behind, especially in Western Europe, China, and southern Africa. Although these people are sometimes referred to as cavemen, they did not live in caves. Instead, they used them for shelter from bad weather and for defense from predatory animals. Deep inside these caves, early people painted pictures of animals and hunting scenes, which may have had a religious significance. Some of the best-known cave paintings are found in Lascaux, France, which were painted some 17,000 years ago.

SPELEOTHEMS

STALAGMITES
Stalagmites are dramatic rock spikes and columns, built up from calcite-rich water dripping onto the cavern floor. As the water evaporates (dries up) in the air of the cavern, it deposits calcite, which slowly accumulates, growing into a higher and higher structure. When a stalagmite grows tall enough to meet a descending stalactite, it forms a pillar as shown here. This 89-ft (27-m)-tall Monarch pillar is from the Carlsbad Caverns, a huge complex of limestone caverns and tunnels, which extends for more than 30 miles (50 km) in New Mexico.

STALACTITES
Stalactites are spectacular iciclelike features that form as water slowly drips down from the cavern roof. A stalactite grows, literally, drip by drip. Before it drops to the cavern floor, each drip clings for a while to the tip of the stalactite and leaves a calcite deposit at the rim. The next drip forms in the same place and also leaves a deposit. Very slowly, these rim deposits build up to form a tube. This is why many stalactites are hollow or partially hollow at their center. The world's longest stalactite, at Poll-an-Ionain in County Clare, Ireland, is 20 ft (6.2 m) long.

CAVE PEARLS
Cave pearls are very rare, appearing as rounded, white pebbles in small pools of water. They form when water dripping into the pool loses carbon dioxide and deposits calcite in layers around a grain of sand or tiny rock fragment. Movement of the water rolls the growing pearl around, and eventually it forms a perfect, polished sphere. All the time the pearl gathers more and more layers of calcite, until after thousands of years it becomes too heavy for the water to move it and becomes fixed. Sometimes spectacular "nests" of these pearls form in cave pools, as shown here.

Stalagmites grow up from the floor

▲ UNDERGROUND PALACE
Limestone caverns can become spectacular natural palaces, such as the Yunshui caverns in Fangshan county, near Beijing, China, shown here lit with colored lights. These caverns are covered in different kinds of calcite (calcium carbonate) deposits, collectively called speleothems. They are created by the constant dripping of water that is saturated in calcite, which has dissolved from the limestone. The larger cave deposits create an interior of pillars and platforms. The colors vary from alabaster white to a dusky red caused by iron deposits. The best-known cave structures are stalactites and stalagmites. Twisting structures are called helictites.

SINKHOLES ▶
When acidic rainwater creates limestone caves close to the ground surface, the cave roof may become so thin that it suddenly collapses, forming a sinkhole. While everything may look solid on the surface, changing conditions, such as urban development or a heavy rainstorm, can trigger the collapse. This large sinkhole has opened up in the arid, treeless Nullarbor Plain in Western Australia.

Sinkhole caused by cavern collapsing near surface

▲ DESERT OASIS
Groundwater is all the water that is stored underground in the soil or in permeable rock—rock that allows water to trickle through it. Typically, groundwater appears on the surface where a hollow in the ground allows the water table to rise, as it does in this oasis in the Namibian Desert in southern Africa. Groundwater can appear when heavy rain or melting snow raises the water table, creating a spring, a well, or even a lake.

HOW FOSSILS FORM

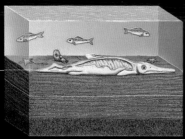

① Ichthyosaurus decays and is buried in soft sediments on the seafloor

② Layers of sediment cover the reptile's bones, which are gradually mineralized

③ Weight of land compresses the fossilized skeleton

④ Forces of erosion wear away the surface, exposing the skeleton

FOSSILS

Nearly all sedimentary rock contains fossils, the preserved remains of plants and animals that lived millions of years ago when the rocks were formed. Fossils are perhaps the geologist's most useful clues to the history behind rock formation. Most of the fossils are shellfish, such as ammonites, which lived in shallow seas. Many of these fossils are characteristic of a particular geological period, so that they can help to date precisely the rock in which they are found.

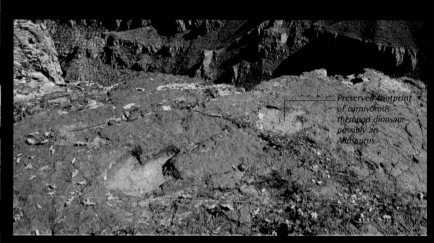

Preserved footprint of carnivorous theropod dinosaur— possibly an Allosaurus

◄ FOSSILIZATION OF AN ICHTHYOSAURUS

Fossils form in a number of ways, but normally only the hard parts of an animal, such as its bones or shell are preserved. Soft parts usually rot before they can be fossilized. This sequence shows how an ancient marine reptile called an *Ichthyosaurus* may have fossilized in mud on the seafloor.

▲ TRACE FOSSILS

Trace fossils are not the fossils of an animal's remains, but preserve the signs left behind by the animal, such as a nest or footprints. Perfectly preserved footprints (shown above) reveal the tracks of a three-toed theropod dinosaur as it tramped across mudflats more than 170 million years ago.

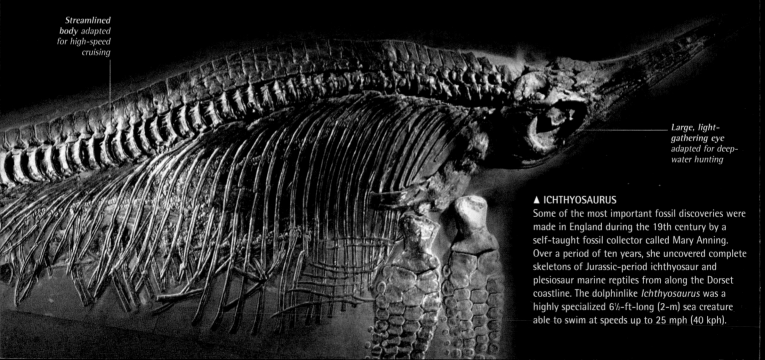

Streamlined body adapted for high-speed cruising

Large, light-gathering eye adapted for deep-water hunting

▲ ICHTHYOSAURUS

Some of the most important fossil discoveries were made in England during the 19th century by a self-taught fossil collector called Mary Anning. Over a period of ten years, she uncovered complete skeletons of Jurassic-period ichthyosaur and plesiosaur marine reptiles from along the Dorset coastline. The dolphinlike *Ichthyosaurus* was a highly specialized 6½-ft-long (2-m) sea creature able to swim at speeds up to 25 mph (40 kph).

SPIDER TRAPPED IN AMBER

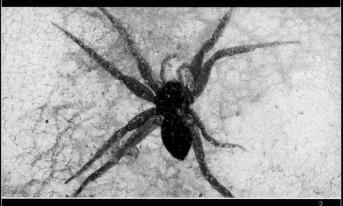

Amber is the fossilized resin (sticky sap) produced by some species of pine tree. Since prehistoric times, its attractive yellow appearance has led to its use in jewelry and religious objects. Insects are so fragile that they are rarely preserved as fossils. However, they can become preserved in amber (along with lichens, small lizards, and frogs) for millions of years. They become trapped in the sticky resin as it drips down trunks and stems before hardening. Sometimes even the delicate veins of insect wings survive. Amber is extremely useful for ancient DNA research since it preserves soft tissue for a very long time. In most fossilized bones, all the organic material is replaced by minerals.

▲ ANCIENT SHELLFISH

Ammonites are extinct shellfish related to cuttlefish and squid. These creatures were on Earth for around 160 million years until the end of the Cretaceous period, 65 million years ago. They were so widespread and varied, evolving rapidly all the time, that they have become a key guide for geologists, indicating exactly when a rock formed.

▲ FOSSIL FERNS

One of the key pieces of evidence that dinosaurs were killed off by a global climatic disaster was the discovery of "fern spikes." Dating from a short period just after the extinction, these are fossils that show large concentrations of ferns. Ferns are often the first plants to return after volcanic eruptions or other geological catastrophes.

A 2-ft-long (70-cm) nose gave T. rex an acute sense of smell

Plaster jacket used to protect exposed T. rex thighbone

Serrated, curved 7-inch-long (18-cm) teeth

Lower jaw hinged in the middle like a door

▲ THE FOSSIL RECORD

Discovering a major fossil like this 80-million-year-old *T. rex* thighbone is an exciting event. In addition to telling us a little more about dinosaurs, it also helps us to build up a fossil record of how life evolved over time. Fossils can also reveal the movements of Earth's landmasses and changes in the Earth's climate, from almost desertlike to the bitter cold of the Ice Ages. Fossils can even reveal the existence of catastrophic events that caused mass extinctions of life, such as the one that killed off the dinosaurs 65 million years ago.

T. REX SKULL ▶

Dinosaur fossils are rare, but when found—in places such as the Badlands of the Midwest and Asia's Gobi Desert—they are often spectacular. Fossils of more than 350 different kinds of dinosaur have been found to date, ranging from tiny two-legged runners to gigantic, lumbering four-legged vegetarians. Fossils are rarely complete skeletons, so the discovery of the complete skull of a *Tyrannosaurus rex*, like this one found in the Black Hills of South Dakota, is a major event. *T. rex* was the second-largest flesh-eater that ever lived—taller than a house and heavier than an elephant.

fossils

Chalk layers built up from the crushed shells of microscopic sea creatures

ROCK FROM LIFE-FORMS

Some of the world's toughest rock, including many kinds of limestone, is made from the remains of living things. There are two kinds of organic sedimentary rock: bioclastic and biogenic. Bioclastic rock, such as limestone, is made from the fragmented remains of plants and sea creatures. Biogenic rock, such as coral, is made from the whole remains of living things. Sometimes the buried remains of living organisms are transformed over millions of years into fossil fuels, such as coal, oil, and natural gas.

◄ WHITE CLIFFS OF DOVER
Chalk, here exposed in England's White Cliffs of Dover, is a soft white rock of almost pure calcite (calcium carbonate). It formed on the seabed some 100 million years ago during the Cretaceous period, when dinosaurs roamed the Earth. Minute algae grew with coccoliths (microscopic plates of calcite). When the algae died, the plates fell on the seafloor along with the shells from tiny animals called foraminifers. These eventually turned into chalk.

sedimentary rock

Foraminiferal shells are microfossils found in chalk formed on the seabed.

▲ FOSSILIFEROUS LIMESTONE
Most limestones are a mixture of organic and chemically formed calcite. But a few, like fossiliferous limestone, are made almost entirely of fossils, like this 420-million-year-old example of Silurian limestone from Wenlock in Shropshire, England. It is rich in sea-creature fossils, such as trilobites (beetlelike creatures, now extinct) and brachiopods—a type of shellfish that was attached to the seafloor by a stalk.

▲ FOSSILIZED ORGANISMS IN CHALK
The fossilized remains of coccoliths (algae plates) and sea creatures (foraminifers—shown here) that make up chalk are so tiny that the rock looks white and powdery. But under a powerful microscope, the organisms can be seen. Unlike most protozoans (single-celled organisms), foraminifers have shells and it is their shells—along with the plates of calcite deposited by algae—that are preserved as calcite in chalk.

CORAL REEFS

Reef, or coral, limestones are made entirely from the fossilized remains of the creatures that lived on coral reefs, including the corals themselves, millions of years ago. Sometimes the shape of the ancient reef may be preserved in the formation of the rock, which forms a small hill called a reef knoll. The best-known coral reef is the Great Barrier Reef off the eastern coast of Australia.

Corals are formed from the external skeletons of marine animals.

THE STORY OF COAL

Vegetation dies and falls into the swamp.

① *Warm swamps in Carboniferous period turn to peat*

PEAT

② *Lignite formed from peat buried deep in mud*

LIGNITE

③ *Bituminous coal produced after hundreds of millions of years of pressure*

BITUMINOUS COAL

④ *Anthracite produced by extreme pressure on coal*

ANTHRACITE

◄ COAL FROM DEAD PLANTS

Coal is made from plants that grew in swamps millions of years ago. As time passed, dead layers of these plants were squeezed dry by the weight of mud above them and they turned to increasingly concentrated carbon. At the top is soft brown peat (60 percent carbon). Lower down is more compressed, dull brown coal or lignite (73 percent carbon), then shiny black, bituminous coal (83 percent carbon). Anthracite (almost 100 percent carbon) only forms under extreme pressure.

▲ MINING COAL

The best coal (bituminous and anthracite) is usually found in narrow layers called seams, far below ground. To get at this coal, engineers sink deep shafts to reach the seam. Miners then tunnel along it to extract the coal from the exposed face. This coal face at Blacksville, Virginia, is 800 ft (240 m) below ground. In the past, coal was dug out by hand with picks and shovels. Most modern pits now use remote-controlled cutting machines, such as the longwall shearer shown here.

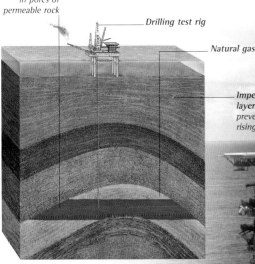

Oil trapped in pores of permeable rock

Drilling test rig

Natural gas

Impervious layer of rock prevents oil rising

▲ OIL TRAPS

Most oil comes from tiny organisms that lived in the sea millions of years ago. When their remains were buried in seabed mud, bacteria turned them to kerogen (a waxy, tarlike substance). Over time, heat and pressure deep below the surface turned the kerogen into oil and natural gas. Most of this oil becomes trapped in a layer of porous rock (rock that holds liquid) under layers of impervious rock (rock that does not allow liquid to pass through it).

Derrick holds the boring pipe. It is lengthened as the drill goes deeper

Excess gas burner

◄ DRILLING FOR OIL

When oil is found under the seabed, a drilling tower, known as a derrick, is set up on an oil rig. Some oil rigs are floating platforms; others are anchored to the seabed, such as this one in the North Sea. The choice of rig depends on the seabed, the depth of water, and the usual weather conditions. Often a single oil rig can open up a number of wells, by sending the drill bits down at an angle into the oil trap.

SPACE ROCK

Earth's geology is far from unique. Earth is one of four rock planets circling the Sun, along with Mercury, Venus, and Mars. The Moon is also rocky. The Earth is continually being struck by space rocks known as meteorites. Some kinds of meteorite, called chondrites, appear to have changed little since they were formed in the earliest days of the solar system. Geochemists believe that when they look at a particular kind of chondrite meteorite, called a carbonaceous chondrite, they are looking at the earliest form of rock.

▲ SHOOTING STARS IN EARTH'S ATMOSPHERE

Most meteorites come from fragments of asteroids—large bodies of space rock. In space these fragments are known as meteoroids. When they enter the Earth's atmosphere they become meteors. Most meteors are so tiny they burn up on entry, creating the glowing trails we call shooting stars. When the Earth passes through the tail of a comet (an icy lump which releases vast clouds of gas and dust as it approaches the Sun), meteor showers (shooting stars) like those shown here can be seen in the night sky. Occasionally, meteors are so large that they crash into the Earth without burning up entirely—these are called meteorites.

Martian rock from meteorite

▲ MARTIAN METEORITES ON EARTH

Twenty-four of the meteorites found on Earth originally came from Mars. They are the only samples of rock that we have from another planet. This one, found in the icy Antarctic desert, caused tremendous excitement when NASA scientists found microscopic structures in it. They believed these could only have been created by living organisms. Future space probes to Mars will look for signs of microscopic life on the planet.

Glassy rock produced by heat of meteor impact

Tektites are often egg-shaped

▲ TEKTITES

Tektites are small blobs of silica-rich glassy rock, which are usually disk- or egg-shaped. They can vary in color from pale yellow to black. Geologists once thought them to be meteorite fragments, but now believe they are produced when molten blobs of terrestrial rock, flung out by the impact of a huge meteorite, cool rapidly .

METEOR CRATER ▶

There are many more meteorite craters on the Moon than on the Earth. Geologists suggest that the reason we do not see as many impact craters here is because continual geological activity covers them up. Nevertheless, some can be seen. The first impact crater to be identified was Meteor Crater in the Arizona desert (shown here). It was created 49,000 years ago by a 336,000-ton (305,000-metric ton)-meteorite that hit the Earth at around 450,000 mph (724,000 kph). Scientists have identified more than 160 large impact sites around the world.

TYPES OF METEORITE

IRONS

Meteorites are made from iron and stone. They are divided into three groups according to how much of each they contain. Irons—or iron-nickels—are less common than stones, but were the first to be identified because their metallic look and weight made them easy to recognize. The largest meteorites are irons.

STONES

Almost 90 percent of the meteorites that fall to Earth are stones. They range from ancient chondrites, as old as the solar system itself, to rocks that have broken off the Moon and Mars. Chondrites, like the one shown here, get their name because they contain chondrules—once-molten globules of pyroxene or olivine.

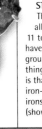

STONY IRONS

These are the least common of all meteorites and less than 11 tons (10 metric tons) of them have been found. The stony-iron group is very varied, but the one thing these rocks have in common is that they are all about half iron-nickel and half stone. Stony irons are divided into pallasites (shown here) and mesosiderites.

VOLANOES IN SPACE

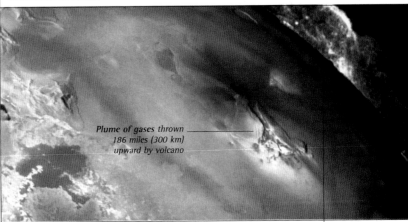

Plume of gases thrown 186 miles (300 km) upward by volcano

Io's surface pulsates as it is squeezed by Jupiter's gravity

Earth is not the only planet in the solar system with volcanoes. Mars has Olympus Mons, the tallest volcano in the solar system, and Venus has more volcanoes than any other planet. But the most spectacular volcanic activity is found on Jupiter's moon Io. It is probably not Io's internal heat that generates volcanic activity, but the closeness of Jupiter. The giant planet's intense gravitational pull creates so much pressure on Io that it melts rock. Some parts of Io brighten regularly as floods of lava erupt from the surface. One volcano, called Loki, has a cauldron of lava 120 miles (200 km) across.

space rock

Reddish tinge comes from high iron content of Martian rock

MARTIAN ROCKS ▲

We know more about the planet Mars than any other planet. The search for signs of life there has prompted a series of exploratory missions to the planet. We know that Mars has a rocky composition very similar to Earth's, with an iron core, a semimolten mantle, and a hard crust. Unmanned missions are revealing more and more evidence that water once flowed on the surface of Mars—and if there was water, there could have been life. Photographs from above the surface have revealed vast valleys that look as if they were carved out by floodwater. In 2004, NASA's robotic Mars rovers *Spirit* and *Opportunity* analyzed Martian rocks, which showed signs that they were once covered in water.

Breccia (rock fragments) fall back into the crater after impact

Rim built up from ejecta—pulverized rock blasted out by the impact

¾ MILE (1.2 KM)

MINERAL CLASSES

To make sense of the 3,000 or so different kinds of mineral, mineralogists organize them into classes, or families, based on their chemical composition. The most widely used system for grouping minerals is the Dana system. First published by Yale University professor James Dana in 1848, this system divides minerals into eight basic classes. The most important groupings are native elements, silicates, oxides, sulfides, sulfates, halides, carbonates, and phosphates. Dana's system is still used today.

Garnet forms in schist rock when certain minerals are altered by high temperatures and pressures

GARNET IN SCHIST

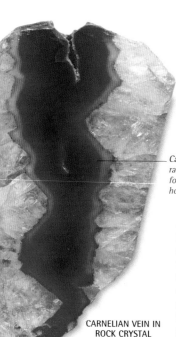

Carnelian is a rare mineral that forms in veins of hot fluid

CARNELIAN VEIN IN ROCK CRYSTAL

▲ HOW MINERALS FORM

Minerals form when the elements in a gas or liquid crystallize into a solid. Different combinations of elements form different minerals. Some form when hot, molten rock from the Earth's interior cools slowly; others form from chemicals dissolved in liquids in the ground. Existing minerals can be altered by chemicals in the Earth or be transformed by being squeezed or heated by geological processes such as mountain building. The rocks of the Earth's crust are made of common minerals; rarer minerals tend to form in veins (cracks) and cavities (holes) in the rocks.

EVAPORITES ▲

When hot, mineral-rich, salty waters evaporate (dry up), the minerals left behind are known as evaporites. Halite, gypsum, and anhydrite form in this way. Most evaporites form around hot springs—spouts of water heated by volcanic activity. At Pamukkale, Turkey (pictured above), mineral deposits from calcite-rich hot springs have created a solid white "waterfall" made from the evaporite, travertine.

MINERAL CLASSES

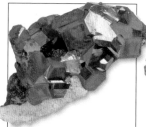

NATIVE (*see* pp.50–53)
Most minerals are made from combinations of chemical elements, but a few elements, such as silver (shown here in a rare crystal form), occur naturally by themselves. These are known as native elements and occur in igneous and metamorphic rocks. Some native elements may survive erosion and end up on stream beds.

SILICATES (*see* pp.56–59)
Silicates are metals combined with silicon and oxygen and are the most common minerals. There are more of them than all the other minerals put together. Quartz and feldspar make up the bulk of silicate-rich igneous rock. Other silicate groups include mica, pyroxene, and garnet (shown embedded in a host rock).

OXIDES (*see* pp.62–63)
Oxides, like the chromite shown here, are a combination of a metal with oxygen. They include dull ores, such as bauxite, and rare gems, such as rubies and sapphires. Hard, primary oxides form deep in Earth's crust. Softer oxides form nearer the surface from sulfides and silicates that have broken down.

SULFIDES (*see* pp.64–65)
Sulfides, like the stibnite shown here, are generally brittle, heavy compounds of sulfur usually combined with a metal. They form as very hot water evaporates underground. They include some important metal ores such as chalcopyrite (a copper ore), cinnabar (a mercury ore), and pyrite (an iron ore).

SULFATES (*see* pp.66–67)
Sulfates are a large and widespread group of minerals that are generally soft, pale-colored, and translucent. They form when metals combine with sulfur and oxygen. They include barite and gypsum, shown here in its "daisy" form. Like a daisy, its crystal "petals" radiate outward from a central point.

CRYSTAL SHAPE ▶
All but a few minerals form crystals, and each mineral forms its own characteristic crystal shape, like this tourmaline crystal. Tourmaline crystals are typically long, striped, hexagonal rods. Crystals that form at the same time as the rock in which they are embedded are so small and so mixed in that their characteristic shapes can be hard to spot. In places where crystals have room to grow freely, their characteristic shapes are much clearer.

Tourmaline crystals are usually trigonal and form in many colours

Feldspar is a silicate

Stalactites made of travertine rock form on the overhang of rock terraces

Amethyst crystals fill the inside of this geode

Agate often grows in cracks in lava flows or seabed limestones

Pillowlike formations give Pamukkale ("Cotton Castle") its name

minerals

SPECTACULAR CRYSTALS ▲
Large, well-defined crystals are rare and often grow in rock cavities, known as geodes, and veins, where mineral-rich water cools slowly. When the minerals are concentrated and crystals have enough space to grow in regular shapes, they may form valuable gems and spectacular crystals, such as the amethyst and agate shown here. A slow-forming single crystal can grow very big but most crystals form quickly and remain small.

HALIDES (see pp.68–69)
Halides are usually very soft minerals, in which metallic elements combine with halogen elements (chlorine, bromine, fluorine, and iodine). Sodium chloride, or table salt, is the best known. Halides dissolve easily in water, so they can only form under special conditions. The most common are halite (salt) and fluorite.

CARBONATES (see p.70)
Carbonates are minerals that form when metals or semimetals combine with a carbonate (carbon and oxygen). Most are formed by the alteration of other minerals on the Earth's surface. Calcite, or calcium carbonate, shown here in its "nailhead" form, makes up the bulk of limestones and marbles.

PHOSPHATES (see p.71)
Phosphates are one of the smaller, less common families of minerals. They are usually secondary minerals that form when primary ore minerals are broken down by the weather. When combined with other minerals they often have vivid colors, such as the greenish-blue of turquoise or this lime-green pyromorphite.

MINERALOIDS

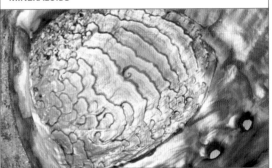

A few substances occur naturally in the Earth and do not fit in with the basic properties of other minerals. They are not members of any of the chemical families (shown left), nor do they form crystals. Such substances are called mineraloids. Some are glassy, like opal and jet (a dense form of coal). Some are formed by living things, such as amber (formed from pine-tree resin) and mother-of-pearl (shown here), which is formed in the shells of certain shellfish.

PHYSICAL PROPERTIES

Although every mineral has a unique combination of features, all share physical properties that help geologists to identify them. They can be grouped according to their habit (how their crystals form); crystal system (the symmetry of their crystal shapes); chemical composition; cleavage (how they split); specific gravity (their density in relation to water); and hardness (how easily they scratch).

ACICULAR
(SOLECITE)

RENIFORM
(HEMATITE)

PRISMATIC
(ORTHOCLASE)

DENDRITIC
(PYROLUSITE)

MASSIVE
(LIMONITE)

BOTRYOIDAL
(HYDROZINCITE)

▲ CRYSTAL HABITS

Crystal habit describes the shapes that minerals form when they grow. Although most minerals have more than one habit, habits are sometimes quite distinctive and common to only a few minerals. The examples shown above are just a small selection of the many different kinds of habit. Acicular crystals form needles; reniform crystals are kidney-shaped; prismatic crystals are symmetrical (one side mirrors the other); dendritic crystals are plant-shaped; and botryoidal crystals look like bunches of grapes. Massive habits have no visible crystals.

CHEMICAL PROPERTIES

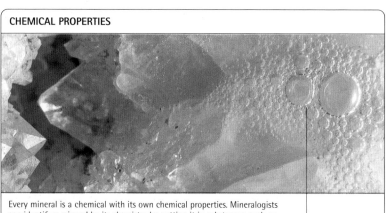

Every mineral is a chemical with its own chemical properties. Mineralogists can identify a mineral by its chemistry by putting it in substances, such as acids or water, to see if it dissolves. Although most minerals will not dissolve in pure water, borax and halite are among the exceptions. But many minerals dissolve in acids, especially hot acids. Calcite, for instance, dissolves in weak hydrochloric acid, which helps to distinguish it from similar-looking quartz, which does not dissolve in the acid.

Dissolving calcite fizzes in weak hydrochloric acid

CRYSTAL SYSTEMS

CUBIC
Minerals are classified into six systems according to the symmetrical arrangement of their planes (flat surfaces). Minerals in the cubic system have the most regular crystal symmetry. These include halite (shown here), galena, and silver.

TETRAGONAL
The tetragonal system is one of the least common. Tetragonal crystals typically come as elongated four-sided prisms (a set of parallel faces), shown right. Minerals include chalcopyrite, rutile, scheelite, zircon, and vesuvianite (or idocrase), shown left.

MONOCLINIC
Almost a third of all minerals belong to the monoclinic system, the most common type of symmetry. Monoclinic crystals are only symmetrical in one plane (shown right). Monoclinic minerals include manganite (shown left), mica, gypsum, and selenite.

TRICLINIC
The least symmetrical crystals are found in the triclinic system. They are also the rarest. Minerals with triclinic systems include anorthite, serpentine, turquoise, kaolinite, and kyanite. Axinite (shown here) gets its name from its distinctive wedge-shaped crystals.

ORTHORHOMBIC
These crystals are very common. They are short and stubby and generally appear prism or matchbox-shaped (shown right). Minerals in this system include aragonite, sulfur, olivine, topaz, peridot, celestine, adamite, cerussite, and barite (shown left).

HEXAGONAL/TRIGONAL
These two systems are grouped together because they have a similar symmetry. Hexagonal crystals have six faces in the prism (shown right), trigonal crystals have three. Quartz, the gemstone beryl (hexagonal, shown left), and tourmaline all fall into this system.

▲ CLEAVAGE
The way that a mineral breaks along well defined planes of weakness is called cleavage. Many minerals can be identified by the way they break. Muscovite, shown here, cleaves (splits) cleanly in one direction, forming flat sheets. Fluorite splits in four directions to form diamond-shaped pieces.

▲ CONCHOIDAL FRACTURE
Not all minerals break cleanly along flat cleavage planes. Some show a distinctive way of fracturing. There are about 12 common fracture patterns. One of the most recognizable is the conchoidal, or shell-like shape, where the mineral breaks into curved flakes. Opal (shown here), flint, and obsidian all fracture in this way.

▲ UNEVEN FRACTURE
Striking a mineral with a hammer and breaking it sometimes reveals a rough, uneven surface. Arsenopyrite, pyrite, quartz, kaolinite, anhydrite, and sillimanite (shown here) all fracture unevenly. If the broken surface has sharp edges, geologists call it a jagged fracture.

physical properties

SPECIFIC GRAVITY ►
Minerals vary in density. Galena, which is rich in lead, is very dense and much heavier than a lump of gypsum the same size. Mineral density can be compared by measuring its specific gravity. This can be a useful clue to identity. A mineral's specific gravity is its weight in relation to the same volume of water. Galena has a specific gravity of 7.5, which means that a lump of galena weighs 7.5 times as much as the same volume of water. Quartz is one of the lighter minerals, with a specific gravity of just 2.65.

Quartz, a silicate, is relatively light

Galena, a sulfide, is very dense

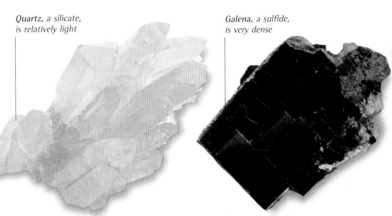

MOHS' HARDNESS SCALE ►
Hardness is a mineral's resistance to scratching. It can be measured on a scale that was devised by German mineralogist Friedrich Mohs in 1822. He selected ten standard minerals against which all minerals could be compared. A mineral's position on Mohs' scale depends on whether it can scratch, or be scratched by, Mohs' chosen minerals.

| 1 TALC | 2 GYPSUM | 3 CALCITE | 4 FLUORITE | 5 APATITE | 6 ORTHOCLASE | 7 QUARTZ | 8 TOPAZ | 9 CORUNDUM | 10 DIAMOND |

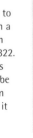 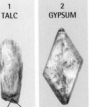        

TALCUM POWDER ►
The softest mineral on Mohs' hardness scale is talc. Every mineral can scratch talc. Its softness has made it a popular mineral for carving since ancient times. The Chinese, Babylonians, Egyptians, and Native Americans all carved ornaments from talc.

Talcum powder is made from talc

DIAMOND PARTICLES ►
The hardest mineral on Mohs' hardness scale is diamond. Diamond is so hard that it will scratch every other mineral—and yet cannot be scratched itself. Besides being highly valued as gemstones, diamonds are also in demand in cutting tools and drills.

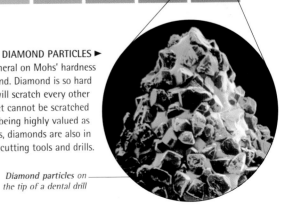

Diamond particles on the tip of a dental drill

OPTICAL PROPERTIES

One of the first clues to a mineral's identity is often the way it looks. Minerals reflect and let light through in different ways. For example, many minerals glint and sparkle, while others barely reflect light at all. Some minerals look greasy, as if they were coated with butter. Some have a distinctive color. Qualities like these are known as optical properties. Color, luster, and clarity are the most obvious, but there are others, including fluorescence and refraction.

Shiny azurite set in dull limonite

LUSTER ►

Luster is the way that light bounces off a mineral's surface. A surface can be as shiny as glass or as dull as soil. Here, bright-blue azurite is instantly distinguishable from the brown limonite in which it is set, not just by color but also by its distinctive glasslike luster. Some minerals can also be distinguished by the way that light bounces around inside it. For example, when light hits an opal, its chemical structure makes it appear to shimmer with the colors of the rainbow.

Tiny malachite crystals form a crust

◄ COLOR

Minerals get their color from their chemical makeup. Some minerals, such as cuprite (a mixture of copper and oxygen, shown here), are colored by the main chemicals in their makeup and always appear the same color. Minerals like these are known as idiochromatic. Other minerals, such as quartz, vary wildly in color. They get their coloring from impurities and are known as allochromatic minerals. Quartz takes its many different colors from trace minerals; rose quartz is pink due to traces of titanium, while chrysoprase is green because of traces of nickel.

Uneven, submetallic luster

DIFFERENT COLORS

CITRINE
Yellow, orange, or brown citrine is a variety of quartz—an allochromatic mineral. Its colors are caused by minute traces of iron. Pale yellow citrine stones are the most highly prized and give the mineral its name, after the Latin word "citrus" for lemon. Heating citrine turns it white.

AMETHYST
Like citrine, amethyst is another variety of quartz that gets its coloring from tiny traces of iron. However, because amethyst forms at lower temperatures, it appears purple. If heated, it turns yellow, while exposure to X-rays restores its original color. The best quality amethysts are found in geodes (rock hollows).

AZURITE
Azurite, an idiochromatic mineral, has a distinctive bright blue color. It is the most common blue mineral and its name comes from the French word "azure", meaning 'blue sky." It is made of a mixture of copper, carbonate, and hydrogen. Painters ground it up to make a vivid blue pigment that was almost as good as lapis lazuli.

STREAK TESTS

ORPIMENT   HEMATITE

A mineral's streak is the mark it leaves when it is dragged across a ceramic tile. Some minerals, such as orpiment (shown above), are the same color as their streak, while others produce a streak of different color. Their streaks help to tell them apart. Hematite (shown above) and chromite both look black, but chromite's streak is black, while hematite's is brownish red. Minerals, such as fluorite, appear in many colors but have the same colored streak. Flourite's is always white.

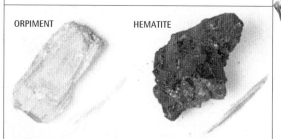

TYPES OF LUSTER

VITREOUS (GLASSY)
The word vitreous comes from the Latin word for "jelly" and describes the texture of an eye. Mineralogists use it to mean a shiny, glasslike luster. Most clear and semitransparent gems are characterized by a vitreous luster, including ruby (shown here), topaz, emerald, tourmaline, aquamarine, corundum, and fluorite.

METALLIC
A metallic luster is a shiny, highly reflective finish that is typical of freshly cut metals and their ores. All native metals have this luster when newly broken or polished. So too do many ores, such as galena, chalcopyrite, pyrite, and magnetite. Graphite (shown here) is not a metal but has a dull metallic luster.

SUBMETALLIC
Some minerals have what is called a submetallic luster. This is an uneven, semimetallic reflection from the mineral's surface—caused by traces of metal in the mineral. It is often seen on dark, almost opaque (nontransparent) crystals, such as chromite, cuprite, rutile, sphalerite, and lepidocrocite (shown here).

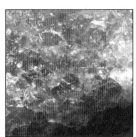

GREASY
Minerals with a greasy luster have an oily appearance. Although they are shiny, they do not show reflections like glass. This kind of luster is common in minerals with microscopically small amounts of mineral impurities. Halite (shown here), quartz, and apatite all have a greasy appearance.

SILKY
Minerals with a silky luster tend to have a fine structure of fibers that makes them shimmer, just like silk. Fibrous asbestos minerals, such as serpentine chrysotile and riebeckite crocidolite all have a silky luster. So do minerals, such as gypsum (shown here), wavellite, tremolite, and fibrous calcite.

optical properties

Azurite crystals have a glassy luster

◄ FLUORESCENCE
When some minerals are exposed to ultraviolet light, they glow in colors that are different from their normal color in daylight. This glow is called fluorescence—a word that comes from the mineral fluorite (shown here), which comes in many colors but which gives off a blue or green fluorescence. Fluorite is thought to fluoresce because it contains minute amounts of uranium or "rare earth" elements—a group of chemically similar metals. Sometimes fluorescence is caused by tiny impurities in minerals. For example, traces of manganese give calcite a bright-red glow.

Fluorite glows bright blue in ultraviolet light

OPAQUE: GOLD

TRANSLUCENT: AQUAMARINE

▲ CLARITY
A few minerals, such as quartz and sapphire are almost as transparent (clear) as glass in their pure state. However, tiny impurities can make them appear less clear. Some minerals, such as moonstone, are semitransparent, so that things seen through them appear blurred. Geologists describe minerals that are not transparent, but which still let some light through them, such as chrysoprase, as translucent. Minerals that block off light completely, such as malachite, are said to be opaque. All metals are opaque.

REFRACTION ►
Some minerals are very clear and transparent but distort the light passing through them. They are said to refract (bend) the light. For example, objects seen through calcite appear twice due to double refraction. The light reflected off this black line is split into two rays, which produce a double image.

Calcite distorts light

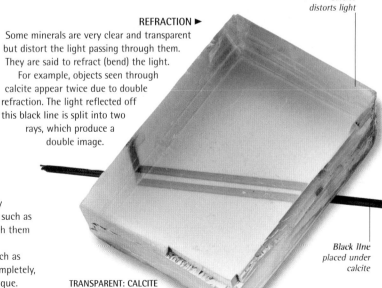

Black line placed under calcite

TRANSPARENT: CALCITE

NATIVE ELEMENTS

Most minerals are compounds, which means they are made up of combinations of chemical elements. But some minerals occur naturally by themselves, and these are called native elements. They are often metals, but also include semimetals, such as bismuth, antimony, and arsenic, and nonmetals, such as sulfur and carbon (in the form of graphite and diamond). Nonmetals are usually found in volcanic features such as underground veins and—with sulfur—in hot springs. Sulfur and graphite are common, but bismuth, antimony, and arsenic occur rarely as native elements—and diamonds are rarest of all.

Chunky orthorhombic crystals

Needlelike monoclinic crystals

▲ TWO HABITS OF SULFUR
Chunky orthorhombic crystals (see p.46) are the most common form of sulfur. Occasionally, though, it is found in monoclinic form (see p.46). Monoclinic sulfur can be the same vivid yellow as ordinary sulfur—though it is more often orange—but the crystals are acicular, which means they are long and needlelike.

Cloth provides some protection from the poisonous sulfur gases

Sulfur deposits found near volcanic hot springs

▲ SULFUR MINING
Native sulfur is recognizable by its bright yellow color. It is often found around the edges of hot volcanic springs and smoky volcanic chimneys called fumaroles. Here, a miner is digging sulfur from the crater of Ijen volcano in eastern Java, Indonesia. In this type of sulfur mining, people collect chunks of cooled sulfur from around the crater and carry them away in baskets. Most of the world's sulfur, however, is mined from underground beds, such as those found under the Gulf of Mexico, using the Frasch process in which very hot water, injected into the beds at very high pressure, melts the sulfur. The molten sulfur is then pumped to the surface. After the water evaporates, pure sulfur is left behind.

◄ PROCESSING SULFUR
While nearly pure sulfur can be extracted from the ground using the Frasch process, sulfur is also found in fossil fuels and ores such as pyrite and galena. In these cases, the sulfur is separated out by heating the mineral to release hydrogen sulfide gas. The gas is then burned to separate the hydrogen, leaving pure sulfur. Most commercially extracted sulfur is turned into sulfuric acid in large chemical plants, such as the one in England shown here. Sulfuric acid has many uses in industry. It is used to make fertilizer, dyes, paper, and cellophane.

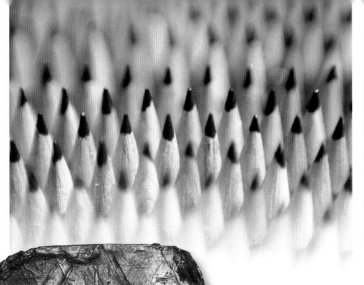

▲ GRAPHITE

Graphite and diamond are both forms of carbon, but the two are very different. Graphite is opaque, dark gray, and one of the softest minerals—so soft it is used as the "lead" in pencils. More recently, scientists have produced a man-made form of graphite called graphene, which may be used in the future, instead of silicon, for ultrafast computer chips. Most graphite forms in rocks (usually marble) through the metamorphism of organic material, such as fossils.

▲ DIAMOND

The world's hardest natural substance, diamond is pure carbon that has been transformed into a clear, hard gemstone by incredible forces of pressure and heat. Most diamonds found today are billions of years old. They formed deep underground and were carried to the surface through volcanic pipes in molten kimberlite magma. They survived because they are so hard. Pressure like this is rare in nature.

GRAPHITE AND DIAMOND CHEMICAL STRUCTURES

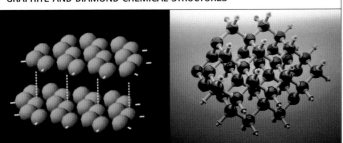

Pure carbon occurs in four forms: graphite, diamond, soot (burned organic matter), and a very rare form called fullerene. In graphite, the atoms form in two-dimensional, sheetlike structures (above left). However, the bonds between the sheets are weak, which is why graphite is so soft. In the diamond form, the atoms are bonded into a strong, three-dimensional framework (above right). This is why diamond is so hard.

native elements

Dull, nonmetallic sheen

Botryoidal (grapelike) clusters

▲ ANTIMONY

Although silvery-gray like a metal, antimony is called a semimetal because it sometimes behaves chemically like a metal, sometimes like a nonmetal. Antimony occurs rarely as a native element—usually in volcanic veins. The main source of antimony is stibnite, a sulfide ore. Ancient Egyptians used it for eyeliner, and medieval artists used it for painting.

▲ BISMUTH

Bismuth is found as a native element only rarely, mostly in volcanic veins. Like antimony, it is a semimetal and expands on freezing as water does. This property makes bismuth very useful for soldering metals together because it expands to fill any gap as it solidifies. Bismuth is usually extracted from the ores bismuthinite and bismite.

▲ ARSENIC

Sometimes, pure arsenic forms botryoidal (grapelike) clusters, such as those shown here. However, arsenic is usually found combined in minerals such as arsenopyrite, orpiment, and realgar. Pure arsenic is poisonous. It can be combined with other minerals in making many things, from electronic transistors to wood preservatives.

METAL ELEMENTS

A few of the less reactive metals, including gold, silver, platinum, and copper, can be found in pure form as metal elements. Nuggets or flakes of these metals can be taken straight from rock, but this is uncommon. In the crust, most of Earth's metals are found mixed up with other elements in ores. Gold, almost uniquely, is mainly found as a native element. Metal elements are very rare in the Earth's crust, but they are more common in the core. Most of Earth's iron, for example, sank to the core very early in Earth's history, because it was so heavy.

Gold in quartz

▲ GOLD

Gold is the least reactive of all metals; it stays uncorroded (not damaged by chemical action) and shiny almost indefinitely. It was one of the first metals to be used because it was found in the ground in pure form, glittering in cracks and on the surface of rocks. It is also soft enough to hammer easily into shape. Many of the world's most beautiful ancient artifacts are made from gold. They have survived unblemished by time.

SILVER ►

Silver was known as "white gold" by the Ancient Egyptians and was once more highly prized than gold. It was first used in Anatolia, Turkey, more than 5,000 years ago. When polished, it is a beautiful, shiny white metal, but exposure to air quickly tarnishes it with a black coat of silver sulfide. This coating makes it hard to spot in the ground. Like gold, it forms in volcanic veins, often with galena (lead ore), zinc, and copper. Unlike gold and platinum, it rarely forms nuggets. Today, silver is mainly used for tableware and in many electrical components, because it conducts electricity very well, even better than copper.

Copper wire coiled up on drums

SILVER ORE

TARNISHED SILVER

◄ COPPER

Copper's distinctive reddish color makes it the most instantly recognizable of all metals. It is quite soft and is often found in its native form. Copper was one of the first metals people learned to use, because they could find and extract it easily. Today, most copper is taken from deposits of chalcopyrite ore. Like silver, it often grows in branching dendritic crystals, and like silver, it tarnishes quickly on exposure to air. However, the tarnish on copper is bright green, not black, so copper deposits are often revealed by bright green stains on a rock's surface, known as copper blooms.

Copper blooms are green from oxidization (exposure to the air)

native elements

PLATINIM NUGGET

Platinum's shiny surface does not tarnish

PLATINUM WEDDING RINGS

Uneven surface full of pits and holes

Tooth fillings made from amalgam (a mercury and silver mixture)

Mercury forms in liquid globules at room temperature

MERCURY

▲ PLATINUM

Platinum is a silvery metal that is rarer than gold and so even more precious. It has been known in South America for more than 2,000 years. Platinum gets its name from the Spanish word "plata" for silver and is one of the softest and heaviest of all metals. Grains of pure platinum used to be found in stream deposits, along with gold. Now, most platinum is mined from sulfide ores, found mainly Montana, and in the Ural Mountains of Russia. Its main uses are in jewelry and catalytic converters to clean car exhaust fumes.

▲ MERCURY

Mercury is rarely found in its native form and is the only metal that exists as a liquid at room temperature. It is usually found in its mineral ore, cinnabar, which mainly forms around volcanic vents and hot springs. Mercury expands with heat and is best known for its use in thermometers (devices used to measure temperature).

NICKEL-SILVER COMMEMORATIVE COIN

NICKEL ORE

Lead covering on roof helps to protect it against the weather

NATIVE LEAD (GRAY) IN ROCK

▲ NICKEL-IRON

Less common than some major elements, nickel forms a natural alloy with iron, called nickel-iron, which is often found in meteorites on Earth's surface. The Ancient Egyptians called it "sky-iron" and used it to make the sacred tools for mummifying pharaohs. Today, nickel is mostly used in alloys with iron and other metals to make stainless steel and with silver to make coins. Both nickel and iron are produced mainly from ores: pentlandite for nickel, and hematite and magnetite for iron.

▲ LEAD

Lead is a very dark, soft metal. Its softness makes it easy to use and shape—which is why the Ancient Romans used it to make water pipes. Lead is also very heavy—one of the densest of all metals. It is rarely found as a native element. More often it is combined with other elements, in galena, anglesite, and cerussite. In fact, even lead pipes are not made from pure lead. Because the metal is so soft, it is usually alloyed (mixed) with other elements.

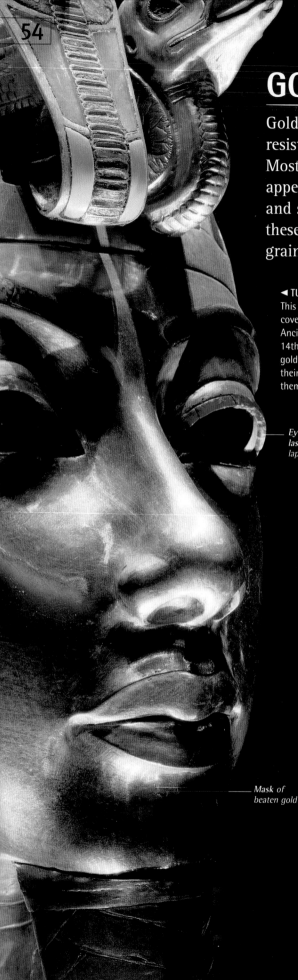

GOLD

Gold is a native element, prized for its bright yellow color and resistance to tarnishing. Gold deposits typically form in two ways. Most gold is formed in hydrothermal veins in the rock, where it appears mixed in with quartz and other minerals (such as silver and sulfides). Most of the world's gold is mined from veins like these. Gold is also found in deposits in riverbeds, where gold grains from weathered rock accumulate.

◄ **TUTANKHAMUN'S FUNERAL MASK**
This stunning gold funeral mask was found covering the mummy of Tutankhamun, an Ancient Egyptian boy-king. He lived in the 14th century BC. For the Ancient Egyptians, gold symbolized everlasting life, so they packed their pharaohs' tombs with gold objects for them to use in the afterlife.

Eyebrows and lashes made from lapis lazuli

Mask of beaten gold

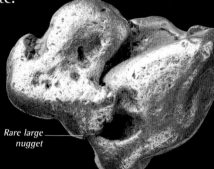

Rare large nugget

GOLD NUGGET ▲
Gold is usually found in branches of tiny crystals covering quartz, or in small grains. Large nuggets are quite rare. The largest nugget ever found was the famous 157-lb (71-kg) "Welcome Stranger Nugget" found in 1869 in Moliagul, Australia.

Rare cubic crystals

◄ **GOLD CRYSTALS**
Gold crystals are typically cubic, but unlike many other minerals, gold rarely forms crystals. When they do occur, they are often distorted or microscopic. The finest specimens found since ancient times have usually been melted down for use. So crystal growths like the one shown here are treasured and worth much more than their weight in gold.

USES OF GOLD

MONEY
Gold has always played a major role in nations' economies. Many of the earliest coins were gold. But gold is rare, expensive, and heavy. Today, its main monetary use is in the gold bars that make up a nation's gold reserves. The largest of these belongs to the US, followed by Germany.

TEETH
Gold is highly resistant to corrosion. The Etruscans of Ancient Italy used gold wire to secure false teeth 2,700 years ago. Since then, gold has been widely used in dentistry, for filling, crowning, or even replacing teeth. It is often alloyed with palladium, silver, zinc, or copper to make it tougher.

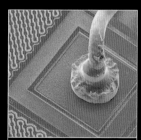

ELECTRONIC CONTACTS
Gold is almost as effective at conducting electricity as copper and silver. Gold-plated connectors and gold wires (shown here) are widely used in electronics, featuring in everything from mobile phones to computers. In 2001, 220 tons (200 metric tons) of gold were used worldwide in electronic components.

River gravels swirled around in a pan to reveal grains of gold

THE GOLD RUSH

In the 19th century, the discovery of gold deposits anywhere in the world inspired hordes of prospectors to descend on the spot in the hope of striking it rich. There were many gold rushes in North America, the most famous of which was the California gold rush of 1849. Here, prospectors use a homemade sluice to wash away silt in the hope of finding gold grains. There was only enough gold to make a few lucky people rich—most prospectors found little or nothing.

◄ PANNING FOR GOLD

When rock containing gold is broken down by the weather, gold grains may be washed into streams or rivers. Gold is very dense so the grains accumulate in deposits on riverbeds. Recovering these grains involves a labor-intensive technique known as panning. This involves scooping shingle from the riverbed into a pan, then carefully swilling the water around until the lighter gravels are rinsed out, leaving the heavier gold grains behind.

STRIP MINING ►

Estimates suggest that all the gold ever mined amounts to around 160,000 tons (145,000 metric tons) and that a further 2,760 tons (2,500 metric tons) or so are dug up each year. In the past, most of this gold came from South Africa. Extracting the gold here means digging expensive, ever-deeper mines. More recently, gold-mining companies have begun to exploit deposits nearer the surface in places such as Indonesia, Russia, Australia, and Papua New Guinea (shown here). Gold can be extracted more cheaply from strip mines, which are large pits in the ground. But their wide-scale excavation poses much more of a threat to the environment.

gold

Excavators used for digging in strip mine

Gold ore excavated from terraces

PYRITE (FOOL'S GOLD)

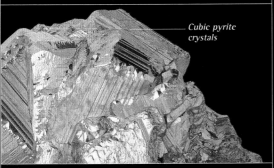

Cubic pyrite crystals

The shiny, yellow mineral called pyrite (an iron sulfide) looks so much like gold that it has fooled many prospectors into thinking they have found the real thing. Yet pyrite, sometimes known as "fool's gold," is among the most common minerals and is found in most environments. Indeed, any rock that looks a little rusty probably contains pyrite. Its crystals form in a number of shapes, including cubes and pentagonal dodecahedrons, which have 12 five-sided faces.

UNDERGROUND MINING ►

To extract gold from the ground, gold-containing ores have to be dug from the surface or out of underground seams. The gold is then separated from the waste ore in a process known as flotation, smelted (a combination of heating and melting), and then refined into 99.5 percent pure gold. This geologist is taking a sample from deep below the surface. Analysis of the sample for gold content will determine whether it is worth continuing to mine.

FELSIC SILICATES

Silicates make up more than 90 percent of the weight of Earth's crust, and most rocks are mainly composed of them. There are more than 1,000 different silicate minerals, split into two types: felsic and mafic silicates. Silicates that form in granites are called felsic silicates. The word felsic is a combination of "fel" for feldspar and "sic" for silica. They are lighter in weight and color than other silicates, because they contain less iron and magnesium. The felsic silicates include quartz (pure silica) and the K-feldspars, which are rich in potassium (K). Micas are a group of silicate minerals that split easily into sheets.

Debris from erosion

Volcanic plug exposed after erosion

POTASSIUM (K-) FELDSPARS

ORTHOCLASE
Orthoclase is an important rock-forming mineral. Orthoclase and plagioclase (*see* p.58) feldspar, make up 60 percent of the Earth's crust. Orthoclase is one of the main minerals in granite rock, along with mica and quartz. When granite erodes, the orthoclase is recycled in arkose (feldspar-rich) sandstones.

SANIDINE
Sanidine (shown here) forms in a variety of volcanic rocks, such as trachyte and rhyolite, and in contact metamorphic rocks, such as marble and hornfels. It is usually colorless or white, with a white streak. It can form in massive or prismatic (shown here) habits (see p.46). The crystals are often twinned (see p.59).

ANORTHOCLASE
Anorthoclase is a K-feldspar similar to sanidine and another K-feldspar called albite. However, unlike them, it is rich in both sodium and potassium. Sanidine contains little sodium, and albite contains very little potassium. Anorthoclase generally forms in igneous rocks in dykes and small intrusions.

silicates

(*see* p.58)

BOARS TUSK VOLCANIC PLUG ▲
Boars Tusk in Wyoming is the core of an ancient volcano. Over millions of years, the softer external rock has worn away, exposing the tougher rock that plugged the volcano's vent. This rock is rhyolite—similar to granite, but formed near the surface, rather than deep underground. The rocks have the same felsic minerals—quartz, potassium feldspar, and mica—but granite can contain microcline or orthoclase (potassium), while rhyolite contains sanidine (potassium and sodium).

MICROCLINE AND PORCELAIN ►
Microcline is the main K-feldspar found in igneous and metamorphic rocks, forming at relatively low temperatures in deep rocks, such as syenite and pegmatite. Microcline crystals in pegmatite are the largest ever found. A specimen from Karelia, Russia, weighed more than 2,000 tons (1,800 metric tons). The Chinese used microcline to make fine porcelain more than 1,500 years ago. When heated, tiny microcline particles help to cement the finely ground kaolin ("white clay") and quartz together into a white, translucent ceramic.

Glaze (a hard, water-resistant coating) also made from microcline

CHINESE PORCELAIN VASE

Amazonite is a gemstone variety of green microcline

MICAS

MUSCOVITE
Muscovite looks brittle but is remarkably tough. It is often found in sands where other minerals have been destroyed. In Muscovy (old Russia) it was used for house windows, giving it its name. Its heat-resistant qualities meant that it was once used in stove windows. Today, it is used for making electrical components.

BIOTITE
Biotite mica is a common mineral and a major ingredient in granites, gneisses, and schists. It is darker than muscovite—usually black or dark brown—and is soft and crumbles easily. Flakes of biotite often stick together in clumps up to 7 ft (2 m) in diameter. These clumps are known as "books," because they resemble pages.

LEPIDOLITE
Lepidolite is a rare mica, forming in thin flakes in acid igneous rocks, such as granite. Its pink, purple, or gray coloring comes from the presence of the metal lithium. It often forms together with tourmaline—the combination of pink lepidolite and red tourmaline is attractive in carved ornaments.

Clear muscovite sheet used as window pane

▲ MICA WINDOW
Mica minerals are found in all kinds of rock. In some pegmatites, they typically form thin, colorless, brittle flakes. Some micas, such as muscovite, are extremely clear and resistant to weathering. As a result, the sheets of mica were once used as window panes, like this one from a Native American dwelling situated high on a rock outcrop in Acoma Pueblo, New Mexico. Mica has heat-resistant properties and is still used in oil stoves and lamps.

Pinky-purple tourmaline is called rubellite

◄ TOURMALINE
Tourmaline minerals occur in a wide range of vivid colors. Quite often, single long crystals have multicolored layers, like an exotic cocktail. Each layer reflects a slight chemical change during its formation. Red tourmaline becomes electrically charged on heating.

TOURMALINE

Quartz matrix

Beryl turned to green emerald by impurities

Quartz vein containing emeralds

Emeralds will be prised out of the rock by hand to avoid damage

BERYL ►
Beryl is a widespread mineral. Pure beryl (goshenite) is colorless, but impurities give it rich colors. When chrome and vanadium turn it to brilliant green, as shown here, it becomes an emerald. Blue beryl is called aquamarine, yellow beryl is called heliodor, and pink beryl is called morganite. Beryl is an important source of beryllium, which is used in nuclear reactors and for making metal alloys.

EMERALD

EMERALD MINING ►
Beryl is found most commonly in pegmatites where it forms gigantic crystals. Archeological excavations show that it has been mined for thousands of years. In 1816, the French explorer Cailliaud discovered Ancient Egyptian beryl mines dating back to 1650 BC. Other discoveries from the Red Sea reveal mines dating back to the time of Queen Cleopatra. The finest emeralds come from South America, especially Chivor and Muzo in Colombia (shown here).

MAFIC SILICATES

The family of silicates known as mafic silicates get their name from a combination of "Ma" for magnesium, and "fic" for iron (from ferric). They typically form in magmas that well up where tectonic plates are pulling apart, such as under the ocean floor, and make up the building blocks of the basic group of igneous rocks (*see* p.27), which includes basalt and gabbro. The mafic silicate minerals olivine and pyroxene, found in basic and ultrabasic rocks, are denser and darker than felsic silicates. Other mafic silicates, called plagioclase feldspars, are characterized by varying proportions of calcium and sodium in their chemical structure.

PLAGIOCLASE FELDSPARS

OLIGOCLASE
Each variety of plagioclase feldspar has a different proportion of sodium or calcium. Oligoclase is a white or yellow mineral that contains more sodium than calcium. In its gem form, it is known as moonstone or sunstone if it has traces of hematite.

ANORTHITE
The plagioclase feldspar with the least sodium and the most calcium is anorthite. This causes the crystal to refract or bend light in a different way than other plagioclase feldspars. In fact, each of the plagioclases can be identified by the way it refracts light.

PERIDOT

◄ OLIVINE
Instantly recognizable due to their dark-green color, olivines are rich in iron and magnesium. In some places, such as Hawaii (shown left), olivine grains can turn river and beach sands green. Olivines are very common in mafic rocks such as basalt and gabbro. The group of igneous rocks known as ultramafic include peridotite and dunite and are almost pure olivine. Since most of the Earth's mantle is made from olivine peridotite, olivine may be the most common mineral in the Earth. However, in the crust it is much less common and rarely occurs larger than microscopic grains. This is the reason why large, green gem crystals called peridots are so highly prized.

Sand contains green olivine grains

ANORTHOSITE ►
Richer in plagioclase feldspar than any other rock—almost 100 percent—anorthosite is closely related to diorite and gabbro. The plagioclase feldspar in anorthosite rock is typically rich in calcium. It is found in a few 1.5-billion-year-old outcrops on the Earth, including the Appalachian Mountains and in southern Scandinavia. But the Highlands of the Moon and the planet Mercury are thought to be largely made of anorthosite rock. The Apollo 16 Mission brought back four-billion-year-old chunks of this rock from the Moon.

Samples of anorthosite rock from the Moon

Anorthosite rock is very light and floated to the surface when the Moon was molten

AUGITE

Rare large crystal

ACTINOLITE

▲ PYROXENES

Among the most common rock-forming minerals are pyroxenes, such as augite (shown here) and diopside. They form stubby, dark-green crystals. Pyroxenes are found in most igneous and metamorphic rocks. Darker mafic rocks, such as gabbro and basalt, contain lots of pyroxene. Pyroxenes form when there is little water present in the rocks. Pyroxene comes from the Greek words for "fire" and "stranger," because mineralogists were surprised to see these dark green crystals in hot lava.

▲ AMPHIBOLES

Like pyroxenes, amphiboles, such as actinolite (shown here) and hornblende, are common rock-forming silicates, rich in iron and magnesium. However, unlike pyroxenes, they form at lower temperatures with water present, and often grow into bladelike or threadlike masses of crystals. Tremolite is whitish-gray and contains calcium, magnesium, and some iron. Green nephrite (a source of jade) combines actinolite and tremolite. Amphibole cleavage meets in a diamond shape, while pyroxene cleavage meets at right angles.

METAMORPHIC

Like most minerals, silicates can be changed by heat and pressure as rocks become metamorphosed. Mild metamorphism changes silicates to hydrous minerals. These are minerals, such as serpentine and chlorite, that contain water. Intense metamorphism dries the silicates out, initially creating minerals such as muscovite and biotite, followed by garnets.

Red garnet crystals can be seen in this sample of eclogite

silicates

Silicate containing aluminum and iron

STAUROLITE

TWINNING

PLAGIOCLASE
Crystals of plagioclase feldspars, such as albite (shown here), are renowned for their "twinning." Twinning is caused by an error during crystallization. Instead of a normal single crystal, the crystals double and seem to grow out of each other like Siamese twins. Twinning follows rules called twin laws.

SPHENE (TITANITE)
There are two kinds of twinning: contact and penetration. Contact twins, like those in sphene (shown here) have a distinct boundary between the two crystals, so they look like mirror images of each other. Penetration twin crystals, like those in neptunite and phenakite, appear to grow right across each other.

LABRADORITE
Twinning is not always seen on the surface. In labradorite, the twinning occurs in sheets inside the mineral. This affects the way that light travels through the crystals, creating a spectacular display of coloring, known as labradorescence. Colors change from blues and violets to greens and oranges.

▲ STAUROLITE CROSS

One of the most amazing examples of twinning is provided by staurolite, which forms in metamorphic rock. Here, two crystals interpenetrate so completely that it looks as if they grew out of each other. In the highly prized variant shown here, the crystals grow at right angles, giving the mineral its name—from the Greek word for cross. Its resemblance to the Maltese cross—the symbol with four arms of equal length adopted by the crusading Knights of St. John—gives the mineral its Christian association and reputation as a good luck charm. In another variety of staurolite, the crystals cross at 60°.

QUARTZ

Quartz, a silicate, is made up of oxygen and silica. It is very common and is a major ingredient of most igneous and metamorphic rock. Quartz is very tough and does not break down, so it provides much of the raw material for clastic (particle) sedimentary rock, such as sandstone and shale. Although pure quartz is colorless, impurities give it a range of colors and forms. Despite being so common, quartz's range of colors mean that some quartz crystals are valued as semiprecious gems.

**MOSS AGATE
CHALCEDONY**

**GREEN CHRYSOPRASE
CHALCEDONY**

▲ CHALCEDONY
When quartz forms at low temperatures in volcanic cavities, the crystals are so tiny that they resemble smooth porcelain. This cryptocrystalline quartz is called chalcedony and comes in an array of colors and patterns, including blood-red carnelian, apple-green chrysoprase, moss agate, and reddish-brown sard. The name chalcedony comes from Chalkedon, Turkey, where the mineral was mined in ancient times.

QUARTZ VARIETIES

ROCK CRYSTAL
Rock crystal is the purest quartz, and the chunky six-sided crystals are as clear as ice. Historically, the crystals were shaped to make fortune-tellers' crystal balls or sparkling chandeliers. Rock crystal is now used in making watches, because it has a natural electric charge that helps to regulate the mechanism.

AMETHYST
Traces of ferric (iron) oxide in quartz give amethyst a purple or mauve color. The name comes from the Greek myth of the maiden Amethyst. When the goddess Artemis turned her into white stone to save her from tigers, Dionysus, the god of wine, poured deep-red wine over her, staining her purple.

MILKY QUARTZ
Quartz crystals can form with things trapped inside. These internal features are called inclusions and can be anything from gas bubbles to insects. Milky quartz contains tiny bubbles of fluid that make it look white. Milky quartz inclusions trapped in other types of quartz are known as "phantoms."

SMOKY QUARTZ
Smoky quartz is a dark brown, transparent gemstone. Other similar varieties include black morion, and black-and-gray coontail quartz. The dark color comes from exposure to radioactive elements (such as radium) under the ground. Smoky quartz is found in the Swiss Alps and the Cairngorm Mountains in Scotland.

ROSE QUARTZ
Rose quartz gets its pink color from traces of iron and titanium. Rose quartz is not treated as a gemstone because it does not often form clear crystals. Instead, it is made into ornaments, and jewelry. The Romans carved it into objects used for stamping wax seals. The best specimens of rose quartz are found in Brazil.

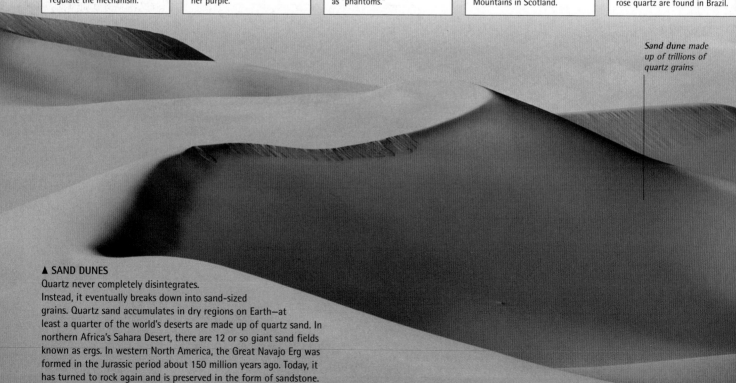

Sand dune made up of trillions of quartz grains

▲ SAND DUNES
Quartz never completely disintegrates. Instead, it eventually breaks down into sand-sized grains. Quartz sand accumulates in dry regions on Earth—at least a quarter of the world's deserts are made up of quartz sand. In northern Africa's Sahara Desert, there are 12 or so giant sand fields known as ergs. In western North America, the Great Navajo Erg was formed in the Jurassic period about 150 million years ago. Today, it has turned to rock again and is preserved in the form of sandstone.

BLUE LACE AGATE

Fine-grained blue lace banding

Agate originates in effusive lava, filling gaps left behind by gas bubbles

▲ AGATE

When traces of iron, manganese, and other chemicals create bands in chalcedony, it is known as agate. Moss agate is white chalcedony with mossy bands of green chlorite. Blue lace agate has alternating bands of mauve-blue and white. Onyx has black-and-white bands. Thunder eggs have star-shaped, brown-and-yellow bands. Although the bands form naturally, agate that is sold commercially is often stained by artificial dyes.

quartz

HOW AGATE IS FORMED ▲

Agates ususally form in basalt lavas, and agate pebbles can be found in beaches or riverbeds in areas of basalt rock, like here in British Columbia, Canada. Frothy basalt lavas solidify quickly when they flood to the surface, trapping gas bubbles. Water moving through the pile of lavas picks up silica and other elements, such as iron, and deposits them in the bubbles. As the lava cools, the dissolved minerals crystallize inside the bubbles. Colored bands are created as the chemistry of the water changes over time.

SILICON CHIPS

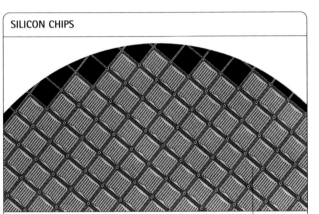

Quartz is a form of silica or silicon dioxide. Silicon is a semiconductor, which means it can transmit electricity. Today, one of its main uses is to make electronic components. Computer microprocessors are made with silicon chips, which were invented in 1958 by an American research scientist, Jack Kilby. These are minute squares of silicon onto which electrical circuits are printed in gold, silver, or copper. The chips are made in large wafers, which are then broken up for use.

Silicon chips are printed in tiny squares on large wafers

Spoil heaps (waste) from opal mine workings cover the landscape

OPAL ▶

Opal does not form crystals and looks more like pearly colored glass than a traditional mineral. Opals form in different ways as silica-rich fluids solidify—often in hot springs or volcanic rocks. Chemically, opals are a combination of silica and water. Heating opal removes the water molecules and can turn it into quartz. Black opal and fire opal are the most prized varieties. Fire opal, which is colored red and yellow, is mined in Querétaro, Mexico.

Opalescence is the term for this shimmering of colors

▲ OPAL MINING IN AUSTRALIA

Ninety percent of the world's opals come from Australia. The first opal field to be exploited was at White Cliffs, New South Wales (shown here), but this is now exhausted. The main field was at the famous Coober Pedy in South Australia. The days are so hot and the nights are so cold here that most people live underground. This earned Coober Pedy its name, which comes from the Aboriginal words for "white man in a hole."

Sapphire *said to have belonged to the 11th-century English king, Edward the Confessor*

IMPERIAL STATE CROWN

Spinel *(Black Prince's Ruby)*

OXIDES

Although 90 percent of the Earth's minerals contain oxygen, the term oxide is generally used to describe minerals that are a simple combination of a metal with oxygen, or a metal with oxygen and hydrogen (an hydroxide). Oxides form a large group, occurring in most geological environments and rock types. Oxide minerals include everything from common cassiterite (tin ore) to precious gems such as sapphires and rubies (forms of corundum). Oxides vary in color from rich-red rubies to dull-black iron ores.

HEMATITE HABITS

RENIFORM
Hematite has been mined since ancient times as an iron ore. It forms in a variety of habits (shapes), including reniform (kidney-shaped), shown above. Hematite comes from the Greek word for blood. When powdered, it makes a red color. According to Greek myth, it formed from blood-stained rocks on battlefields.

MASSIVE
The massive form (no visible crystals) of hematite can be easily weathered and shows a distinctive brownish-red streak, similar to rust. Like rust, this streak is produced when water reacts with iron to produce iron oxide. Small flecks of specular hematite (shiny, reflective crystals) can be seen dotted around the specimen.

SPECULARITE
Specular hematite has gray, metallic, hexagonal-shaped crystals. Lion Cavern in Swaziland, South Africa, is an ancient source of specularite. It is said to be the world's oldest mine, dating back 40,000 years. African bushmen used specularite as a cosmetic. They rubbed it on their heads to make them shimmer.

▲ SPINEL
Spinels are a group of minerals that are made from combinations of metal oxides. The semiprecious gem spine is magnesium aluminum oxide. Traces of other metals give it a variety of colors, including blue, green, purple, and brown, but the typical color is a red that rivals the red of ruby. Many gems once thought to be rubies have proved to be spinels. The most famous example is the large Black Prince's Ruby, set in the British Imperial State Crown (shown here). The "ruby" was given to Edward the Black Prince (of Wales) in 1366 by Pedro the Cruel of Spain. Gem-quality spinels are still found in Sri Lanka, India, and Thailand.

SPINEL

MAGNETITE ▶
Magnetite is a naturally magnetic iron ore. The word magnet comes from the Ancient Greek town of Magnesia, where large quantities of magnetic iron ore were found. The Ancient Chinese were the first to exploit these magnetic properties. Feng shui practitioners use a direction-finding compass to advise people where to position graves or new buildings in order to maximize the flow of "chi" (Earth energy) around them and create a better setting. At first the Chinese used spoons shaped from magnetite to indicate a north-south direction, but later they used magnetized needles, as in the feng shui compass shown here.

Iron needle *magnetized by rubbing it with magnetite*

Chinese feng shui compass divided into "24 mountains" (15° segments)

oxides

MAGNETITE

◄ SAPPHIRE

Sapphire is a precious form of corundum, one of the hardest minerals. The blue color is caused by traces of iron and titanium. Sapphires are often found in river gravels, where they accumulate after the rocks in which they form are broken up. Kashmir, in India, and Australia are famous for their sapphires. Besides jewelry, sapphires are also used in mechanical engineering and for making lasers.

◄ RUBY

Ruby is another precious corundum and is colored by traces of chromium. The ancient Hindus called it *Rajnapura*, meaning "king of gems." For centuries, the finest rubies came from the Mogok region of Myanmar (Burma), where they formed in marble and other metamorphic rocks. Star rubies (and star sapphires) appear to contain three- or six-pointed stars inside the stone, in an effect known as asterism.

CASSITERITE ►

Cassiterite is the richest tin ore. Tin was one of the first metals used by humankind. It was mixed with copper to make bronze 8,000 years ago, allowing the manufacture of hard tools and weapons. This discovery was so important it gave its name to a new era—the Bronze Age. Most tin comes from cassiterite, which is found in veins in igneous rock, as well as in sediment deposits.

Tin cans are made of aluminum or steel, coated in a layer of tin

RUTILE ►

Rutile is the most important source of titanium. Titanium is three times as strong as steel and twice as light, making it ideal for use in the manufacture of missiles and aircraft. Today, 95 percent of the world's titanium is used to make titanium dioxide, the main ingredient of white paint (used here for road markings).

RUTILATED QUARTZ

Rutile needles form in quartz

Storage tank for used nuclear fuel rods

Uraninite is known as "pitchblende" when it forms in a massive habit

◄ URANINITE

Uraninite is a radioactive mineral. It is the main ore for uranium and radium. Uranium is used to generate nuclear power. More than 110,000 tons (100,000 metric tons) of uraninite must be mined to produce 28 tons of reactive uranium. This is the amount a typical nuclear power station uses every year. Today, much of the uranium used is recycled from dismantled nuclear bombs. Uraninite is mostly found in compact clusters known as pitchblende.

Cobalt used to color the glass bright blue

SULFIDES

The minerals in this group are made up of sulfur combined with another mineral, usually a metal. Sulfides include some of the world's most important metal ores, such as cinnabar (mercury ore), galena (lead ore), sphalerite (zinc ore), and chalcopyrite (copper ore). Most sulfides are dense, brittle, and look a little like metal. A few sulfides, such as orpiment and realgar, are clear, light, and shiny. Sulfosalts are compounds of sulfur, in which sulfur bonds directly with a semimetal such as arsenic, bismuth, or antimony.

◄ CINNABAR
Usually a bright, brick-red crimson, cinnabar typically crystallizes around hot springs or in volcanic veins. Because it contains so much mercury (up to 85 percent or more), it is our main source of mercury. Mercury is used in thermometers (shown right) and other scientific instruments. Powdered cinnabar was once widely used as a red paint pigment called vermilion. This pigment is no longer used because, like all mercury compounds, it is poisonous.

◄ LEAD-FRAMED WINDOWS
Lead is a soft, easily worked metal that was widely used in the past for pipes, roofs, and paint pigments. It is now used in electrical batteries, metal alloys, and to shield against X-rays. Lead is easy to shape, so it was used to put together stained-glass windows. H-sectioned bars of lead were bent to fit around the fragments of glass in the window and hold them together.

Lead frames hold the stained glass together

Chunk of galena showing cubic and octahedral (eight-sided) crystals

sulfides

Mercury in thermometer

Massive galena forms in volcanic veins

▲ GALENA CUBIC CRYSTALS
Made from sulfur and lead, galena sometimes forms distinctive gray cubic crystals, making it one of the most recognizable minerals. Galena is a natural semiconductor (transmits electricity) and the forerunner of most electronic gadgets we know today. Galena crystals were used in the very first crystal radio sets. The best crystals come from Germany, France, Mexico, and the Tri-State Mining District (Kansas-Missouri-Oklahoma).

GALENA (LEAD ORE) ▶
Around three million tons of lead ore are mined every year, mostly from large massive habits found in hydrothermal veins. The main producers are Australia, China, and the US. Once the ore has been brought to the surface, 90 percent of the material needs to be removed before the metal can be separated by smelting (heating and melting). However, most of the lead we use today is recycled from scrap, which uses far less energy.

▲ CHALCOCITE

Chalcocite is a mixture of copper and sulfur. Typically 80 percent copper, its sulphur content is fairly easy to separate off. Unfortunately, chalcocite (also known as chalcosine) is very rare. The best deposits are virtually mined out. Today, the main copper-producing ore is chalcopyrite, less rich in copper than chalcocite, but more widely found.

▲ ORPIMENT

Lemon-colored orpiment is one of the Earth's most strikingly colored minerals. It was once used as a yellow pigment in paint. Highly unstable, orpiment disintegrates over time. The Greek philosopher Theophrastus gave orpiment the name *arsenikon*. The deadly poison it contains—arsenic—got its name from this word. Like all arsenic-rich minerals, it smells of garlic when it is heated.

▲ REALGAR

Bright red realgar is as distinctively colored as orpiment, just as unstable, and just as deadly. Like orpiment, it is a sulfide of arsenic. The Ancient Chinese carved it into ornaments, which have now disintegrated. Realgar's name comes from the arabic, *rahj al ghar*, meaning "powder of the mine."

PRESERVED IN PYRITE

Pyrite replaces organic materials

Living things can be preserved in many ways, but one of the most common is by pyritization. In this chemical process, iron sulfide minerals, called pyrites, gradually form. As buried organic material slowly disintegrates, it is replaced, molecule by molecule, by pyrites. Over millions of years organic remains, like this ammonite, retain their shape but are transformed into pyrites.

TELLURIDES AND ARSENIDES ▶

In tellurides and arsenides, tellurium and arsenic virtually take the place of sulfur in the chemical structure. They are otherwise so similar to sulfides, however, that they are classified with them. Tellurides, in particular sylvanite and calaverite, are among the few minerals that contain gold. The 1890s gold rush to Cripple Creek in Colorado was based on a find of telluride gold minerals, such as sylvanite.

SYLVANITE

SULFOSALTS

ENARGITE

This rare mineral is a compound of arsenic, copper, and sulfur. It is rich in copper. Good crystals are found in places like Butte, Montana, Sonora in Mexico, and the Cerro de Pasco in Peru. Enargite often forms very distinctive, star-shaped, twinned crystals known as trillings.

PROUSTITE

Proustite is a compound of silver, antimony, and sulfur. One of the few sulfide minerals that is neither metallic nor opaque, it forms beautiful wine-red crystals that are sometimes cut to make gemstones. This mineral is sometimes called "ruby silver." It is often found in silver mines.

BOURNONITE

A combination of copper, lead, antimony, and sulfur, bournonite forms chunky, prismatic (tablet-shaped) crystals. Sometimes it develops remarkable twinned crystals in the shape of a cog wheel, leading to its English name of "cog wheel ore." Copper, antimony, and lead can all be extracted from it.

Lilac-blue anhydrite

ANGELITE BOX

Massive habit of anhydrite colored pink by traces of iron

SULFATES AND OTHERS

Sulfates are compounds in which one or more metals combine with sulfate (a combination of sulfur and oxygen). Sulfates typically form when sulfates are exposed to air as evaporites or as deposits left by hot volcanic water. All are soft and pale, often with transparent to translucent crystals. There are more than 200 different kinds of sulfate, of which the most common is gypsum. This is a soft, sedimentary rock-forming mineral, with many industrial uses. However, most sulfates are rare and occur only in a few places.

▲ ANHYDRITE

Anhydrite is a translucent, brittle mineral, that ranges in color from white to brown and forms in thick beds. It is often found mixed in with gypsum, halite, and limestone. In fact, some beds of anhydrite form when the gypsum dries out. When anhydrite dries, it shrinks, so layers of anhydrite are often contorted or riddled with cracks and cavities. Anhydrite crystals are rare, because water usually turns them back to gypsum. Lilac-blue anhydrite is called angelite, because of its "angelic" color.

FORMS OF GYPSUM

DESERT ROSE
In hot deserts, water often evaporates from shallow, salty basins. Here, gypsum can grow around grains of sand to form flowerlike clusters of flat, bladed crystals, called "desert roses." Cockscomb barite forms similar roses, but the gypsum petals are better defined. Namibia in southern Africa is famous for its desert roses.

SATIN SPAR
Although gypsum usually looks dull and powdery, it sometimes forms clear or silky white, threadlike crystals. This form, called satin spar, is treasured for its satin look and is used for carved jewelry and ornaments. Geologists use the word spar to describe any white or light-colored crystals that are easily broken.

DAISY GYPSUM
When gypsum forms from small pockets of moisture on the surface of rocks, it can often grow in radiating, overlapping patterns of crystals. They are called daisy gypsum because they look like daisies. Sometimes, they even have a tiny yellow spot in the center to complete the daisy effect.

Porous texture makes it easier to paint

Facial features carve easily because alabaster is soft

◄ GYPSUM (ALABASTER)
Gypsum forms in thick beds where saline (salty) water from shallow seas or salt lakes has evaporated. Gypsum comes in many different varieties, each with its own name (see above). When anhydrite deposits are moistened by surface water, they form fine-grained gypsum. When heated and dried, this is the form that is used as the base for most plasters, including plaster of Paris. Left alone, it is better known as alabaster. This white, ornamental stone has been used in fine carvings since Ancient Egyptian times. This alabaster sculpture comes from the medieval tomb of a knight.

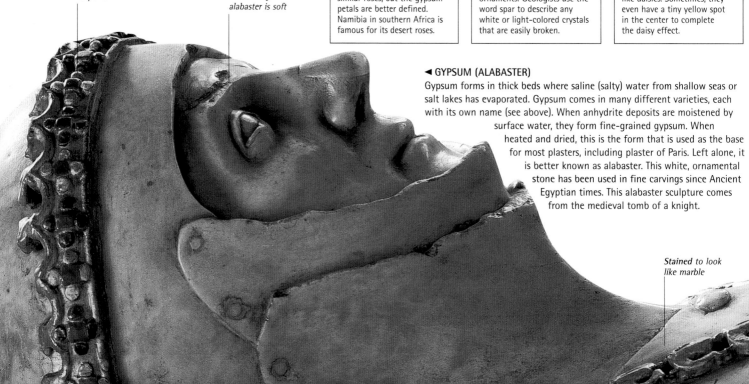

Stained to look like marble

EPSOM
SALTS

TUNGSTEN
FILAMENT

COPPER PANS

EPSOMITE ►
Epsomite is one of
only a few sulfate
minerals that dissolve in water.
As a result, large crystals are rare. It tends to
form as a white deposit on limestone cave walls
or around hot springs. Its chemical form is
hydrated magnesium sulfate, but it is better
known as Epsom salts from the mineral waters
in Epsom, England, where it was discovered.
Epsom salts are used to treat mild indigestion.

WOLFRAMITE ►
Tungstates are closely related
to sulphates. Tungsten replaces sulfur
and the resulting tungsten-oxygen
pairing then combines with another
metal. Wolframite and scheelite are
the main ores for tungsten, which is
used for, among other things, making
lightbulb filaments. Tungsten's melting
point, 6,170°F (3,410°C), is higher than
any other metal.

CHALCANTHITE ►
Bright blue
chalcanthite occurs
where copper ores are
exposed to air. It is the natural form
of copper sulfate. Because it dissolves in
water, it is usually only found in dry regions.
Large deposits were once mined in Chile. This
reddish metal is used for making everything
from copper pans to electrical wires, because
it conducts heat and electricity well.

FORMS OF BARITE

COCKSCOMB
Barite (barium sulfate) is a
common mineral. It often forms in
hot volcanic waters. Sometimes it
grows in thin, bladelike crystals
that cluster in a formation that
looks like the crest of a cock or a
rooster (shown here). When these
crested barite cockscombs are
stained red with iron, they are
known as "barite roses."

CRYSTALLINE
Barite crystals can also form in
sheets, fibers, or transparent,
colorless, prismatic crystals (shown
here), which can be very large.
Large masses of barite are
exploited for the metal barium.
Barium is useful because it is inert
(chemically inactive). The main use
of barium is as a filler in paints,
glass, and toothpaste.

sulfates

Lead ore forms a
dark groundmass

CROCOITE

WULFENITE

*Splinterlike
crystals*

*Thin, square
crystals*

◄ CROCOITE
Chromates are a combination of chromium and
oxygen. When metallic elements combine with
chromates, they produce rare and brightly colored
minerals. Crocoite, a combination of chromate and
lead, is a chromium ore. The most famous examples
come from Dundas in Tasmania, Australia, where
some specimens have slender, prismatic crystals up to
8 in (20 cm) long. Most specimens are made up of
small splinterlike crystals or have no crystals at all.

WULFENITE ▲
Molybdates combine molybdenium and oxygen.
When metallic elements combine with molybdates,
they form dense and brittle compounds. Wulfenite,
a combination of molybdate and lead, is easily
identified by its striking square-shaped crystals, which
resemble interlocking plastic tiles. Usually yellow,
they can also be white, red, or orange. The brightest
orange crystals came from Chah-Karbose in Iran.

Sea-salt stacks piled up to dry

HALIDES

Halides are minerals that form when a metal combines with one of the five halogen elements—fluorine, chlorine, bromine, iodine, and astatine. The best known is halite, or rock salt (sodium chloride), from which we make table salt. Like rock salt, many of the halides are soluble (they dissolve easily in water), which is why they often occur only under special conditions. Halite is so common that, despite its solubility, it is found in huge deposits all around the world and has a wide range of industrial uses.

▲ SALT MOUNTAINS
Most halite is mined from thick beds of salt left behind as ancient oceans dried out. It is then left in huge mounds to dry. Some halite forms as water evaporates in salty lakes, such as Utah's Salt Lake. Salt is also used to preserve meat and fish and to make food tasty. Although the human body relies on a regular intake of naturally occurring salts to keep its system balanced, too much salt is unhealthy.

TYPES OF HALITE

ORANGE HALITE
When halite crystallizes, it usually forms cube-shaped crystals. These cubic crystals can often be seen in unrefined sea salt. In nature, however, large halite crystals are rare because the minerals dissolve so easily in water. Where they do occur, they come not only in white but also in colors such as orange and pink.

BLUE HALITE
Some colour changes in halites are produced by bacteria. Some are caused by exposure to natural radiation. Gamma rays turn halite first amber, then deep blue. The blue colour comes from specks of sodium metal. These specks are created when radiation knocks the electrons about within the crystal's structure.

HOPPER CRYSTAL
One of the most striking halite habits is the hopper crystal. The cube-shaped hopper crystals get their name because their sides are indented in a way that resembles the hoppers (containers) on a mine conveyor belt. The indentation occurs because the edges of the crystal face grow faster than the center.

HARVESTING SEA SALT ►
Some countries, especially tropical islands, such as the West Indies and Cape Verde, still harvest salt from the sea—the oldest and most labour-intensive method. Sea water is pumped into large, shallow pans and then left to evaporate in the sun. The salt left behind (a tiny proportion) is harvested by hand and sent to a refining plant, where most of it is turned into other chemicals, such as chlorine.

halides

ATACAMITE

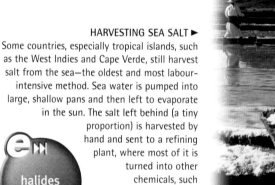

Atacamite is a bright-green copper chloride halide. It gets its name from the Atacama Desert in Chile, one of the driest regions in the world, where the best specimens are found. Atacamite forms only in very dry places where copper sulfide minerals are exposed to the air. Typically, it forms in association with malachite, azurite, and quartz, as well as rarer minerals such as chrysocolla, connellite, pseudomalachite, cornetite, and brochantite. Atacamite is very absorbent.

Bright-green malachite, often found with atacamite

Blue John showing bands of colored crystals

◄ BANDED FLUORITE

Fluorite, another halide, is the only mineral, aside from quartz, that comes in such a variety of colors. In pure form it is colorless, but impurities turn it every shade of the rainbow, from intense purple to bright green. It also glows in the dark under ultraviolet light, giving us the word "fluorescent." Most fluorites are a single color, but some form in colored bands. One of the best-known banded fluorites is Blue John, a corruption of its French name, *Bleu Jaune* (Blue Yellow). It is also known as Derbyshire Spar, after the English county in which it is found. It was discovered in the 18th century by miners looking for sources of lead in Derbyshire's caves. It was fashionable to have objects, like this goblet, made of Blue John.

Molten metal helped to flow by flux made from fluorite

FLUORITE ►

Fluorite gets its name from the Latin word meaning "to flow," because it is mainly used as a flux—a substance that lowers the melting point—in steel and aluminum processing. It helps the molten metal flow more easily, and, at the same time, it helps to remove impurities such as sulfur from the metal. Fluorite is a common mineral found in hydrothermal veins and limestones. It is the only source of fluorine, a chemical that is often added to drinking water and toothpaste (as fluoride) to strengthen teeth.

Glasslike, cubic crystals

SYLVITE ►

Sylvite is a chloride chemically very similar to halite. Like halite, it formed in massive beds on ancient seabeds, but unlike halite, it contains potassium (or potash) rather than sodium. Ancient sylvite beds are a major source of potash, which is a main ingredient in fertilizers, used by farmers (see right) all over the world. A quarter of the world's sylvite is mined in Saskatchewan, in Canada. Sylvite crystals do occur (as shown above), but they are very rare.

CARBONATES AND OTHERS

Carbonate minerals form when a carbonate (carbon and oxygen) combines with metals or semimetals. Minerals in this group are soft and dissolve easily in acidic substances. Many carbonates form when minerals on Earth's surface are altered by the acidity of the air and rain. Nitrate, borate, and phosphate minerals form when nitrate, borate, or phosphate combine with one or more metallic elements. Phosphates tend to be soft, brittle, and colorful.

▼ CALCITE FORMATIONS

Calcite is made from calcium, carbon, and oxygen. It is one of the Earth's most common rock-forming minerals. Calcite, formed from the tiny shells of dead sea creatures, is the main ingredient in limestone. Mounds of travertine (a form of calcite) form where hot, mineral-rich waters erupt on the Earth's surface in geysers. These mounds at the Fly Geyser in the Black Rock Desert, Nevada, have formed around mining pipes that are no longer used. Calcite stalactites and stalagmites also form in caves.

Travertine calcite is colored brown by rusty water

◀ ARAGONITE

Aragonite, a white mineral, was first discovered in Aragon, Spain. It is chemically identical to calcite, but its crystals form different shapes, including pointed needles. Aragonite often forms in hot springs or on cave walls where it grows in strange coral-like shapes known as "flos ferri" (flower of iron). Some sea creatures release aragonite naturally. The pearly substance inside oyster shells is made from aragonite.

Flos ferri crystals look like corals

◀ MALACHITE

Malachite is named after the Greek for "mallow," since it has the same color as a mallow leaf. It is a copper carbonate and usually forms as a tarnish or crust on copper ore. Malachite often has distinctive green bands. It has been carved for ornamental use since ancient times. When copper occurs in other minerals, it can give a blue (azurite or chrysocolla) or red (cuprite) coloring.

Malachite is prized for its rich green color

◀ RHODOCHROSITE

Rosy pink rhodochrosite often forms inside the bubbles of volcanic mineral veins, containing silver, lead, and copper. The small lumps have a black crust of manganese oxide, while the insides show banding in shades of pink. Rhodochrosite is one of the ores of the metal manganese and is usually found as granular (rough) pieces, rather than crystals.

Pink bands are revealed when rhodochrosite is sliced

CALCITE CRYSTALS

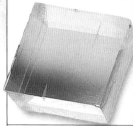

ICELAND SPAR

There are more than 300 different forms of calcite crystal. Pure calcite has been valued for its light-refracting qualities since the 17th century. Iceland spar crystals are used to make optical equipment, such as microscopes. Today, most Iceland spar comes from Mexico.

DOGTOOTH SPAR

Dogtooth spar is named after its resemblance to a dog's pointed teeth. They often form clusters in pools in limestone caves. The pointed shape is called a scalenohedron, because the sides form scalene triangles—triangles in which each side is a different length. Often two crystals form together as twins.

NAILHEAD SPAR

Nailhead spar, or tack-head spar, forms crystals that look like nails. The "nails" are made of two rhombohedra—a long rhombohedron topped with a flat rhombohedron. Nailhead spar often forms in caves and mines. The Jewel Cave in South Dakota's Black Hills gets its name from the sparkling nailhead crystals on the walls.

◄ PHOSPHATES (WAVELLITE)
Wavellite belongs to the class of minerals known as phosphates, which contain a mix of oxygen and the metal phosphorus. Wavellite forms balls of crystals in limestone, chert rock, and granite. When the balls are broken, they show patterns of spoked disks, such as those shown here.

WAVELLITE

PHOSPHATES (APATITE) ►
Apatite is also a phosphate. It is named after the Greek word for trickery because it comes in many colors and is often mistaken for other minerals such as beryl or peridot. Apatite crystals form in metamorphic rock, but most are too small to see. Large crystals, like the one shown here, are rare. Apatite forms an important part of animal teeth and bones. Its main industrial use is in fertilizers.

APATITE

e ►►
carbonates

Lignite forms the black in the mask

AZTEC MASK DECORATED WITH TURQUOISE TILES

◄ PHOSPHATES (TURQUOISE)
Turquoise is a phosphate and gets its blue-green color from the presence of copper. It often forms in deserts—the Ancient Egyptians mined turquoise from the Sinai Desert more than 5,000 years ago. It was imported to Europe through Turkey in the Middle Ages—the word turquoise comes from the French for "Turkish." In Central America, turquoise mining began about 1,000 years ago. The Aztecs used it as raw chunks in jewelry, or made it into tiny mosaic tiles as shown in this mask.

TURQUOISE

NITRATES (NITRATINE) ►
Nitratine (sodium nitrate) belongs to the nitrate family. It resembles calcite but is softer and lighter. Nitrates are rare because they dissolve in water. So they are mainly found in dry regions, such as Chile and California. Nitratine mainly comes from Chile's Atacama Desert. It is used for making fertilizers (magnified above) and explosives.

NITRATINE

BORATES (ULEXITE) ►
Ulexite belongs to the borate group of minerals. Sometimes, ulexite occurs in closely packed threadlike fibers known as "TV rock." The fibers act in the same way that fiber optics (used in telecommunications) do, transmitting light along their lengths by internal reflection. Ulexite is often found with borax, a water-soluble mineral found in everything from food preservatives to fiberglass.

ULEXITE

EARLY USES OF MINERALS

Our earliest ancestors used stone tools to help them hunt and kill animals, slice meat, and build shelters. Around the same time, they discovered the rich color pigments in minerals and used them to create cave paintings. With the rise of the first civilizations some 9,000 years ago, the variety of uses of rocks and minerals began to expand dramatically. People learned how to build in stone, how to use clay to make pots, how write on clay tablets, and how to use metals to fashion everything from weapons and armor to tools, bowls, and ritual objects.

FLINT ARROWHEADS

FLINT SCRAPER

▲ STONE TOOLS

Prehistoric humans were chipping flint to give them sharp edges for knives and handaxes more than two million years ago. Recently, archaeologists found flint knives dating back as far as 2.6 million years at Gona, Ethiopia. Flint provided our ancestors with their first tools, so the period up until the discovery of bronze (c. 9000 BC) is known as the Stone Age.

MINERAL PIGMENTS ▶

People learned long ago to make colored pigments by grinding minerals into a paste. Cave paintings dating from 20,000 years ago show the use of four main mineral pigments: red ocher from hematite, yellow ocher from limonite, black from pyrolusite, and white from kaolin (china clay). With the development of the first civilizations, people learned how to use more minerals to create a much wider range of colors—red from realgar, yellow from orpiment, green from malachite, blue from azurite, and ultramarine from lapis lazuli. The rarest pigments, such as lapis lazuli, were highly prized.

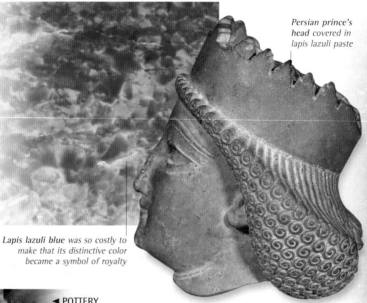

Persian prince's head covered in lapis lazuli paste

Lapis lazuli blue was so costly to make that its distinctive color became a symbol of royalty

"Terracotta Army," made up of 7,000 life-sized figures sculpted from earthenware (the earliest pottery), was buried with China's first emperor

◀ POTTERY

More than 30,000 years ago, people discovered how to mold soft clay into small statues of humans and animals and to bake them hard in furnaces. No one knows when they learned to shape the clay to make pots, but primitive clay bowls were being made in the Middle East more than 8,000 years ago. Archeological finds of increasingly sophisticated pottery tell us much about early civilizations. These life-sized earthenware figures of soldiers and horses were buried near the first Chinese Emperor, Qin Shi Huang, in 206 BC. They were intended to guard him in the afterlife.

Sandstone façade protected from erosion by overhanging rock

early uses

ROCKS FOR BUILDING ▶

The earliest shelters built by humans were temporary structures, made from sticks and mud. As soon as people began to settle—to farm or to live in towns— they wanted houses that lasted. In the earliest cities, such as Catal Huyuk (modern Turkey), built around 9,000 years ago, people constructed their houses from air-dried mud bricks. The world's oldest stone buildings—the Great Pyramids—were designed as tombs for the ancient Egyptian pharaohs. Sometimes, buildings were carved into the rock, such as those from the 4th-century BC city of Petra, Jordan (shown here).

◄ METAL MONEY
With the first human settlements, trading became part of human life. People needed units of currency (money) with a fixed value. The first currencies were made from shells or beads. These were later replaced by durable, valuable metals, such as gold and silver, which could be easily melted and formed in regular shapes. The earliest coins, dating from the 7th century BC, were found in Lydia (modern Turkey) and were made from electrum (a mix of gold and silver). Doubloons and other Spanish coins were made from gold taken from Central America.

16TH-CENTURY SPANISH DOUBLOON

Petra Treasury modeled on Greek architectural style

DANGEROUS MINERALS

Some minerals, such as the poison arsenic, have been known to be dangerous since the earliest times. Others, such as lead, have been more stealthy killers. The Romans were probably poisoned by the lead that lined their water pipes. In 16th-century Europe, noble women, including Queen Elizabeth I (shown here), applied a paste made from cerussite (white lead) on their faces to achieve a fashionably pale look. However, cerussite was so caustic that it burned the face, leaving marks and scars.

Scales used to weigh the salt

▲ PRECIOUS SALT
Salt (from halite) has been treated as a precious mineral since ancient times, both for health and as a food preservative. A Chinese book on pharmacy, *Peng-Tzao-Kan-Mu*, written some 4,700 years ago, recommended the consumption of salt for health reasons. Ancient Egyptian art showed salt-making as an important activity. Roman soldiers were paid a regular salt allowance, called a salarium. Even in medieval times, people were being paid a salary—in salt—as this 14th-century painting illustrates. Salt also denoted a person's social status at local banquets, when the less privileged sat "below (beyond) the salt" at the dining table. Throughout history, wars have been fought over access to precious salt reserves.

GEMSTONES

Most minerals are dull or made of small crystals. However, a few are richly colored and form large, striking crystals. The color, sparkle, and rarity of these gemstones has made them treasured across cultures and ages. There are more than 3,000 minerals, but only 130 form gemstones. The most valuable of these—diamonds, emeralds, rubies, and sapphires—are known as precious gemstones and are prized for their brilliance (brightness), rarity, and hardness. The more common gemstones, such as beryls, garnets, and peridots, are referred to as semiprecious gemstones.

Light is reflected through the front of the stone

**BELLE EPOQUE
DIAMOND NECKLACE (1900s)**

Colorless, brilliant-cut diamond

◄ DIAMOND MINE
Natural diamonds are incredibly old. Most formed deep in the Earth under extreme heat and pressure up to three billion years ago. Most of these are then brought up to the surface in volcanic pipes filled with kimberlite rock. However, the Argyle mine in Western Australia (shown here)—the world's largest diamond mine—extracts its diamonds from lamproite rock.

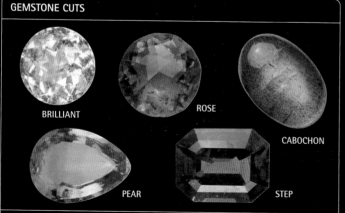

83-CARAT UNCUT DIAMOND

DIAMOND JEWELRY ►
Most diamonds are clear and colorless, but they hide within them a rainbow of colors that can flash dramatically as light hits them at different angles—causing refraction and dispersion of the light. When jewelers cut diamonds to make jewels like those in this necklace, they aim to make the most of this sparkling "fire."

GEMSTONE CUTS

BRILLIANT

ROSE

CABOCHON

PEAR

STEP

Different styles of cutting are used to bring out a stone's best qualities. Opaque or translucent semiprecious gemstones are typically cut into a smooth oval, which is rounded on top and flat underneath. This is called cabochon. Clear precious gemstones, such as diamonds, are usually cut with a series of mirrorlike facets (surfaces) to make them sparkle. Colored stones, such as emeralds and rubies, are step-cut to bring out the rich hues (colors) in the stone. All other cuts are variations of these two. Pear cuts, for example, are pear-shaped with a large flat top.

◄ EXAMINING A STONE
Gemstones often look like dull pebbles until they are cut and polished by a skilled lapidarist (gem-cutter). It is very close and detailed work, usually done under a magnifying glass. To cut smooth facets, a rough gemstone is typically glued to a stick and held against a rotating, polishing wheel.

gemstones

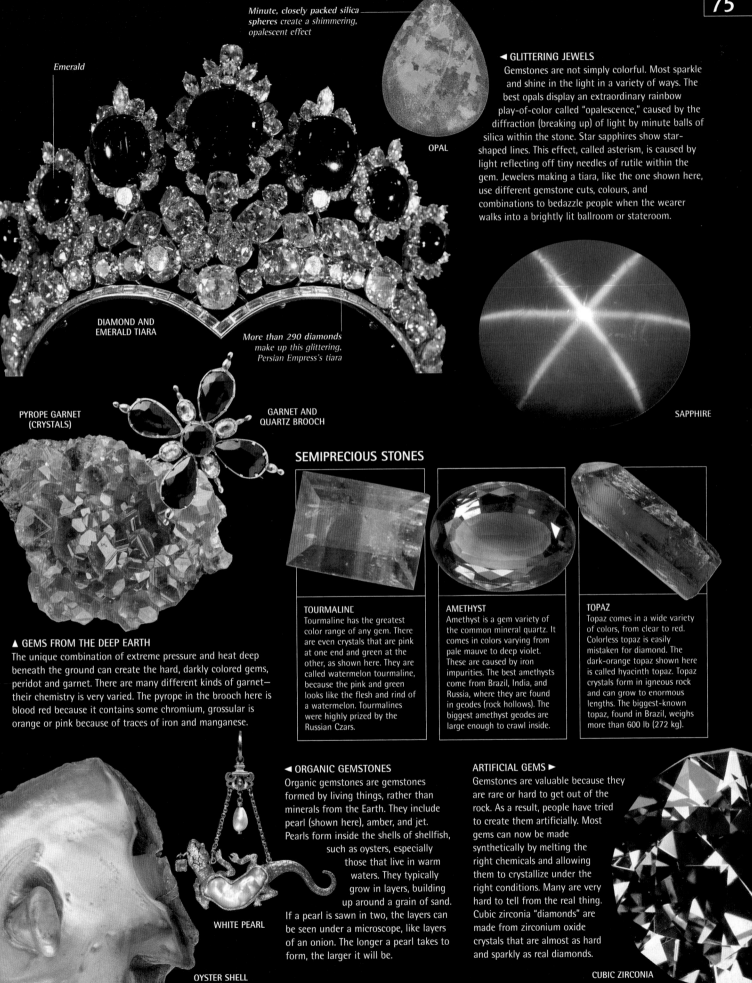

Minute, closely packed silica spheres create a shimmering, opalescent effect

Emerald

OPAL

◄ GLITTERING JEWELS

Gemstones are not simply colorful. Most sparkle and shine in the light in a variety of ways. The best opals display an extraordinary rainbow play-of-color called "opalescence," caused by the diffraction (breaking up) of light by minute balls of silica within the stone. Star sapphires show star-shaped lines. This effect, called asterism, is caused by light reflecting off tiny needles of rutile within the gem. Jewelers making a tiara, like the one shown here, use different gemstone cuts, colours, and combinations to bedazzle people when the wearer walks into a brightly lit ballroom or stateroom.

DIAMOND AND EMERALD TIARA

More than 290 diamonds make up this glittering, Persian Empress's tiara

SAPPHIRE

PYROPE GARNET (CRYSTALS)

GARNET AND QUARTZ BROOCH

SEMIPRECIOUS STONES

▲ GEMS FROM THE DEEP EARTH

The unique combination of extreme pressure and heat deep beneath the ground can create the hard, darkly colored gems, peridot and garnet. There are many different kinds of garnet—their chemistry is very varied. The pyrope in the brooch here is blood red because it contains some chromium, grossular is orange or pink because of traces of iron and manganese.

TOURMALINE
Tourmaline has the greatest color range of any gem. There are even crystals that are pink at one end and green at the other, as shown here. They are called watermelon tourmaline, because the pink and green looks like the flesh and rind of a watermelon. Tourmalines were highly prized by the Russian Czars.

AMETHYST
Amethyst is a gem variety of the common mineral quartz. It comes in colors varying from pale mauve to deep violet. These are caused by iron impurities. The best amethysts come from Brazil, India, and Russia, where they are found in geodes (rock hollows). The biggest amethyst geodes are large enough to crawl inside.

TOPAZ
Topaz comes in a wide variety of colors, from clear to red. Colorless topaz is easily mistaken for diamond. The dark-orange topaz shown here is called hyacinth topaz. Topaz crystals form in igneous rock and can grow to enormous lengths. The biggest-known topaz, found in Brazil, weighs more than 600 lb (272 kg).

◄ ORGANIC GEMSTONES

Organic gemstones are gemstones formed by living things, rather than minerals from the Earth. They include pearl (shown here), amber, and jet. Pearls form inside the shells of shellfish, such as oysters, especially those that live in warm waters. They typically grow in layers, building up around a grain of sand. If a pearl is sawn in two, the layers can be seen under a microscope, like layers of an onion. The longer a pearl takes to form, the larger it will be.

WHITE PEARL

OYSTER SHELL

ARTIFICIAL GEMS ►

Gemstones are valuable because they are rare or hard to get out of the rock. As a result, people have tried to create them artificially. Most gems can now be made synthetically by melting the right chemicals and allowing them to crystallize under the right conditions. Many are very hard to tell from the real thing. Cubic zirconia "diamonds" are made from zirconium oxide crystals that are almost as hard and sparkly as real diamonds.

CUBIC ZIRCONIA

DECORATION

Besides gemstones, many other rocks and minerals are used for decoration. Although never clear or sparkling like gems, they often have vivid colors and patterns. Ornamental stone is quarried to decorate the façades (fronts) of buildings. Almost any rock can be ornamental, as long as it polishes well and resists weathering. Typical examples of ornamental stone include marble, limestone, travertine, slate, and granite. Colorful nonprecious minerals, used for carving ornaments, statues, and more functional objects, include agate, onyx, jade, and jasper.

AGATE

18TH-CENTURY SNUFFBOX

AGATE ▲
Agate, a form of banded chalcedony, is one of the most popular minerals for ornamental work. In the 16th century, a large agate ornament industry grew up around the Idar-Oberstein district of Germany. Ring agate, with its circular bands, is particularly effective in ornaments like this 18th-century snuffbox. Today, much of the agate used in ornamental work has been artificially stained.

▼ ONYX
Onyx is a variety of agate with black-and-white alternating bands. Carnelian onyx has white-and-red bands. Sardonyx (shown below) has brown-and-white bands. Onyx has been popular for carving since Roman times. Indeed, the Romans called any beautiful stone for carving, onyx. This carved snuff bottle was made in China in the 19th century.

JASPER ►
Jasper is a mottled brick-red stone related to quartz. It is actually a kind of chert (sedimentary) rock, which forms hard nodules in limestone. Red jasper (shown below) gets its color from traces of iron, while green jasper gets its color from tiny fibers of the mineral actinolite. It is fairly dull when found but polishes well. Jasper pebbles glisten attractively when wet.

18TH-CENTURY VASE

SARDONYX

JASPER

JADE ►
Jade is the ornamental variety of not one but two minerals—nephrite and jadeite. Both these minerals can be white, colorless, or red, but the most sought-after kind is pale emerald green. Jade is particularly cherished in China, where it has been carved into jewelry, ornaments, and small statues for thousands of years. One of China's best-known archaeological finds was the tomb of the Han prince Liu Sheng and princess Tou Wan, dating from 113 BC. Each body is completely encased in a suit of armor made from more than 2,000 small plates of jade, sewn together with gold wire. The Chinese believed that jade would protect their bodies from decay—and perhaps evil spirits, too—and give them immortality.

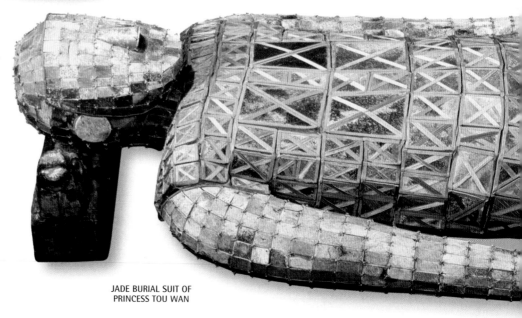

JADE BURIAL SUIT OF PRINCESS TOU WAN

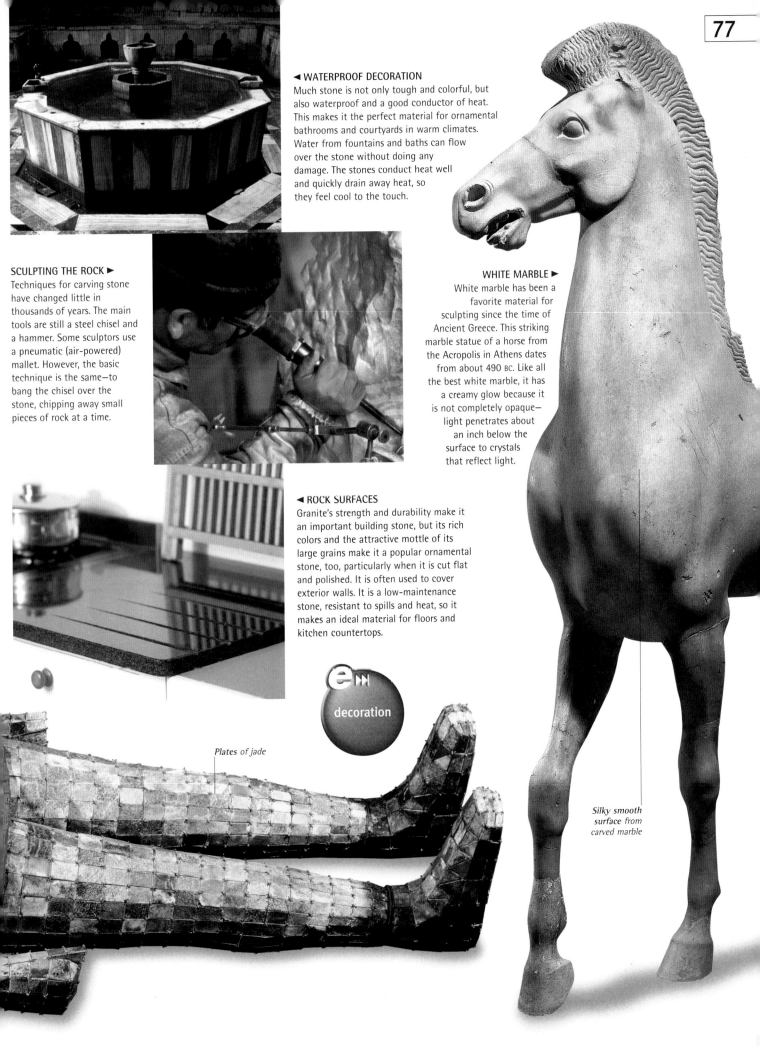

◄ WATERPROOF DECORATION

Much stone is not only tough and colorful, but also waterproof and a good conductor of heat. This makes it the perfect material for ornamental bathrooms and courtyards in warm climates. Water from fountains and baths can flow over the stone without doing any damage. The stones conduct heat well and quickly drain away heat, so they feel cool to the touch.

SCULPTING THE ROCK ►

Techniques for carving stone have changed little in thousands of years. The main tools are still a steel chisel and a hammer. Some sculptors use a pneumatic (air-powered) mallet. However, the basic technique is the same—to bang the chisel over the stone, chipping away small pieces of rock at a time.

WHITE MARBLE ►

White marble has been a favorite material for sculpting since the time of Ancient Greece. This striking marble statue of a horse from the Acropolis in Athens dates from about 490 BC. Like all the best white marble, it has a creamy glow because it is not completely opaque— light penetrates about an inch below the surface to crystals that reflect light.

◄ ROCK SURFACES

Granite's strength and durability make it an important building stone, but its rich colors and the attractive mottle of its large grains make it a popular ornamental stone, too, particularly when it is cut flat and polished. It is often used to cover exterior walls. It is a low-maintenance stone, resistant to spills and heat, so it makes an ideal material for floors and kitchen countertops.

decoration

Plates of jade

Silky smooth surface from carved marble

Handle of bone lashed together with sealskin

Butchering knife made from hand-beaten copper

METALS IN HISTORY

Ancient civilizations first used metal about 6,000 years ago, when they hammered native gold and silver into ornaments. Different cultures soon discovered that rocks held many other metals, including copper, tin, iron, and lead. Each had its own unique characteristics. What made metals special were their durability and malleability—they could be shaped into anything from simple weapons and tools to huge machines, and they lasted. These qualities have helped metal to play a key part in the progress of human technology.

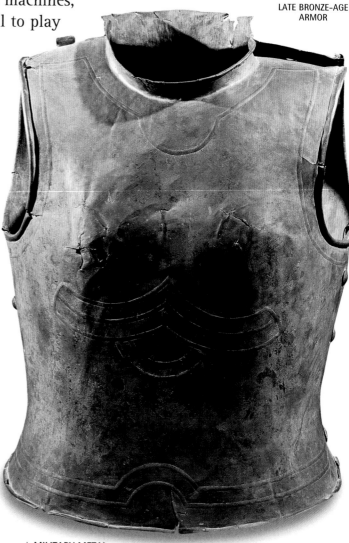

▲ BEATEN COPPER
Copper was one of the first metals to be used for making everyday objects, because it is easily extracted from the ground. Like gold, it can be beaten into shape, like this ornate Inuit blade. Evidence from around Lake Superior shows that ancient peoples, known as the "Old Copper Culture," began mining copper about 6,000 years ago. Copper remained the main metal used by Native Americans for thousands of years.

LATE BRONZE-AGE ARMOR

▲ THE DISCOVERY OF BRONZE
Learning to mix copper with arsenic—and later with tin—to make bronze, was a breakthrough in metalworking. The Bronze Age lasted from around 3000 BC, when bronze was discovered in Southwest Asia, until around 1000 BC, when iron was first widely used. The bronze frieze shown here, which dates from c. 840 BC, covered the huge, wooden gates that led into the Assyrian city of Balawat in modern-day Iraq.

◄ COPPER SMELTING
The first metals used by humankind were native metals. Native metals are rare, so it was a great leap forward when metalworkers first discovered how to obtain metals from ores (rocks containing minerals) about 5,000 years ago. They heated the ore until the metals inside melted and ran out in a liquid form. This process, known as smelting, is shown in this woodcut. The workman loading the ore into the furnace wears a safety mask as protection against the fumes. Copper was the first metal to be smelted, from copper-rich sulfide minerals, such as chalcopyrite.

▲ MILITARY METAL
Copper is too soft to make a blade that stays sharp. Early cultures found that adding tin to copper made it much tougher. This alloy is known as bronze. The first swords and suits of armor were bronze. When the Ancient Greeks famously attacked the city of Troy in Asia Minor, they may have wanted to win control of the city's famous bronze trade. Bronze was brought to the rest of Europe—where this chest armor was made—by roving Greek merchants.

| 5000 BC | Beaten copper used in Europe and Asia | 4000 BC | Bronze used in Middle East | 3000 BC | Bronze used in Europe | 2000 BC |

◄ IRON PILLAR, NEW DELHI

The problem with making bronze is that tin is rare and costly. About 4,500 years ago, people—perhaps the Hittites in Anatolia (modern Turkey)—learned how to smelt iron. Iron ore was relatively common and cheap. Ironworking started in India about 3,500 years ago. This 23-ft-high (7-m) iron pillar in New Delhi, India, was erected during the Gupta dynasty in the 5th century AD. The quality of the iron used for making the pillar is very pure and it has not rusted at all, despite the warm, moist climate.

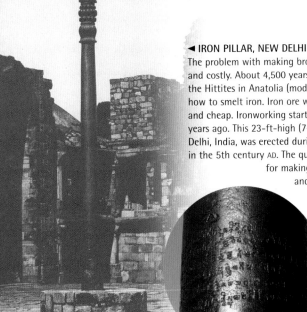

Sanskrit inscription shows that the pillar was raised in memory of King Chandragupta

e ▶▶ metals in history

ALCHEMY

Early knowledge of chemistry, including the properties of metals and acids, came from the work of alchemists. These early "scientists" were interested in finding the secret of turning base metals, such as lead, into precious metals, such as silver or gold. Some alchemists even tried to find the secret of immortality through their experiments. Alchemists were especially interested in mercury, which could be combined with other metals to make colored powders. The study of alchemy began in Ancient Egypt and had spread across Asia and into Europe by the Middle Ages.

THE AGE OF IRON AND STEEL ►

Iron can be turned into a tougher metal, called steel, by heating it and alloying (mixing) it with carbon. Indian metalworkers discovered this process more than 2,000 years ago. However, it was only at the end of the 18th century that a process for mass-producing iron and steel was developed in England, leading to the Industrial Revolution. England's first ironworks factory (shown here) was built at Coalbrookdale. Out of this came the whirring, clanking, smoking machines of the modern age—from steam locomotives to weaving machines.

Chimneys spewed out noxious pollution

Cast iron allowed engineers to create larger, stronger structures

Ironworks were usually situated close to supplies of coal and iron ore

◄ IRON IN CONSTRUCTION

Early iron was usually wrought (hammered) into shape by hand. The process of casting—pouring liquid metal into shaped molds—dates back to the 6th century BC in China. But the increased demand for iron during the Industrial Revolution led to the development of large-scale casting techniques. Although early cast iron was more brittle than wrought iron, it was used for mass-produced machine parts. Engineers also found that cast iron was so strong it could be used to build bridges, buildings, and other weight-bearing structures. This 18th-century arched bridge at Coalbrookdale, England, was the world's first iron bridge.

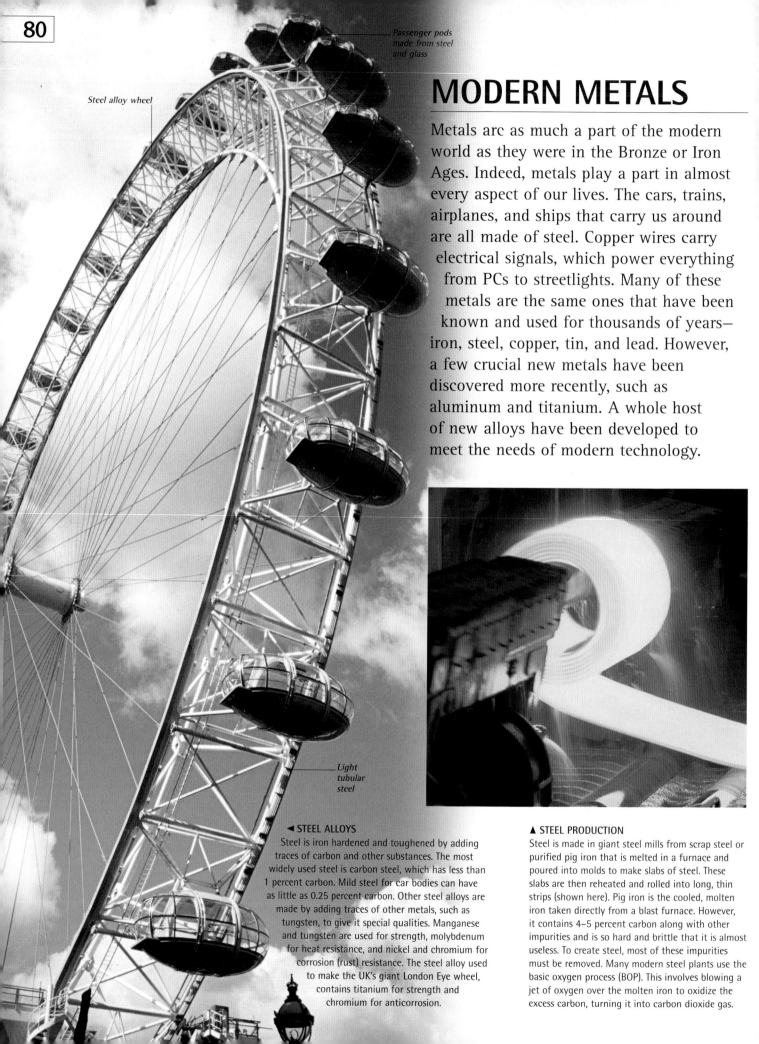

Steel alloy wheel

Passenger pods made from steel and glass

MODERN METALS

Metals arc as much a part of the modern world as they were in the Bronze or Iron Ages. Indeed, metals play a part in almost every aspect of our lives. The cars, trains, airplanes, and ships that carry us around are all made of steel. Copper wires carry electrical signals, which power everything from PCs to streetlights. Many of these metals are the same ones that have been known and used for thousands of years— iron, steel, copper, tin, and lead. However, a few crucial new metals have been discovered more recently, such as aluminum and titanium. A whole host of new alloys have been developed to meet the needs of modern technology.

Light tubular steel

◄ STEEL ALLOYS

Steel is iron hardened and toughened by adding traces of carbon and other substances. The most widely used steel is carbon steel, which has less than 1 percent carbon. Mild steel for car bodies can have as little as 0.25 percent carbon. Other steel alloys are made by adding traces of other metals, such as tungsten, to give it special qualities. Manganese and tungsten are used for strength, molybdenum for heat resistance, and nickel and chromium for corrosion (rust) resistance. The steel alloy used to make the UK's giant London Eye wheel, contains titanium for strength and chromium for anticorrosion.

▲ STEEL PRODUCTION

Steel is made in giant steel mills from scrap steel or purified pig iron that is melted in a furnace and poured into molds to make slabs of steel. These slabs are then reheated and rolled into long, thin strips (shown here). Pig iron is the cooled, molten iron taken directly from a blast furnace. However, it contains 4–5 percent carbon along with other impurities and is so hard and brittle that it is almost useless. To create steel, most of these impurities must be removed. Many modern steel plants use the basic oxygen process (BOP). This involves blowing a jet of oxygen over the molten iron to oxidize the excess carbon, turning it into carbon dioxide gas.

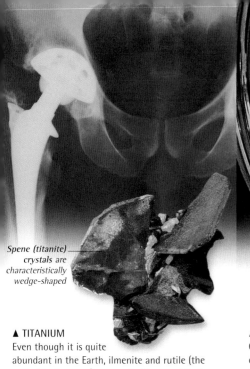
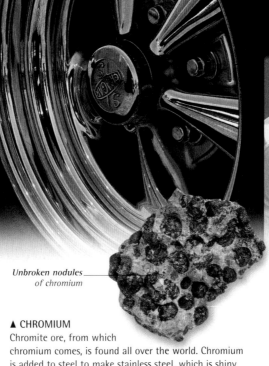

Spene (titanite) crystals are characteristically wedge-shaped

Unbroken nodules of chromium

Sphalerite crystals range in color from black to white

▲ TITANIUM
Even though it is quite abundant in the Earth, ilmenite and rutile (the main titanium ores) were only discovered in the 1790s. Now titanium is one of the most important metals for modern technologies. It resists corrosion, is stronger than steel and almost as light as aluminum. It is used in everything from aircraft alloys to artificial hip replacements (shown above).

▲ CHROMIUM
Chromite ore, from which chromium comes, is found all over the world. Chromium is added to steel to make stainless steel, which is shiny, tough, and very resistant to corrosion. The chromium content varies from 10 to 26 percent. Chromium is also used to plate everyday metal objects, such as faucets, car hubcaps (shown above), and espresso coffee machines, to give them a lasting, shiny look.

▲ ZINC
Sphalerite and smithsonite are the main zinc ores. Zinc has been used since Roman times, when it was combined with copper to make brass. Today, zinc is mainly used for galvanizing steel—a thin coating stops the steel from rusting. A zinc compound is also used as a sunscreen (shown above), reflecting harmful rays away from the skin.

◀ ALUMINUM
Aluminum is the most abundant of all the Earth's metals and one of the most widely used. Its high electrical conductivity, low weight, and resistance to corrosion means it is valued for everything from overhead power cables (shown here) to food packaging. However, bauxite (its ore) was not discovered until 1808, and a way of extracting aluminum from its ore was not found until 1854. Bauxite is not solid rock like some ores, but a kind of laterite— a loose, weathered material found in the tropics.

modern metals

PROBLEMS OF MINING

Modern mining methods have left vast areas marked by huge craters and have poisoned lakes and vast stretches of streams. Here, a stream polluted with waste-water runoff from a local coal mine flows into the Ohio River. Iron pyrites from the mine causes the reddish-brown color. In the US alone, the metal-mining industry released around 16,500 tons (15,000 metric tons) of toxic waste into the environment in 2000.

Titanium-rich alloy wings are tough and light

▲ MODERN ALLOYS
The demands for tougher, lighter metals by the aerospace industry has led to the development of numerous new alloys. Many involve titanium or aluminum. A fighter plane, like the F-16XL shown here, may be up to 10 percent titanium by weight and include a dozen or more different specialized alloys, each performing a different task. For the new A380 Super-Airbus alone, three brand-new aluminum alloys were created, using the metals cobalt, hafnium, molybdenum, and titanium, to give added strength and flexibility, while protecting against stress and corrosion.

MINERALS IN INDUSTRY

Many minerals are used in industry. Some minerals, such as quartz, silica, and gypsum, are extracted in bulk (vast quantities) from sedimentary rocks, such as limestone, clay, and shale. Many of these are important for building, providing materials for making cement and aggregate (pieces of crushed stone or gravel), which, along with cement, make concrete. Others help to purify metals or prepare coal for power stations. Bulk minerals are also used in glass, paint, ceramics, electronics, drugs, and many other products.

GYPSUM

◄ CALCITE (CHALK)

Most limestone is mainly made up of calcite (calcium carbonate). Chalk is almost pure calcite. Calcite is an incredibly useful mineral, known since ancient times. It is a key ingredient in cement and fertilizer. Pure, finely ground calcite is called "whiting" and is widely used as a filler or pigment in ceramics, paints, paper, cosmetics, plastics, linoleum, and putty.

CALCITE

◄ CEMENT

Cement is the "glue" that holds bricks together in buildings. The Ancient Romans used it to make the world's first concrete dome for the roof of the Pantheon in Rome, Italy, in AD 126. To make the cement, they mixed wet lime with volcanic ash, taken from near the city of Pozzuoli. Today, cement is made from a mixture of limestone (calcite), silica, alumina, gypsum, and iron oxide. Cement also helps to combine aggregates, such as sand and gravel, into concrete.

Pantheon's dome is made from concrete—a mix of cement, sand, and gravel

industrial minerals

▲ GYPSUM PLASTER

Most modern plaster is made by grinding gypsum to a powder, heating it to dry it, and then adding water. Gypsum plaster was used by the Ancient Egyptians to plaster the Great Pyramid of Giza. Until recently, many buildings in Europe and North America used traditional lime plaster (made from heated limestone), which gives a softer, smoother, whiter finish—but takes a long time to dry. Lime plaster was also used as a surface for frescoes and for making ornamental moldings. Today, most builders use gypsum plaster (shown above) because it dries quickly to a tough finish.

▲ NEUTRALIZING ACID LAKES WITH LIME

When limestone is heated in limekilns, it turns to lime, known as quicklime. When quicklime is mixed with water, it becomes hot and swells, making it look "quick," an old-fashioned word for alive. After water is added, it is known as slaked lime and will not react to the water because its thirst has been slaked (satisfied). Lime is widely used as a fertilizer and in water and sewage treatment to reduce acidity. Recently, lime has been used to try to counteract some of the effects of acid rain. Huge quantities of quicklime are sprayed into acid-affected lakes in an effort to neutralize the acidity that kills off life in the lake. This has only been successful in small lakes.

◄ KAOLIN

Kaolin, or China clay, is a soft, white clay named after a hill in China, where it was mined for centuries. It provides the basic material in porcelain and the whiteness in paper. It is made mainly of the mineral kaolinite, but contains traces of other minerals such as feldspar. Deposits form mainly from the weathering of feldspar-rich rocks. In South America, parrots lick kaolin clay to counteract toxins in some of the tropical plant fruit and seeds they eat.

PORCELAIN VASE

CONCRETE ►

Concrete is the cheapest, toughest, and most versatile of all building materials. Almost every major construction project uses concrete. It is made from chunks of hard material called aggregate, bound together by cement. The character of the concrete depends partly on the cement mix, but mainly on the kind of aggregate used. Common aggregates include sand, crushed or broken stone, gravel, boiler ash, and burned clay.

Concrete used to create a runoff ditch as a flood-control measure

Glass is made from silica

Molten glass flows like treacle and can be easily shaped and blown into shapes

▲ SILICA

Silica is the name for a group of minerals made of silicon oxide—a combination of the two most abundant elements in the Earth's crust (silicon and oxygen). Silica occurs in a variety of forms, the most common of which is quartz. Quartz is so common that it is found in nearly all mined and quarried materials and is one of the key ingredients in many modern technologies. It is used for glassmaking (shown here), paints, plastics, glues, ceramics, foundry casting, aggregates, oil drilling, farming, and electronics.

COMMONLY USED INDUSTRIAL MINERALS

TALC
Talc is the Earth's softest mineral. It often occurs in a soft rock called soapstone. Soapstone has a long history of being carved and made into ornaments. Powdered soapstone (talcum powder) is used on its own as a drying agent, but it is also used to help make cosmetics, paint, lubricants, and ceramics.

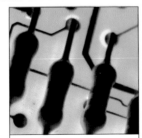

MICA
Mica is a very important mineral, occurring in almost every kind of rock. The most commonly used forms are muscovite and phlogopite—they easily cleave into thin sheets, and resist heat and electricity. This makes mica an ideal choice for insulating electrical components, such as this circuit board.

BORAX
Borax is a soft, light chemical made from minerals, such as colemanite and kernite. Much of it comes from crusts formed in evaporite deposits around lakes in California. Borax has a wide range of industrial uses, including ceramics, glassware, and metalware (shown here). It is used to fuse metal seams.

MINERALS IN THE HOME

A modern home is built almost entirely out of materials taken from minerals. The only exception is lumber, which is used for providing roofs, floors, and structual supports. The foundations that support the house are made of concrete (gravel, sand, and cement). The walls are made of bricks (clay) bound with mortar (limestone). Roof tiles (clay) and plastic guttering (oil) divert the water outside. Inside, water is pumped around the house in metal pipes (copper) for heating and washing. Ceramic (clay) or metal (stainless steel) basins, bathtubs, and heaters hold the water. Windows made from glass (silica) provide natural light, while electrical wiring (copper) provides artificial light, as well as telecommunications and power.

MINERALS USED IN THE HOUSE ▶
Every modern house is made from processed bulk industrial minerals, such as gypsum and limestone, and metals, such as copper and steel. Natural rock, such as granite and marble, is often used decoratively in kitchens and bathrooms. While in the past houses were built from identifiable, local materials, it is almost impossible to trace the origins of the minerals used in a modern house. Just the sink may contain borates from California, K-feldspar from Russia, and kaolinite from the Czech Republic.

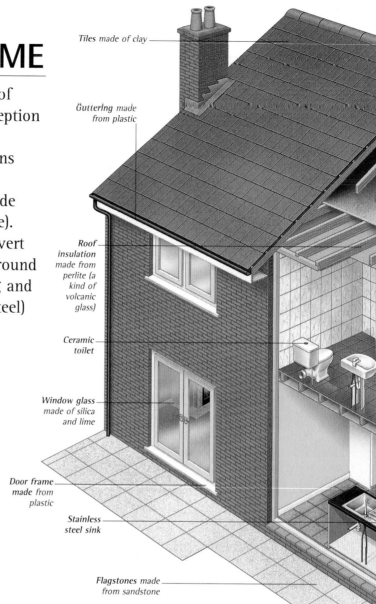

Tiles made of clay

Guttering made from plastic

Roof insulation made from perlite (a kind of volcanic glass)

Ceramic toilet

Window glass made of silica and lime

Door frame made from plastic

Stainless steel sink

Flagstones made from sandstone

▲ MORTAR (CEMENT, SAND)
Mortar—a mixture of cement, sand, and water—is used in building to bind bricks or stone together. The cement used is usually Portland cement, invented in 1824. It is a mixture of fine lime (calcium hydroxide from heated limestone) with clay or shale.

▲ TILES (CLAY)
In the past, many roofs were covered in slate. Today, roofs are sometimes covered in molded clay tiles. Traditionally, clay tiles were made by hand and retained their natural color variation. Modern tiles are machine-made, all colored the same, and fired in high-temperature kilns.

▲ PIPES (COPPER)
Pipes providing hot water for the bathroom and central heating are usually made from copper because it is cheap and easy to shape. But copper is not very good for drinking-water pipes, because too much copper is toxic for babies.

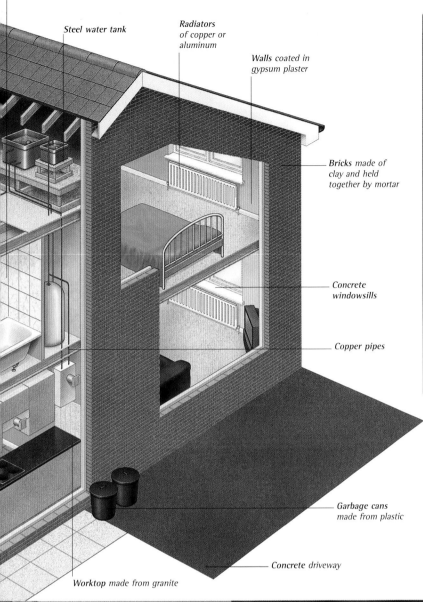

Ceramic tiles

Steel water tank

Radiators
of copper or
aluminum

Walls *coated in
gypsum plaster*

Bricks *made of
clay and held
together by mortar*

Concrete
windowsills

Copper pipes

Garbage cans
made from plastic

Concrete *driveway*

Worktop *made from granite*

ENVIRONMENTAL BUILDING

Many houses are still built from bricks. In recent years, a range of alternative building materials has been tried. This environmentally friendly house is partly made of straw bales, which insulate it so well it needs very little heating. The upper floors are covered with quilted sheets of fiberglass cloth to block out noise. The house is raised up on cement-filled sandbags. The wattle and metal fence, a mixture of natural and recycled materials, provides privacy. The house is partly solar-powered.

BRICKS ►

The first bricks were made from mud taken from the riverbank. The mud was molded into blocks and dried in the sun. The idea of heating clay in a kiln to make harder bricks was first thought of 3,500 years ago. Today, the basic process is the same, but a wider range of clays is used, including river clays, shales, and fire clays mined from the ground.

▲ GLASS (SILICA)
The sheet glass in windows is made from silica, soda ash, lime, and a tiny amount of magnesia (magnesium oxide). Other materials, such as selenium or cobalt oxide, are added to remove the green tinge caused by traces of iron. This helps to give a clear view.

▲ PAINT (TITANIUM DIOXIDE)
In the past, people mixed their own housepaints. But for the last century or more, most houses have been decorated in ready-mixed paints, made with linseed oil, turpentine, colored pigments, and a base. The base used to be lead, but, because lead is poisonous, the base is now titanium dioxide.

▲ BUILT-IN KITCHEN (GRANITE, CLAY)
The best-quality kitchens tend to have work surfaces made from granite. Granite is valued for its durability, heat resistance, and looks. Glazed ceramic tiles (clay) protect the walls from water and grease. Stainless steel (iron) is used for making stoves and sinks.

MINERALS FOR LIFE

Every plant and animal on the Earth depends on minerals for their nutrients— substances essential for life and for growth. Plants get their main nutrients from phosphorus, calcium, and potassium. These are supplemented by much smaller quantities of iron, cobalt, zinc, boron, nickel, manganese, and copper. The plants absorb these minerals from the soil through their roots. Animals, including humans, rely mainly on minerals such as iron, calcium, sodium, and potassium. They get most of these from the food that they eat.

Black humus made from rotting plants and organic matter

Topsoil rich in humus (rotting plants) and minerals

Subsoil is poor in humus

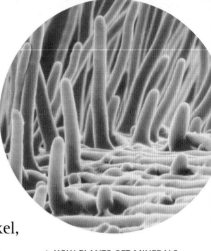

▲ HOW PLANTS GET MINERALS
Plants have a vast surface area of branching roots, which they use to absorb mineral-rich water from the soil. Each root is covered with microscopic root hairs, which draw in the water and send a continuous supply up the stem to the leaves where it is needed.

▲ MINERALS IN SOIL
Soils are a mix of organic matter with minerals, such as silica and iron oxides. Most soils contain all the minerals a plant needs. However, these minerals are not always available in the right amounts. This is why some soils are more fertile than others. As a soil matures, it develops distinct layers with different mineral contents. In areas of heavy rain, minerals are often leached (washed down) through the soil to a deeper layer.

▲ HERBIVORES
Herbivores, such as hippopotamuses and cows, rely entirely on plants for the minerals that they need. Amazingly, plants provide almost all these minerals, though herbivores can sometimes lack calcium and phosphorus. Herbivores often lick salt deposits to make up for a lack of salt (sodium and chloride).

▲ CARNIVORES
Carnivores, such as lions and bears, rely on meat for their minerals. Meat is rich in most of the minerals the animals need to stay healthy, including calcium, chromium, copper, iron, selenium, sulfur, and zinc. However, meat is short of other vital minerals, such as salt, potassium, iodine, and manganese. Carnivores usually supplement their diet with plant foods containing these, in order to stay healthy.

Olive oil contains sodium

Pepper has vitamin C, which improves calcium absorption

Pulses contain magnesium, potassium, and manganese

Milk contains calcium

Nuts contain manganese, phosphorus, and copper

Fresh fruit and vegetables contain phosphorus, sulfur, and potassium

Dark-green leafy vegetables contain iron, calcium, and molybdenum

◄ MINERALS IN FOOD
Scientists have identified 16 minerals that people need to have in their diet to stay healthy. Large amounts of the basic nutrient minerals—calcium, sodium, chloride, magnesium, phosphorus, and potassium—are needed. Small amounts of iron and zinc are also needed. Certain minerals, such as selenium, magnesium, and iodine, are only needed in miniscule amounts. Different foods contain different amounts of minerals. However, the same food can contain varying amounts of minerals depending on the type of soil it grew in. The picture here shows which foods supply which basic minerals and vitamins.

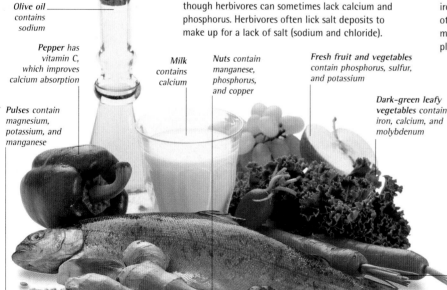

Carrots contain beta carotene, which is converted into vitamin A

Fish contains phosphorus, chromium, iodine, and selenium

Chillis contain vitamin C

minerals for life

Mineral deposits from osteoblast cells

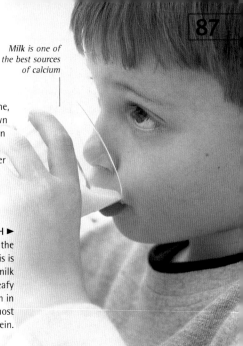

Milk is one of the best sources of calcium

◄ BONE FORMATION

More than a tenth of your skeleton is replaced each year. Bone cells called osteoclasts clear away dead bone, while cells called osteoblasts create new ones, as shown here. Osteoblasts create rubbery collagen and lay down deposits of calcium and phosphorus, which give the bone rigidity. In young children, osteoblasts outnumber osteoclasts, and more bone is created than destroyed. As you grow older, the balance reverses.

CALCIUM FOR GROWTH ►

Calcium and phosphorus are crucial in the growth of children's bones and teeth. This is why children are encouraged to drink milk and eat cheese and dark green, leafy vegetables. These foods are all rich in calcium. Phosphorus is found in most plant and animal protein.

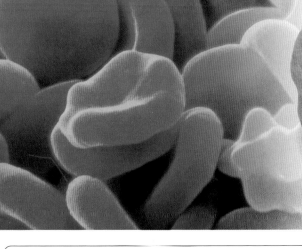

◄ BLOOD AND IRON

Red blood cells (shown here, greatly magnified) are the cells that carry oxygen around the body. The oxygen is carried inside each cell by a unique molecule called hemoglobin, which contains iron. In the lungs, oxygen attaches itself to the iron and is deliverd to all the tissues by the blood. Hemoglobin glows bright red when it is carrying oxygen, giving oxygen-rich blood its color. If there is a shortage of iron, the red blood cells cannot carry as much iron and symptoms of breathlessness occur, as the heart pumps faster and the lungs try to make up for the lack of oxygen.

Spinach leaf provides essential iron

◄ SOURCES OF IRON

Iron is essential for all body cells. Although iron is found in a variety of foods, its absorption by the body differs significantly depending on the food. Iron in meat and fish is absorbed much more easily than the iron in fruit, beans, grains, and dark green vegetables such as spinach. Absorption of the iron in these foods can be increased by combining them with sources of vitamin C.

MINERALS FOR HEALTH

People have bathed in mineral-rich waters and natural hot springs to improve their health since the earliest times. The earliest known spa, in Merano, Italy, dates back 5,000 years. At its height in the 18th century, spa-bathing was an upper-class social phenomenon. However, there is some evidence that spa-bathing may have real benefits for diseases like cirrhosis, lead-induced gout, rheumatoid arthritis, and high blood-pressure. Bathing in mineral-rich waters can also be good for the skin—and can be very relaxing. Today, sales of mineral water for drinking are at an all time high.

MINERAL SUPPLEMENTS ►

Lack of iron in the diet over a long period can lead to iron-deficiency anemia, which makes people look tired and pale. Most people who eat a balanced diet, including red meat such as beef, will not suffer from this. However, vegetarians are more at risk. People often take tablets containing iron to correct iron deficiency, but most doctors believe it is better to eat the right food.

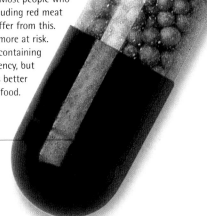

Iron granules housed in edible case

GEOLOGY IN THE FIELD

Geologists collect mineral specimens directly from the landscape, then identify and analyze them using scientific tests. Geologists and other Earth scientists do not just test their theories in laboratories or with mathematical calculations. Instead, they collect their data and test their specimens in the real world—facing bitter winds on mountain tops or braving erupting volcanoes close-up. The word used to describe this hands-on outdoor work is fieldwork. For the geologist, the field can mean anything from an Arctic glacier to a deep underwater ocean trench—in fact, anywhere on Earth.

◄ RADIOMETRIC DATA

A geologist uses a Geiger counter or radiometer to measure the amount of radioactivity produced by rock formations. Natural (background) levels of radioactivity result from the decay of the element uranium, which is present in almost all rocks and soils. When uranium decays, it produces the radioactive gas radon, which comes out of the ground continuously. The reading from the Geiger counter can be used to identify the rocks in a particular area, because each rock type has a different radiometric reading.

▲ MEASURING WITH SATELLITES

Tectonic plates can move a lot over millions of years. During a lifetime these movements are very small. Until recently, geologists could not measure such tiny movements. But since the invention of laser measuring systems using satellites, geologists can detect the widening of an ocean by even a few millimeters. Now with the addition of the global positioning system (GPS), geologists can measure how far land moves in a short time. GPS measurements showed that this spot in California (shown above) moved upward by 15 in (38 cm) and northeast by 8 in (21 cm) in the 1994 Northridge earthquake.

Gas mask protects from poisonous fumes

Pickaxe used to retrieve rock samples

PREDICTING VOLCANOES ►

An unforeseen eruption can have devastating consequences, so vulcanologists try to identify geological signs that can predict when eruptions will occur. Here, vulcanologists collect gas samples from the top of Colima Volcano, Mexico. They are looking for increased levels of carbon dioxide gas—one of the tell-tale signs of an impending eruption. Other signs include an increase in ground temperature, changes in gravity, or a variation in electrical or magnetic fields. However, vulcanologists still cannot predict eruptions accurately.

Scuba-diving geologist examining stromatolites

Fossilized mats of bacteria

geology

◄ UNDERWATER GEOLOGY

Geologists sometimes venture to dangerous or difficult places, including the bottom of the ocean. The geologist here is scuba diving in the Caribbean, looking at living stromatolites. Stromatolites, which look like giant stone mushrooms, are ancient communities of bacteria that live in shallow, tropical waters on limestone rock. Each community contains so many bacteria that they build up thick mats of organic matter over the rock. Fossilized stromatolites found in Western Australia date back over 3.5 billion years, providing the earliest evidence of life on Earth.

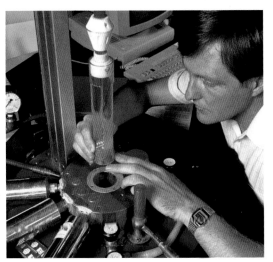

◄ UNDERSTANDING EARTH'S MAGNETIC FIELD

Rock samples are often brought back to the laboratory for testing. This basalt sample is being loaded into a cryogenic magnetometer to measure the strength and alignment of its magnetic field. The basalt contains grains of iron oxide that indicate the direction of the Earth's magnetic poles when the lava hardened. Geologists use this data to understand changes in Earth's magnetic field over millions of years.

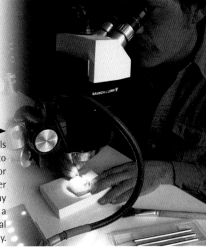

IDENTIFYING SAMPLES ►

High-powered microscopes can help to identify minerals by revealing their crystal structures. They are also used to prepare samples of minerals and fossils (shown here) for further study. Minerals that cannot be identified under a microscope can sometimes be identified by X-ray crystallography. This involves beaming X-rays through a sample. Every crystal has its own unique chemical structure, which diffracts (breaks up) the rays differently.

ESSENTIAL FIELD EQUIPMENT ►

You can collect your own rock and mineral samples, when you stroll along the beach or take a walk in the countryside. To get the best out of a rock-hunting expedition, it helps to take some basic equipment with you. You will need a hammer and chisel for extracting rock samples, and goggles and gloves to protect your eyes and hands. Specimens, especially delicate crystals, should be wrapped in newspaper or other protective material, to prevent chipping and scratching, and packed in a secure container.

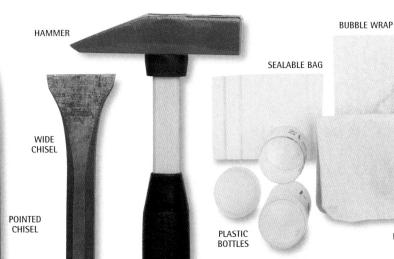

HAMMER

WIDE CHISEL

SEALABLE BAG

BUBBLE WRAP

NEWSPAPER

POCKETKNIFE

POINTED CHISEL

PLASTIC BOTTLES

MUSLIN BAG

PROPERTIES

Rocks and minerals can be organized and identified by a variety of different properties. Listed here are some of the most important properties for a range of common rocks and minerals. Rocks are grouped here by their origin (where they formed), minerals by their chemical composition. Sometimes, a single property can identify a specimen; more often, a combination of properties is needed. Basalt rock, for example, is classified as a basic, extrusive igneous rock and identified by its dark color and fine grain.

properties

ROCKS

NAME	ORIGIN	GRAIN SIZE	CLASSIFICATION	WHERE FORMED	COLOR
IGNEOUS					
Granite	Intrusive	Coarse	Acid	Pluton	Light, Medium
Diorite	Intrusive	Coarse	Intermediate	Pluton, Dyke	Medium, Dark
Syenite	Intrusive	Coarse	Intermediate	Pluton, Dyke	Light, Dark
Gabbro	Intrusive	Coarse	Basic	Pluton	Medium
Dolerite	Intrusive	Medium	Basic	Dyke, Sill	Dark
Rhyolite	Extrusive	Fine	Acid	Volcano	Light
Obsidian	Extrusive	Very Fine	Acid	Volcano	Dark
Peridotite	Intrusive	Coarse	Ultrabasic	Pluton, Dyke, Sill	Dark
Andesite	Extrusive	Fine	Intermediate	Volcano	Medium
Basalt	Extrusive	Fine	Basic	Volcano	Dark
Tuff	Pyroclastic	Fine	Acid to basic	Volcano	Medium
Pumice	Extrusive	Fine	Acid to basic	Volcano	Medium

NAME	ORIGIN	GRAIN SIZE	CLASSIFICATION	PRESSURE	TEMPERATURE	STRUCTURE
METAMORPHIC						
Slate	Mountain ranges	Fine	Regional	Low	Low	Foliated
Schist	Mountain ranges	Medium	Regional	Moderate	Low to Moderate	Foliated
Gneiss	Mountain ranges	Coarse	Regional	High	High	Foliated, Crystalline
Amphibolite	Mountain ranges	Coarse	Regional	High	High	Foliated, Crystalline
Marble	Contact aureoles	Fine, Coarse	Contact	Low	High	Crystalline
Hornfels	Contact aureoles	Fine	Contact	Low to High	High	Crystalline
Metaquartzite	Contact aureoles	Medium	Contact	Low	High	Crystalline

NAME	ORIGIN	GRAIN SIZE	CLASSIFICATION	FOSSILS	GRAIN SHAPE
SEDIMENTARY					
Conglomerate	Marine, Freshwater	Very coarse	Clastic	Very rare	Rounded
Sandstone	Marine, Freshwater, Continental	Medium	Clastic	Invertebrates, Vertebrates, Plants	Angular, Rounded
Shale	Marine, Freshwater	Fine	Clastic	Invertebrates, Vertebrates, Plants	Angular
Mudstone	Marine, Freshwater	Fine	Clastic	Invertebrates, Plants	Angular
Clay	Marine, Freshwater, Continental	Fine	Clastic	Invertebrates, Vertebrates, Plants	Angular
Limestone	Marine	Medium, Coarse	Chemical	Invertebrates	Rounded
Chalk	Marine	Fine	Organic	Invertebrates, Vertebrates	Rounded, Angular
Dolomite	Marine	Medium, Fine	Chemical	Invertebrates	Crystalline
Travertine	Continental	Crystalline	Chemical	Rare	Crystalline
Anthracite	Continental	Medium, Fine	Organic	Plants	Amorphous

MINERALS

NAME	CHEMICAL FORMULA	HARDNESS	SPECIFIC GRAVITY	CLEAVAGE	FRACTURE
NATIVE ELEMENTS					
Gold	Au	$2_{1/2}$–3	19.3	None	Hackly (with rough edges)
Silver	Ag	$2_{1/2}$–3	10.5	None	Hackly
Copper	Cu	$2_{1/2}$–3	8.9	None	Hackly
Sulfur	S	$1_{1/2}$–$2_{1/2}$	2.0–2.1	Imperfect basal	Uneven to conchoidal
Diamond	C	10	3.52	Perfect octahedral	Conchoidal
Graphite	C	1–2	2.1–2.3	Perfect basal	Uneven
SULFIDES					
Galena	PbS	$2_{1/2}$	7.58	Perfect cubic	Subconchoidal
Pyrite	FeS_2	6–$6_{1/2}$	5.0	Indistinct	Conchoidal to uneven
SULFATES					
Gypsum	$CaSO_4.2H_2O$	2	2.32	Perfect	Splintery
Barite	$BaSO_4$	3–$3_{1/2}$	4.5	Perfect	Uneven
Wolframite	$(Fe,Mn)WO_4$	4–$4_{1/2}$	7.1–7.5	Perfect	Uneven
HALIDES					
Halite	$NaCl$	2	2.1–2.2	Perfect cubic	Uneven to conchoidal
Fluorite	CaF_2	4	3.18	Perfect octahedral	Conchoidal
OXIDES					
Spinel	$MgAl_2O_4$	$7_{1/2}$–8	3.5–4.1	None	Conchoidal to uneven
Hematite	Fe_2O_3	5–6	5.26	None	Uneven to subconchoidal
Corundum	Al_2O_3	9	4.0–4.1	None	Conchoidal to uneven
Perovskite	$CaTiO_3$	$5_{1/2}$	4.01	Imperfect	Subconchoidal to uneven
CARBONATES, NITRATES, AND BORATES					
Calcite	$CaCO_3$	3	2.71	Perfect	Subconchoidal
Malachite	$Cu_2CO_3(OH)_2$	$3_{1/2}$–4	4.0	Perfect	Subconchoidal to uneven
Nitratine	$NaNO_3$	$1_{1/2}$–2	2.27	Perf. rhombohedral	Conchoidal
Ulexite	$NaCaB_5O_6(OH)_6.5H_2O$	$2_{1/2}$	1.96	Perfect	Uneven
PHOSPHATES					
Turquoise	$CuAl_6(PO_4)_4(OH)_8.4H_2O$	5–6	2.6–2.8	Good	Conchoidal
Apatite	$Ca_5(PO_4)_3(F,Cl,OH)$	5	3.1–3.2	Poor	Conchoidal to uneven
SILICATES					
Quartz	SiO_2	7	2.65	None	Conchoidal to uneven
Opal	$SiO_2.nH_2O$	$5_{1/2}$–$6_{1/2}$	1.9–2.3	None	Conchoidal
Olivine	Fe_2SiO_4-Mg_2SiO_4	$6_{1/2}$–7	3.27–4.32	Imperfect	Conchoidal
Garnet	$Mg_3Al_2(SiO_4)_3$	$6_{1/2}$–$7_{1/2}$	3.4–4.3	None	Uneven to conchoidal
Beryl	$Be_3Al_2Si_6O_{18}$	7–8	2.6–2.9	Indistinct	Uneven to conchoidal
Hornblende	$Ca_2(Mg,Fe)_4Al(Si_7Al)O_{22}(OH,F)_2$	5–6	3–3.41	Perfect	Uneven
Diopside	$CaMgSi_2O_6$	$5_{1/2}$–$6_{1/2}$	3.22–3.38	Good	Uneven
Muscovite	$KAl_2(Si_3Al)O_{10}(OH,F)_2$	$2_{1/2}$–3	2.77–2.88	Perfect basal	Uneven
Kaolinite	$Al_2Si_2O_5(OH)_4$	2–$2_{1/2}$	2.6–2.63	Perfect basal	Uneven
Orthoclase	$KAlSi_3O_8$	6–$6_{1/2}$	2.55–2.63	Perfect	Uneven to conchoidal
ORGANIC					
Amber	Mixture of organic plant resins	$2_{1/2}$	1.08	None	Conchoidal

GLOSSARY

Abrasion The process of grinding or rubbing away a surface, such as a rock.

Acid Relating to rock with a high silica content.

Alloy A combination of two or more metals. Commonly used alloys include bronze (copper and tin) and stainless steel (iron and chromium).

Amygdale A hole in lava or pyroclastic rock containing minerals, such as calcite or quartz.

Asteroid A chunk of rock smaller than a planet, which orbits the Sun.

Asthenosphere The hot, partially molten layer of rock in the Earth's upper mantle, just below the lithosphere.

Atmosphere The layers of gases surrounding the Earth or another planet.

Basic Relating to rock with low silica content.

Batholith A vast igneous intrusion in the crust of more than 39 sq miles (100 sq km).

Bed A thin layer of sedimentary rock.

Bedding plane The boundary between beds of sedimentary rock that formed at different times.

Bedrock Solid rock that lies beneath loose deposits of soil and other matter.

Canyon A deep, steep-sided valley, typically cut by a river.

Cement A material that hardens on drying to bind particles together in sedimentary rock. Cement is also a material used for building, made from crushed lime and clay.

Cementation The stage in lithification when cement glues the sediment particles together.

Chondrite A stony meteorite containing tiny granules of pyroxene and olivine. These rocks are among the oldest objects ever found.

Clastic sediment Rock and mineral particles formed from eroded fragments of broken rock.

Cleavage The way a mineral or rock breaks in a certain plane (direction).

Compaction The stage in lithification when water and air is squeezed out of the buried sediments by the weight of overlying deposits.

Contact aureole The area around a large igneous intrusion where the rock has been altered by the heat of the magma.

Continental drift The slow movement of the Earth's continents on its surface.

Core The Earth's hot, dense iron-rich center—liquid on the outside and solid at the center.

Country rock The rock that surrounds a mineral deposit or igneous intrusion.

Crust The Earth's rigid outermost layer. It is divided into thicker, older continental crust (mainly granite) and thinner, more recent oceanic crust (mainly basalt).

Crystal A solid substance with a regular form and symmetrical faces. Crystals grow in many ways, such as when molten material cools, or when a solution containing a dissolved mineral evaporates. Large crystals grow very slowly.

Delta A fan-shaped area of sediment deposited where a river slows down and splits into many channels, before entering a lake or the sea.

Deposition The dropping of loose sediment carried by water, wind, or moving ice, when they slow down and lose their energy.

Dyke A thin, sheetlike igneous intrusion that cuts across older rock structures.

Element A substance, such as gold, that cannot be broken down into more simple substances.

Erosion The slow wearing away of rocks by moving water, ice, and wind.

Evaporite A natural salt or mineral left behind after the water it was dissolved in has dried up.

Extrusive igneous rock Rock that forms when lava from a volcano cools and solidifies.

Fault An extended fracture in rock along which rock masses move.

Felsic Relating to igneous rocks rich in feldspar and quartz minerals.

Flint A hard nodule of chert (a fine-grained quartz sedimentary rock) that forms in limestone. It fractures well and was used by Stone Age people to make knives and arrows.

Flood plain The flat area each side of a river that is covered in water when the river floods.

Fold Bends in rock strata (layers) caused by tectonic plate movement.

Foliation Banded patterns caused by the alignment of crystals within metamorphic rocks.

Fossil Mineralized impression or cast of ancient plant or animal.

Fossil fuel A fuel, such as coal, oil, and natural gas, which formed from decomposed plant matter buried deep beneath the ground.

Fracture The distinctive way a mineral breaks.

Gemstone A mineral, usually crystalline, such as diamond or ruby that is valued for its color, sparkle, rarity, and hardness.

Geode A small rock cavity lined with crystals or other mineral matter.

Geologist Someone who studies the Earth.

Glacier A slowly moving mass of ice formed by the compaction of snow on mountains or near the Earth's poles.

Groundmass Compact, fine-grained mineral material in which larger crystals are embedded.

Habit The general shape of a mineral.

Hot spot Site of volcanic activity in the Earth's crust away from the plate boundaries, created by magma rising from the upper mantle.

Hydrothermal vein A crack in the rock through which very hot mineral waters circulate due to volcanic activity. As the waters cool, minerals start to crystallize, forming some of the Earth's most valuable gemstones and ores.

Ice Age A very cold period in the Earth's history, when vast ice sheets covered large parts of the world. The most recent glacial period, which lasted about 100,000 years and ended 12,000 years ago, affected much of North America and northern Europe.

Idiochromatic A mineral that is always the same color because of its chemical composition. A mineral (such as quartz) that changes color is known as allochromatic.

Igneous rock Rock formed as magma cools and hardens in the Earth's crust.

Inclusion A tiny crystal or mineral fragment embedded in another mineral.

Intrusive igneous rock Igneous rock that forms beneath the Earth's surface.

Joint A crack in the rock, usually vertical, caused by tiny movements in the rock due to shrinking and expansion.

Karst landscape A limestone landscape, full of dramatically eroded cliffs, gorges, and caves.

Lava Magma that has flowed onto the Earth's surface through a volcanic opening.

Lithification The process of turning loose sediments into rock through compacting and cementing them together over milllions of years.

Lithosphere The hard, topmost layer of the Earth. It is made up of the crust and the upper part of the mantle.

Loess Large deposits of uncemented, fine, wind-blown sediment.

Luster The way in which light reflects off the surface of a mineral.

Mafic Relating to silicate minerals, rich in magnesium and iron, typically formed in basalt and other basic or ultramafic rocks.

Magma Molten rock beneath the Earth's crust that forms as parts of the mantle melt.

Magma chamber Underground reservoir of magma. It can erupt onto the Earth's surface as lava or harden to form a pluton.

Magnetosphere Magnetic forcefield in and around the Earth, created by the movement of iron in the core. It protects the Earth against charged particles streaming from the Sun.

Mantle The middle layer of the Earth, between the core and the crust. Geologists believe it consists of hot, dense rocks, such as peridotite.

Massive formation A mineral habit with no definite shape or crystal faces.

Matrix The fine mass of material in which larger crystals are set.

Metamorphic rock Rock formed when other rocks are transformed by heat and pressure.

Meteor Once a meteoroid (rock and dust debris in space) enters the Earth's atmosphere, it becomes a meteor or shooting star.

Meteorite A meteor that crashes onto the Earth's surface.

Midocean ridge A long chain of undersea mountains that forms along the ocean bed where tectonic plates are moving apart.

Mineral A naturally occurring solid with certain regular characteristics, such as chemical composition and crystal shapes. Earth's rocks are made up of minerals.

Native element An element found naturally as a mineral in its pure form. It does not form part of a compound.

Nodule A hard, rounded, stony lump found in sedimentary rock, typically made from calcite, silica, pyrite, or gypsum.

Normal fault A fault in two blocks of rock, which are being pulled apart, allowing one of them to slip down.

Oolith Small, rounded grains that make up some sedimentary rocks.

Opaque Describes material that does not let light pass through it.

Ore A rock or mineral from which a metal can be extracted for a profit.

Organic Relating to living things.

Placer A deposit of sand or gravel in the bed of a river or lake, containing grains of valuable minerals, such as gold or diamonds.

Plate boundary Where tectonic plates meet in the Earth's crust. There are three types of plate boundary: convergent (where plates collide), divergent (where plates pull apart), and transform (where plates slide past each other).

Pluton Any body of intrusive igneous rock.

Porphyritic Igneous rock containing large, well-formed crystals mixed into a groundmass.

Precipitation Chemical process in which a substance is deposited in solid form from a solution.

Prism A solid geometric figure with a set of faces parallel to one of the axes. An axis is an imaginary line which divides something in half.

Pyroclastic Materials such as rock and ash thrown out by an explosive volcanic eruption.

Radioactivity The spontaneous emission of bursts of radiation (alpha, beta, or gamma rays) caused by the disintegration of the unstable atoms of certain elements, such as the metal uranium. Some radiation is harmful to people.

Refraction The bending of light rays as they pass through a transparent substance.

Regional metamorphism The creation of new metamorphic rocks over a wide area by heat and pressure, typically during mountain-building.

Rock Solid mixtures of minerals. There are three types: igneous, metamorphic, and sedimentary.

Seafloor spreading The gradual widening of an ocean as new oceanic crust forms along the midocean ridge.

Sediment Particles of rock, mineral, or organic matter that are carried by wind, water, and ice.

Sedimentary rock Rock formed from sediment that has been buried and squeezed solid by pressure from above.

Sill A thin, sheetlike, typically horizontal, igneous intrusion, inserted between rock layers.

Spar A crystalline, easily cleavable, translucent or transparent mineral.

Specific gravity Comparing a mineral's weight with the weight of an equal volume of water.

Speleothem A structure, such as a stalactite or stalagmite, formed in a cave by the precipitation of minerals from water.

Strike-slip fault A fault in which blocks of rock slide sideways past each other. A very large strike-slip fault occurring on the boundary of two tectonic plates is known as a transform fault.

Stromatolite Layered mounds of sediment formed by colonies of ancient types of bacteria.

Symmetry When two forms mirror each other on opposite sides of an imaginary dividing line.

Tectonic plate One of about 20 huge, floating rock slabs that make up the Earth's lithosphere.

Thrust fault A fault in which one block is thrust up and over another. If the angle is steeper than 45°, it is a reverse fault.

Translucent A substance that lets light through, but breaks the light up so that you cannot see through it clearly.

Transportation The carrying of loose sediment by rivers, wind, waves, and ice.

Trench A deep trough in the ocean floor.

Twinning When two or more crystals of the same mineral grow together.

Ultrabasic Relating to igneous rock with less than 45 percent silica.

Ultramafic Relating to igneous rock with no quartz and little or no feldspar, made mostly of minerals such as olivine and pyroxene.

Unconformity A noticeable break in a sequence of sedimentary rock layers, due to an interruption in the laying down of sediments.

Uplift When rock structures are raised upward by the movement of tectonic plates. Sediments formed on the seabed may be uplifted to become mountains and plains.

Volcano The site of an eruption of lava and hot gases from within the Earth. Magma flows up a central passage and erupts as lava.

Weathering The slow breakdown of rock by prolonged exposure to the weather, including moisture, frost, and acidic rainwater.

INDEX

A page number in **bold** refers to the main entry for that subject.

ACKNOWLEDGMENTS

Dorling Kindersley would like to thank Marion Dent for proof-reading; Michael Dent for the index; Margaret Parrish for Americanization; Judith Samuelson and Andrew Kerr-Jarrett for editorial support; and Leah Germann for design support.

Dorling Kindersley Ltd. is not responsible and does not accept liability for the availability or content of any web site other than its own, or for any exposure to offensive, harmful, or inaccurate material that may appear on the Internet. Dorling Kindersley Ltd. will have no liability for any damage or loss caused by viruses that may be downloaded as a result of looking at and browsing the web sites that it recommends. Dorling Kindersley downloadable images are the sole copyright of Dorling Kindersley Ltd. and may not be reproduced, stored, or transmitted in any form or by any means for any commercial or profit-related purpose without prior written permission of the copyright owner.

Picture Credits

The publisher would like to thank the following for their kind permission to reproduce their photographs:

Abbreviations key:
t-top, b-bottom, r-right, l-left, c-center, a-above, f-far

8: Corbis/R.L.Christiansen (l), Reuters/Will Burgess (br); 8–9: Corbis/Liz Hymans (t); 9: Corbis (r), Georgina Bowater (cl), Peter Guttman (detail, c), Sally A.Morgan/Ecoscene (b); 10: Corbis/Layne Kennedy (l); 11: GeoScience Features Picture Library (tc), FLPA/Minden Pictures (r); 12: Lonely Planet Images/Andrew MacColl (bc), British Geological Survey (b); 13: www.bridgeman.co.uk/Chartres Cathedral, France (bc); Corbis/Jonathan Blair (tl), Sandro Vannini (br), Werner Forman Archive/University of Philadelphia Museum (bcl); 14: Corbis/Raymond Gehman (acr), Science Photo Library/Alfred Pasieka (fbcl), Dirk Wiersma (acl, bcl), Stephen & Donna O'Meara (bl); 15: Corbis/Bjorn Backe/Papilio (t); 16: Science Photo Library/Bernhard Edmaier (br), Tom Van Sant/Planetary Visions/Geosphere Project (tr); 17: Ardea.com/Francois Gohier (bl), Corbis (tr), GeoScience Features Picture Library (crb, bcr), Marli Miller/Department of Geological Sciences, University of Oregon (fbcr), Science Photo Library/Geospace (tl); 18: Corbis/ O. Alamany & E.Vicens (bcl), Roger Antrobus (bl); 18–19: Impact Photos/Pamla Toler (t), Corbis/Jonathan Blair (c), W. Wayne Lockwood, M.D. (b); 19: Ardea/Alan Weaving (tr), Corbis (bcr), Phil Schermeister (br), Yann Arthus-Bertrand (acr); 20: Corbis/Homer Sykes (tr), Science Photo Library/2002 Orbital Imaging Corporation (acl); 21: Ardea/Jean-Paul Ferrero (tl), Bryan Sage (tc), Corbis/David Muench (c), Corbis/Digital image © 1996, courtesy of NASA (tcl), Gary Braasch (tcr), GeoScience Features Picture Library (tr), Science Photo Library/ B.Murton, Southampton Oceanography Centre (bcr); 22: Corbis/Reuters (l); 23: Natural Visions/Soames Summerhays (acr), Corbis/Alberto Garcia (bl), Corbis/Digital image © 1996, courtesy of NASA (cr), Roger Ressmeyer (tl, tr), FLPA/USDA (cl);

24: Corbis/Roger Ressmeyer (r); 25: Corbis/Ric Ergenbright (t), Galen Rowell (cl); Geoscience Features Picture Library/RIDA (bcl), Marli Miller/Dept of Geological Sciences, University of Oregon (fbcl); 26: The Art Archive/Staatliche Sammlung Ägyptischer Kunst Munich/Dagli Orti (c); 26-27: Corbis/Joseph Sohm/Visions of America (b), 27: Corbis/David Muench (tl); 28: Corbis/ Galen Rowell (r), GeoScience Features Picture Library (acl); 29: Corbis/Detail of David by Michelangelo/Arte & Immagini srl (br), Wild Country (bl); 30: Corbis/Hubert Stadler (b); 31: Corbis/Steve Austin/Papilio (tr), Richard Klune (cl), Sean Sexton Collection (cr), FLPA/Ken Day (br); 32: FLPA/Christiana Carvalho (l); 33: Science Photo Library/Martin Bond (tl), Ardea.com/Francois Gohier (tr); 34: Corbis/ Digital image © 1996, courtesy of NASA (tr), M. L. Sinibaldi (br), GeoScience Features Picture Library (c); 35: FLPA/Mark Newman (t), Natural Visions (cr, br); 36: Corbis/Gianni Dagli Orti (br); 36–37: Getty Images/The Image Bank (t); 37 Ardea.com/Jean-Paul Ferrero (br). Ian Beames (bcr), Bruce Coleman Ltd/Jules Cowan (tr, acr), Corbis/Sharna Balfour/Gallo Images (bl); 38: Ardea.com/Francois Gohier (acr), Corbis/Jonathan Blair (b); 39: Natural Visions (tl), Ardea.com/Francois Gohier (bcl, bcr), John Cancalosi (tc); 40: Natural Visions/Heather Angel (acr), Ardea.com/Kurt Amsler (br), Corbis/ Bob Krist (tl), Science Photo Library/Andrew Syred (bl); 41: Corbis/Michael St. Maur Sheil (br), Roger Ressmeyer (acr); 42: Robert Visser (acr); GeoScience Features Picture Library (cl, c); 42–43: Science Photo Library/Jerry Lodriguss (t), Corbis/Charles & Josette Lenars (b); 43: Corbis/NASA/JPL/Cornell/Zuma (bcr), Science Photo Library/David Parker (tl), Nasa/US Geological Survey (tr); 44–45: Corbis/Christine Osborne (t); 47: Science Photo Library/Manfred Kage (br); 50: Corbis/Ludovic Maisant (c), Science Photo Library/Simon Fraser (b); 51: Corbis/Michael Prince (tl), Tom Stewart (tr), Science Photo Library/Charles D. Winters (c), Chemical Design (cl); 52: Natural Visions/ Heather Angel (cr), Ardea.com/E. Mickleburgh (bl), Royalty-Free/Corbis (bcl); 53: Corbis/ Douglas Whyte (tc), Gleb Garanich (cl), Nik Wheeler (bcr), Science Photo Library/Charles D. Winters (br), Scott Camazine (tl); 54: Corbis/ Mike Simons (bc), Sandro Vannini (l), Science Photo Library/Andrew Syred (br), Rosenfeld Images Ltd (bcl); 55: Corbis/Bettmann (tr), Paul A. Souders (br), Wayne Lawler/Ecoscene (cr); 56: Corbis/Jeff Vanuga (t), Royal Ontario Museum (bcr), Science Photo Library/Roberto de Gugliemo (bcl); 57: Corbis/Lowell Georgia (tl), Reuters (br); 58: Corbis/James L Amos (bl), Neil Rabinowitz (cl), NASA (br), 60: Corbis/ Sergio Pitamitz (b); 61: Corbis/Dave G. Houser (br); 62: Corbis/Tim Graham (tl); 63: Corbis/ Koopman (cl), Ron Watts (cr), Roger Ressmeyer (bl); 64: Corbis/Sandro Vannini (l); 64–65 Geophotos/Tony Waltham (b); 66: British Museum/Dorling Kindersley (tl), Corbis/Angelo Hornak (b), Maurice Nimmo/Frank Lane Picture Agency (cr), GeoScience Features Picture Library (acl); 67: Corbis/Owen Franken (acr); 68: Corbis/Kevin Shafer (t), Impact Photos/Alain Evrard (cr), Science Photo Library/David Nunuk (bc); 69: © Christie's Images Ltd (tc), Corbis/ Richard Hamilton Smith (br), William Taufic (cl); 70: Science Photo Library/Arnold Fisher (cl), Keith Kent (acr); 71: INAH/Dorling Kindersley

(c), Science Photo Library/Biophoto Associates (cl), Lawrence Lawry (br), Sidney Moulds (bl); 72: Alamy Images/Keren Su/China Span (bl), Corbis/Francis G. Mayer (cr), Jose Manuel Sanchis Calvete (cl), Maurice Nimmo/Frank Lane Picture Agency (t); 73: www.bridgeman.co.uk/ Osterreichische Nationalbibliothek, Vienna, Austria (br), Leeds Museums and Art Galleries (Temple Newsam House), UK (tr), Corbis/Archivo Iconografico, S.A (tl), Richard T. Nowitz (bl); 74: © Christie's Images Ltd (tr), Corbis/Jack Fields (br), Reuters (bcl), Roger Garwood & Trish Ainslie (fcl); 75: The Art Archive/Central Bank Teheran/Dagli Orti (tl), Judith Miller/Dorling Kindersley/Fellow & Sons (acl), V & A Images/Victoria and Albert Museum (bcl); 76: www.bridgeman.co.uk/Hermitage, St Petersburg, Russia (tr, fcr), Oriental Museum, Durham University, UK (cl); 76–77: Corbis/Asian Art & Archaeology, Inc (b); 77: Construction Photography.com/Adrian Sherratt (bcl), Corbis/Hans Georg Roth (ac), The Art Archive/Acropolis Museum Athens/Dagli Orti (r), Impact Photos/Alan Keohane (tl); 78: Werner Forman Archive/British Museum (l), Akg-images/Erich Lessing (cr), Corbis/Bettmann (bl), Werner Forman (cl); 79: Akg-images/British Library (tr), Corbis/David Cumming/Eye Ubiquitous (tc), Hulton-Deutsch Collection (tl), Robert Estall (bl), Stapleton Collection (cr); 80: Corbis/Alex Steedman (l), Paul A. Souders (r); 81: Action Plus/Glyn Kirk (tr), Corbis (bcr), Charles E. Rotkin (bl), Guy Motil (tl), James L. Amos (cl), Photomorgana (tl); 82: Corbis/Bill Ross (l), Macduff Everton (tr), Ted Spiegel (br), ImageState/Pictor/StockImage (bl); 83: Judith Miller/Dorling Kindersley/Sloans & Kenyon (tc), Corbis/Charles E. Rotkin (cl), Christina Louiso (bcl), Jan Butchofsky-Houser (bc), Morton Beebe (r), Michael and Patricia Fogden (tl); 84: Construction Photography.com/Chris Henderson (br), Royalty-Free/Imagestate (bc), Royalty-Free/Getty Images/Photodisc Blue (bl); 85: Corbis/Brownie Harris (br), Edifice (tr), Royalty-Free/Corbis (cr, bl, bc); 86: Corbis/Peter Johnson (cr), OSF/photolibrary.com (cl), Science Photo Library/Microfield Scientific Ltd (tr); 87: Corbis/Layne Kennedy (bl), Royalty-Free/ Corbis (br), Science Photo Library/Innerspace Imaging (tl), Insolite Realite (tl); 88: Corbis/ Roger Ressmeyer (tr, br), Science Photo Library/Paolo Koch (cl); 89: Corbis/ Jonathan Blair (tl), Layne Kennedy (cr), Science Photo Library/Geoff Lane/CSIRO (cl).

Jacket images
Front: Corbis: Joseph Sohm/ChromoSohm Inc. (crr); Science Photo Library: Lawrence Lawry (cr); Dirk Wiersma (cll). **Spine:** Corbis: Joseph Sohm/ChromoSohm Inc. (c). **Back:** Corbis: Jonathan Blair (cll); Science Photo Library: John Walsh (cr); Dirk Wiersma (cl, crr).

All other images © Dorling Kindersley.
For further information see:
www.dkimages.com